FILIPINO
AMERICAN
PSYCHOLOGY

FILIPINO AMERICAN PSYCHOLOGY

A Handbook of Theory, Research, and Clinical Practice

KEVIN L. NADAL

WILEY

John Wiley & Sons, Inc.

Library of Congress Cataloging-in-Publication Data:

Nadal, Kevin L.
    Filipino American psychology: a handbook of theory, research, and clinical practice / Kevin L. Nadal.
        p. cm.
    Includes bibliographical references and index.
    ISBNs 978-0-470-95136-1; 978-1-118-01975-7; 978-1-118-01976-4;
978-1-118-01977-1; 978-1-118-09474-7
        1. Filipino Americans—Ethnic identity.   2. Filipino Americans—Psychology.
    3. Filipino Americans—Social conditions.   I. Title.
    E184.F4N33 2011
    155.8'49921073—dc22

                                                                            2010049506

Printed in the United States of America

10 9 8 7 6 5 4 3 2 1

To my parents and elders, who pursued their dreams and sacrificed so much to make a better life for me and other Filipino Americans in the United States.

To the new generation of Filipino Americans in my life, especially Noah Cruz, Jamielyn, Jessiemae, Julianna, Faith, Emmaline, Danielle, Jordan, Gavin, Noah Zachary, Delaney, Bubby, Cammy, Jarad, Malcolm, Umahon, Ryley, Lani, Elijah, Tristan, Tyler, Riley, Regan, Kaylen, Madison, Ella, and Alexander. I hope they remember where they come from and continually fight for their voices to be heard.

Contents

Foreword   Derald Wing Sue   *ix*
Preface   *xiii*
Acknowledgments   *xvii*

CHAPTER ONE
Introduction to Filipino American Psychology   1

CHAPTER TWO
Filipino and Filipino American Cultural Values   35

CHAPTER THREE
Racial and Ethnic Identity Development for Filipino Americans   63

CHAPTER FOUR
Colonial Mentality of Filipino Americans   89

CHAPTER FIVE
Filipino American Groups and Communities   109

CHAPTER SIX
Filipino Americans and the Model Minority Myth:
Contemporary Experiences in Education, Health, and Society   137

CONTENTS

CHAPTER SEVEN
Filipino American Experiences With Gender and Sexual
Orientation   161

CHAPTER EIGHT
Multiracial, Multiethnic, and Adopted Filipino Americans   193

CHAPTER NINE
Mental Health Experiences and Psychotherapy With
Filipino Americans   225

References   *265*
Appendix A: Historical References in the Poem "Ikaw"   *289*
Appendix B: Further Readings and Resources   *293*
Glossary   *297*
About the Author   *305*
Author Index   *307*
Subject Index   *311*

Foreword

Filipino American Psychology: A Handbook of Theory, Research, and Clinical Practice is destined to make a major contribution to the field of Asian American psychology and to the larger field of multicultural psychology. No other, more comprehensive text exists that discusses the totality of the Filipino American experience in such an analytical, scholarly, and humane manner. Professor Kevin Nadal should be commended for doing such an outstanding job of providing readers with a unique and refreshingly integrative analysis of Filipino Americans that goes beyond simply describing differences and similarities in cultural values, lifestyles, and racial/ethnic experiences in the United States. He takes us beyond the Black-White and Asian American–Filipino American binaries by reminding us that racial/ethnic diversity in the United States is more than just the experiences of European immigrants, White Americans, Black Americans, and even specific Asian American groups.

Some 40 years ago, when I began work on Asian American personality, identity, and mental health, I believed, along with other ethnic researchers, that it was important to elucidate the experiences of Asian Americans, to raise awareness that the field of psychology was ethnocentric, and to suggest that the "model minority" descriptor given to us was a myth. At that time, no one could have convinced Asian American researchers that they themselves might be ethnocentric and that their good intentions were somehow oppressing and stereotyping of other Asian American groups. But that is precisely the conclusion I have come to after reading Professor Nadal's text. As he reminds us, the Asian American population includes many Asian groups, from Chinese and Japanese to Cambodians as well as Vietnamese, Koreans, Pacific Islanders, Asian Indians, Pakistanis, and many others. Filipino Americans are now the second largest Asian American group in the United States and may become the majority in 2010. When one looks, however, at the research and professional literature on Asian Americans, it is focused predominantly on two groups: Chinese Americans and Japanese Americans. Going further, one would have to conclude that the current knowledge base of Asian American psychology is derived primarily from only two Asian ethnic groups. Certainly, as multicultural psychologists, we must entertain the notion that many of the concepts and principles derived from this body of literature might not be completely applicable to groups like Filipino Americans.

Not only do Professor Nadal's own research and scholarly contributions challenge the universality of the laws and principles of psychology itself, but he asks us to consider the universality of the Asian American experience as well. Step by step he takes readers into the life experiences of Filipino Americans, describes their unique history of colonization, analyzes the impact of religion and Catholicism, phenotype and skin color, and provides us with a new framework of Filipino American identity. His proposed model is captivating and informative because it integrates many sociodemographic and sociopolitical forces into identity development, entertains the notion of diversity within such identities, and discusses the interplay of gender and sexual orientation in the model.

This book is a valuable reference for Filipino Americans themselves who wish to explore their identities as racial/cultural/ethnic beings. *Filipino American Psychology*, however, is definitely an essential reference for scholars, educators, mental health practitioners and students. As Professor Nadal states, he is interested in providing researchers, educators, and mental health providers with awareness, knowledge, and skills when working with Filipino Americans. Becoming culturally competent in working with this population is the primary goal of the text. Each chapter is filled with valuable information. Readers will find particularly helpful the numerous case vignettes that illustrate cultural, social, political, economic, and mental health issues confronting Filipino Americans. The cases not only deal with culture-specific issues and practices but offer suggestions regarding the integration of Western practices with indigenous forms of healing.

Professor Nadal is a master at relating sociodemographic and sociopolitical topics to the everyday lives of Filipino Americans, speaking directly to educators and helping professionals about what they need to do to become culturally competent with this population, grounding his research and theory to actual practical implications, and pointing to new directions for Asian American psychology and the broader society. This book is must reading for everyone.

Derald Wing Sue, PhD
Teachers College, Columbia University
New York

Preface

Growing up in a large Filipino American community in the San Francisco Bay Area, I was taught from an early age to be proud of my culture. My parents and extended family exposed me to an array of Filipino customs and traditions, ranging from learning to dance through *tinikling* bamboo sticks to eating chicken *adobo*, *lumpia*, and *pancit*. I also learned about Filipino values, such as respecting one's elders, always offering to help (especially when you are not asked), and putting family first before everything else.

I always knew I came from a fairly typical Filipino American family. Both of my parents worked full-time (with my mother, of course, being a nurse). My parents had accents and interchanged their *p*'s and their *f*'s. My siblings and I took piano lessons. We sang karaoke at every family party. I had 18 first cousins and hundreds of second and third cousins, and somehow I felt close with all of them. We had a Santo Niño (Baby Jesus statue) shrine in the hallway near my bedroom. I referred to every Filipino adult as "Uncle," "Auntie," "Tito," or "Tita," regardless of our actual blood relationship. And there was always a rice cooker steaming in the kitchen. I loved being Filipino and told everyone about my ethnicity whenever I had the chance.

Despite all of these positive aspects, I also noticed many second-generation Filipino Americans were not attaining levels of higher education or achieving the American dream our parents had hoped for us, and I often wondered why. For as long as I can remember, I noticed a lot of my friends not attending or finishing college, becoming teenage mothers, or getting themselves into trouble with drugs, gangs, or crime. I also always wondered why Filipinos were treated differently from other Asian groups—from the first time a police officer pulled me over for no reason, to the numerous times people would speak to me in Spanish. I always felt as if Filipinos were different from all other racial and ethnic groups, and I learned to develop a deep sense of pride in that.

Having lived in various cities—including Fremont and Irvine, California, East Lansing, Michigan, and my current home in New York, New York—I started to recognize how Filipino Americans everywhere seemed similar. Certain values seemed to govern the ways we communicated, behaved, thought, and felt. There seemed to be common mentalities and thought processes people shared, which influenced how they made decisions and the way they lived their everyday lives. And there seemed to be common experiences with race and ethnicity that existed no matter where Filipino Americans lived in the United States. Although Filipino Americans are all exceptional with their own individualities and personalities, I appreciated that there was a culture that bound us together and connected us all as a Filipino American people.

When I first started learning about multicultural issues in psychology as an undergraduate student at the University of California, Irvine, I recognized that Filipino Americans often were omitted from the literature—in psychology, social sciences, humanities, and across all other fields—and I never really understood why. I thought about how there were very few Filipino American professors in the country, and perhaps this was the reason why we were not being represented. So with great mentorship that steered me in the right direction, I made myself two major promises: (1) I would attain my PhD to increase the number of Filipino American college professors and to do my best to represent the Filipino American community in academia; and (2) I would write a book on Filipino American psychology and mental health issues to serve as a resource for counselors, clinicians, and educators who work with our population. A decade later, both of these promises have been fulfilled, and I could not be happier.

This book is intended to share insights about the lives of Filipino Americans. To the Filipino Americans who read this, I hope this volume sheds light on some of your experiences and perhaps answers some of the questions you have always wondered (e.g., What does it mean to be Filipino? Why does my family communicate in a certain way? Why do Filipinos feel different from other Asian groups? Do other people experience the same things that I do?). If some of the material seems foreign, new, or even controversial, I encourage you to take a step back and understand the purpose of this book: to provide awareness about our culture. In doing so, my aim is for our people to be appreciated more and pathologized less, and for all of us to advocate for improvements in our community, our families, and our inner selves.

To the counselors, clinicians, and other practitioners who read this, I hope this book provides you with some knowledge, awareness, and skills that you can utilize to become effective and culturally competent when working with your Filipino American clients and patients. As of now, limited resources in psychology, education, and other social sciences highlight Filipino American culture and experiences. As you read more about our community, I encourage you to become conscious of ways you can work more effectively with your clients and patients in your professional lives.

And to the general readers, I hope this book presents you with an enlightening education about a group that is often invisible, misunderstood, or forgotten. Fred Cordova, cofounder of the Filipino American National Historical Society, once referred to Filipino Americans as the "forgotten Asian Americans." I dream that someday we will not be forgotten and instead be recognized for the valuable presence we have had in both American and global society.

I leave you with a quote by Dr. José Rizal, the national hero of the Philippines: "Ang hindi marunong lumingon sa pinanggalingan ay hindi makararating sa paroroonan," which translates to "One who does not look back at her or his past will not reach her or his destination." I share a part of my life story with you, to help you to understand my personal journey behind writing this book. Much like many aspects of my life, this book has been a work in progress and a dream accomplished. I hope it encourages you all to follow your passions and your dreams too. And I hope all of you can recognize that you can do your part to save the world.

Maraming salamat (many thanks).

Kevin Leo Yabut Nadal, PhD

Acknowledgments

This book would not have been possible without several people. First of all, I'd like to thank the team of individuals at John Wiley & Sons, particularly Rachel Livsey and Kara Borberly. An infinite amount of respect and appreciation is given to my mentor, Dr. Derald Wing Sue, for writing a wonderful foreword for this book and for inspiring me to become a better psychologist and professor. I would not be where I am today without the help of all of my mentors throughout the years including Dr. Jeannett Castellanos, Dr. Elizabeth Fraga, Dr. Alfiee Breland, and Dr. Maureen O'Connor.

I would like to thank my family for teaching me to be proud of my Filipino American heritage. My deepest gratitude goes to my parents, Leo and Charity Nadal; my brothers, Earl and Lloyd Nadal; and my numerous aunts, uncles, cousins, and in-laws, who have taught me the importance of family. My greatest appreciation and love must go to the H. Tamayo family, Prado family, R. Yabut family, Rino family, Punzalan family, Yabut-Hernandez family, LaGue family, Vasquez family, Perez family, Rynne family, L. Tamayo family, H. Nadal family, C. Nadal family, Villarina family, Lozada family, Escober family, Tarantan family, Legaspi family, Adams family, Meza family, B. Tamayo family, Iquina family, Zabal family, Calderon family, Ramirez family, and Ruiz family. Special gratitude is paid particularly to Christiano Tomas Nadal, Michelle Balancio, Jackie Chan, Agnes Fajutagana, David Gonzalez, Brad LaGue, Lisa LaGue, Maria Legaspi Adams, Steven Perez, Dana Prado, Gail Prado, Jed Prado, Ryan Punzalan, Fiel Rino, Terri Rino,

Debbie Rino Santos, Mateo Rynne, Stephanie Rynne, Tomas Rynne, Dave Santos, Julian Ian Tamayo, Pamela Tamayo, Gayle Teofilo, Goldie Vasquez, Max Vasquez, Jan Rodolfo Yabut, Joni Yabut, Loyen Yabut, Margie Yabut-Hernandez, Rodney Yabut, Wesley Yabut, Althea Zabal, Glenn Zabal, Juliet Zabal, the entire Yabut clan in California, and the entire Tamayo clan in New York. To Evelyn Tamayo, Elna Prado, and Evan Prado, who have been my second parents in New York, thank you for opening up your homes and hearts to me and for teaching me the importance of generosity and selflessness. To my loved ones who watch over me in heaven, especially my uncle Rodolfo "Nonong" Yabut II; my grandparents, Maria L. Nadal, Discoro Nadal, Rodolfo Yabut I, and Oliva R. Yabut; and my family members Kenneth Perez, Franklyn "Toto" Yabut, Emelie J. Yabut, Hector R. Tamayo, Marco Meza, and Jallah Ballayan, rest in Paradise.

Finally, I want to acknowledge all of the friends who have motivated me to become a better person and who have walked alongside me through this journey of life. Eternal gratitude is sent particularly to Ryan Abugan, Laila Alchaar, Clarissa Aljentera, Tracy Barlow Meyer, Jason Barrios, Annalisa Burgos, Michelle Camaya, Melissa Cariño, Sharon Chia Claros, Melissa Corpus, Hanna Crespo, Lorial Crowder, Ryan Cantorna, E. J. R. David, Aubrey Deperio, Mathilda De Dios, Mimi Docena, Maria Doherty, Beverly Fontillas, Ronni Fontillas, JoAnn Garcia, Debbie Green, Thea Green, Kathleen Claire Guiang, Cara Jacobson, Marc Johnston, Angela Kim, Cara Koerber, Sophia Kong, Kate Krontiris, Hernani Lantin, Melanie Lantin, Kelsey Lebrun, Lilian Liu, Marcia Liu, Andrea Lozada, Ben Macaraeg, Pam Macaraeg, Kristine Magat, Bernadette Manzano, Dina Maramba, Silvia Mazzula, Jeff Myers, Risë Nelson, Yael Nitkin-Kaner, Marie Obaña, John Pasquarello, David Rivera, Laura Romo, Sidney Smith, Jonathan Stefiuk, Melissa Lara Valdez, Bryant Williams, and Yeun Mi Yim. The friends I made as a child in the San Francisco Bay Area, in college in Southern California, in graduate school in the Midwest, and in my adult years in New York City have influenced who I am today as a person, and for that I will be eternally thankful. *Maraming salamat* (many thanks) from the bottom of my heart.

CHAPTER ONE

Introduction to Filipino American Psychology

Figure 1.1 First- and second-generation Filipino American cousins at a holiday party
Photo courtesy of Ian Tamayo

Portions of this chapter are taken from K. L. Nadal (2008c), *Ethnic group membership, phenotype, and perceptions of racial discrimination for Filipino and Chinese Americans: Implications for mental health* (Unpublished doctoral dissertation), Teachers College, Columbia University.

INTRODUCTION

In the United States, race is often viewed as a Black and White issue, with members of general American society tending to concentrate on the historical and contemporary racial conflicts between African Americans and White Americans (Nadal, 2008c). This phenomena can be exemplified by the recent election of President Barack Obama in 2008, in which the mainstream media concentrated primarily on the voting patterns of Blacks and Whites without much regard to the opinions or voting practices of Latinos, Asian Americans, or other racial/ethnic groups. This is also demonstrated in many interpersonal dialogues on race (e.g., in academia, legal systems, and workplaces) that tend to focus on racial relations between Blacks and Whites without examining experiences of race for Latino Americans, Asian Americans, or other racial/ethnic groups. Because of this emphasis on Black versus White in American society, the existence of these other racial/ethnic groups is often minimized, forgotten, or made invisible (Yoo & Lee, 2005).

Perhaps this tendency to disregard or forget about other racial groups is due to the historical views of race in the United States, in which individuals were originally divided into three categories: "Black," "White," and "Other" (Gibson & Jung, 2002). The "Other" groups, which included Asians and Native Americans, were not measured until 1860 because their numbers were too insignificant in comparison to Whites and Blacks. For example, in 1860, there were approximately 35,000 Asian Americans and Pacific Islanders (0.10% of the U.S. population), compared to the 4.4 million African Americans (14.1% of the U.S. population). And in 1890, there were approximately 100,000 Asians and Pacific Islanders in the United States (0.20% of the U.S. population), in comparison to the 7.5 million African Americans (or 11.1% of the U.S. population; Gibson & Jung, 2002; U.S. Census Bureau, 1989). So while the number of Asian Americans had doubled during that time, so did the number of African Americans. As a result, as a group, Black/African Americans continued to grow and remain the largest racial minority group in the United States.

However, the "Other" groups have slowly grown and diversified over the years. According to the U.S. Census, Hispanics and Latinos have surpassed African Americans and have become the largest minority group in the United States at almost 13% of the total population (Bernstein, 2008). Although Hispanic is considered an "ethnic" group and not a "racial" group (it is divided into "White Hispanic" and "Black Hispanic"), it is important to acknowledge the growth of this minority population. In addition to escalation of the Latino community, Asian Americans have become one of the fastest-growing minority groups in the United States with a 72% growth between 1990 and 2000 (Barnes & Bennett, 2002). Asian Americans contribute greatly to immigration, accounting for one-third of all arrivals since the 1970s, and are projected to reach 11% of the U.S. population by the year 2050 (Ghosh, 2003). Because of immigration increases in both the Latino and Asian American populations, the total U.S. population is projected to become about 50% "non-Hispanic White" and 50% persons of various racial/ethnic minority groups (Bergman, 2004). As a result, it is likely that the United States will move beyond a "Black and White" paradigm and there will be a greater presence of Latinos and Asian Americans.

As a result of this increase in racial diversity, it is important for counselors, clinicians, educators, and other practitioners to become aware of the unique experiences of *all* the major racial minority groups, including African Americans, Latinos, Asian Americans, and Native Americans. It is also necessary for practitioners to gain an understanding of other invisible ethnic minority groups, such as Arab Americans, Pacific Islanders, Jewish Americans, and multiracial and multiethnic people. Previous authors have purported that most research and training in mental health (including psychology, counseling, and social work) focuses on White, middle-class American values, and people of color are often misunderstood and ineffectively treated in psychological treatment (see Sue, Arredondo, & McDavis, 1992; D. W. Sue & Sue, 2008 for a review). Moreover, the American Psychological Association (APA) has published "Guidelines on Multicultural Education, Training, Research, Practice, and Organizational Change for Psychologists," which primarily focuses on ways of being culturally competent toward oppressed racial and ethnic minority groups (APA, 2003). Therefore, in order to become ethical psychologists and work effectively with various people of color and other minority groups, one must attain appropriate cultural knowledge, awareness, and skills.

The purpose of this book is to examine the experiences of Filipino Americans—an ethnic group that is often invisible in academia.

Filipino Americans are the second largest Asian American group in the United States and become the largest Asian American ethnic group in the upcoming analyses of 2010 Census. Therefore, it is imperative for practitioners in all fields to become multiculturally competent when working with this group. In the next chapters, readers will have an opportunity to gain knowledge about Filipino Americans, awareness of different dynamics that may impact interpersonal relationships with Filipino Americans, and skills on how to work with Filipino Americans in psychotherapy and counseling settings.

This first chapter reviews the history of Asian Americans as a racial group while exploring how the historical experiences of Filipino Americans may be different from other Asian American ethnic groups. Moreover, this chapter introduces socioeconomic demographics and contemporary experiences of Filipino Americans—a group that has been present in the United States since 1587. Finally, this chapter reviews psychological experiences of Filipinos in the Philippines and current mental health issues of Filipino Americans in the United States.

EXPERIENCES OF ASIAN AMERICANS

According to the most recent U.S. Census, Asian Americans are the fastest-growing racial/ethnic minority group in the United States (Barnes & Bennett, 2002; Reeves & Bennett, 2004). Although Asian Americans make up only 3.6% of the entire U.S. population, the group has multiplied eightfold from 1.4 million in 1970 to 11.9 million in 2000. Between 1990 and 2000, Asian Americans had the largest percentage growth (72%), outpacing every other racial/ethnic group in the country (Barnes & Bennett, 2002). The U.S. Census projects that by 2050, Asian Americans will expand from 10.7 million to 33.4 million (a projected 213% growth), and their proportion of the nation's population to double from 3.8% to 8% (Bergman, 2004). Given this development, Asian Americans are projected to have a more noticeable presence in American society, in that 1 in every 12.5 Americans will be of Asian descent in the year 2050.

The term "Asian American" refers to persons who have common ancestral roots in Asia and the Pacific Islands, with a similar physical appearance and comparable cultural values (Nadal & Sue, 2009). The Asian

American racial category comprises over 40 distinct ethnicities, which includes Chinese, Filipino, Korean, Asian Indian, Vietnamese, Japanese, Cambodian, and Hmong (Nadal & Sue, 2009; D. W. Sue & Sue, 2008). Sometimes Pacific Islanders are lumped into this category when discussing multicultural issues, forming broader racial categorizations such as "Asian/ Pacific Islander" (API), "Asian Americans/Pacific Islanders" (AAPI), or "Asian Pacific Americans" (APA). However, in the U.S. Census, Pacific Islanders constitute a separate category (Nadal & Sue, 2009).

When using the term "Asian American," it is important to understand the heterogeneity of the Asian American community. Three points are significant.

1. There are hundreds of languages within the Asian American racial group, including Cantonese, Mandarin, Tagalog, Vietnamese, Japanese, and Farsi (Nadal & Sue, 2009).
2. There are over 20 major religions within the Asian American racial group, ranging from Buddhism, Catholicism, Hinduism, Sikhism, Taoism, and Confucianism (Nadal & Sue, 2009).
3. There are many differences in phenotype (physical characteristics/ attributes) between the major Asian subgroups. Most East Asians (e.g., Chinese, Japanese, and Korean) may have a lighter peach skin tone, Filipino Americans and Southeast Asians (e.g., Vietnamese, Cambodian, Laotian) may possess a light to dark brown skin tone, and South Asians (e.g., Asian Indians, Pakistanis) may have a very dark brown skin tone (Nadal, 2008c; Nadal & Sue, 2009). Eye shapes are also different between different Asian groups, with East Asian Americans typically having smaller eyes, while South Asians having larger eyes. Because of this heterogeneity, it is common for Asian Americans to identify themselves in terms of their ethnicity (e.g., "Chinese," "Indian," "Filipino"), instead of the broader racial category of Asian or Asian American (Nadal & Sue, 2009).

The largest Asian American ethnic groups in the United States include Chinese Americans, Filipino Americans, Asian Indian Americans, Korean Americans, Vietnamese Americans, and Japanese Americans (Reeves & Bennett, 2004). In terms of specific numbers, there are approximately

2.86 million Chinese Americans, 2.39 Filipino Americans, 1.86 Asian Indian Americans, 1.23 Korean Americans, 1.21 Vietnamese Americans, and 1.15 million Japanese Americans. Other smaller Asian American groups include Cambodian Americans, Hmong Americans, Pakistani Americans, and Thai Americans.

Asian American History and Demographics

Among Asian Americans, Filipinos were the first documented group to land in the United States. In 1587, several Filipino men escaped Spanish galleon ships en route to Spain and landed in what is now Morro Bay, California (Posadas, 1999). However, the first Asian Americans to arrive to the United States in large numbers were the Chinese Americans who settled on the West Coast (primarily in California) in the mid-1840s (Takaki, 1998). These Chinese immigrants are credited with building the transcontinental railroads in the United States while enduring very poor living conditions and facing blatant racial discrimination from Whites. Japanese Americans arrived shortly after and also worked as laborers in transcontinental railroads as well as in fish canneries and mines. Like the Chinese, these Japanese immigrants also experienced blatant discrimination from Whites for much of the end of the 19th century.

Because of this anti-Chinese and anti-Japanese sentiment, the U.S. government aimed to limit the number of Asian immigrants into the country by enacting the Chinese Exclusion Act of 1882 and the 1924 Immigration Act (Takaki, 1998). Both of these acts limited the number of Chinese immigrants and later forbade Chinese immigrants altogether. It was not until the 1965 Immigration Act, in which quotas were no longer based on race, that Asian immigration into the United States began to increase again. These post-1965 immigrants came from various Asian countries, such as China, Japan, the Philippines, India, and Korea. Most of the post-1965 Asian American immigrants were professionals, including doctors, nurses, and engineers, who were recruited by U.S. agencies such as hospitals and manufacturing companies. These immigrants came to the United States for better employment opportunities and a superior future for their children while searching for the

"American Dream," which was advertised throughout various Asian American countries.

Another major category of Asian American immigration includes the 2 million Southeast Asian refugees (primarily from Vietnam, Cambodia, and Laos) who began arriving in the United States in 1975 (Takaki, 1998). Although other Asian immigrants have time to prepare for their move, refugees often escape from persecution and other tragic conditions in their home countries and come to the United States without education, money, or resources. Refugees have been relocated all over the continental United States, in areas where other Southeast Asians and refugees reside (e.g., parts of the West Coast) and also in areas where there were few Southeast Asians and refugees (e.g., parts of the Midwest). Although refugees came primarily in the 1980s and 1990s to seek political and economic refuge, a sizable number of refugees move to the United States every day (D. W. Sue & Sue, 2008).

Asian Americans are often described by their generational status (Nadal & Sue, 2009; Uba, 1994). The first generation of Asian Americans consists of Asians who immigrated to the United States in late adolescence or adulthood (e.g., a Korean American who immigrates when she is 18 years old). This generation often maintains many of the values from their country of origin and often has difficulty becoming accustomed to the new values in the United States. Second-generation Asian Americans are individuals who are U.S. born and have foreign-born parents (e.g., a Pakistani American who was born in the United States and whose parents were born in Pakistan). These individuals often are taught the cultural values, language, and customs of their parents' home countries while learning the values and norms of being American in the United States. The 1.5 generation consists of those foreign-born who arrive in the United States prior to age 13 (e.g., a Thai American who was born in Thailand and immigrated to the United States at 11 years old). Members of this group often are characterized as being somewhere in the middle since they maintain characteristics of both the first and second generations (Nadal & Sue, 2009; Uba, 1994). Because they spent their childhood in their home country, they were able to develop many of their values, beliefs, and personality before immigrating to the United States; however, because they immigrated during adolescence, they still have the ability to further develop their values, beliefs, and personality in the United States. The third generation includes Asian Americans whose grandparents immigrated to the United States, and the fourth generation includes Asian Americans whose great-grandparents immigrated to the United States.

Asian American Mental Health

Out of all the major racial groups, Asian Americans are the least researched, studied, or discussed in the fields of psychology, education, and health (David & Okazaki, 2006a; Uba, 1994; Wolf, 1997). Many hypotheses have been offered to explain this fact. One reason is that it has been found that Asian Americans utilize mental health services the least out of all racial groups (Uba, 1994). Some authors have argued that this may indicate lower rates of psychopathology for the Asian American population (Lin & Cheung, 1999). Other literature, however, suggests that these lower rates of mental health utilization for Asian Americans should be attributed to cultural stigmas, reluctance to seek out services, patient suspiciousness, and a different understanding of the manifestation of psychological problems (Uba, 1994). Although Asian Americans are not seeking mental health services, they are as susceptible to mental health problems and psychopathology as other racial groups. Moreover, because of the stigma of mental health treatment, it is likely that those Asian Americans who *do* have mental health problems are not seeking help and therefore are not being treated.

Another reason why Asian Americans are invisible in psychology (and other fields) is the model minority myth. This myth contends that all Asian Americans are well-educated, successful, and law-abiding citizens in the United States, in comparison to other racial/ethnic minority groups of color (e.g., African Americans, Latino Americans, and Native Americans) who are stereotyped to be the opposite of the model: uneducated, unintelligent, or prone to crime (Nadal & Sue, 1999; Uba, 1994). The model minority myth is based on census data, which reveals that Asian Americans attain higher educational statuses and have higher family or household incomes than the general U.S. population (Reeves & Bennett, 2004). However, these statistics are misleading in a number of ways. For example, although many Asian Americans have attained higher levels of education, a large group have not attained a high school diploma. Due to the model minority myth, members of society at large hold false perceptions that all Asian Americans are succeeding educationally (D. W. Sue & Sue, 2008). Moreover, Asian Americans tend to have higher levels of family or household income because more people are contributing to the household income than there are with other racial groups (Reeves & Bennett, 2004).

Because of the prevalence of this myth, psychologists, educators, and researchers tend to assume that Asian Americans are doing well and fail to notice that many have a contrary experience. For example, there are a number of health and educational disparities that are prevalent in many Asian American subgroups (particularly Southeast Asian Americans, Pacific Islanders, and Filipino Americans). These issues range from poverty, lower educational achievement, HIV/AIDS, teen pregnancy, and gang involvement (Nadal, 2008c). However, because of the myth, the experiences of these Asian American subgroups continue to go unnoticed. Chapter 6 discusses the negative outcomes of the model minority myth in more detail.

When considering Asian Americans, it is also important to note that research tends to focus on East Asian Americans, namely Chinese, Japanese, and Korean Americans (Agbayani-Siewert, 2004; David & Okazaki, 2006a; Nadal, 2004; Root, 1997a). This practice in academia parallels the tendency of American society to generalize the experience of East Asian Americans (especially the experience of Chinese Americans) to all Asian Americans (Nadal, 2008c). For example, when the general American population thinks of "Asian," they tend to think of "Chinese" or "Japanese" first (Cordova, 1983), despite the fact that Filipino Americans and Asian Indian Americans are the second and third largest Asian American groups in the United States. Because East Asian Americans are viewed as the dominant Asian American group, non–East Asian American groups often feel marginalized or invisible in the Asian American community. Moreover, because psychologists, educators, and other practitioners are not being trained or taught about the experiences of these marginalized Asian American groups, members of these groups continue to receive culturally inappropriate mental health services and continue to be underserved.

There are some benefits to categorizing Asian Americans into one racial group. One advantage may include attaining power in numbers for community organizing; another reason may involve collectivist social support. However, it is important to understand the problems involved in lumping Asian Americans into a homogenous group.

Hierarchies are formed within the greater racial community, in that some individuals are assumed to be the "norm" while all others may be viewed as marginal, different, or even pathological. For example, within the Asian American community, East Asian Americans are often viewed as the top of the hierarchy in that they have higher educational attainments, technologically advanced home countries, and are likely to have a lighter skin tone. Contrarily, Filipino Americans and Southeast Asian Americans are viewed as the bottom of the hierarchy in that they have lower educational attainments, home countries that are extremely poor, and tend to have darker skin tones (Nadal, 2008c). This hierarchy within the Asian American racial group may also lead to a personal sense of normality for East Asians while resulting in a sense of internalized hatred or self-deprecation for Filipino Americans and other marginalized Asian American subgroups. It also has an impact on racial/ethnic identity development (see Chapter 3), colonial mentality (see Chapter 4), group and community dynamics (see Chapter 5), and disparaging sociocultural experiences (see Chapter 6).

By failing to disaggregate racial categories, many marginalized groups are forgotten or made invisible. For example, Cordova (1983) has referred to Filipino Americans as the "forgotten Asian Americans" because people tend to consider Chinese and Japanese Americans when discussing Asian American history. Because Filipino Americans have a unique colonial history and cultural values that are markedly different from other Asian American groups, they may not fit into the Asian American community and may align closely with other racial/ethnic groups like Latinos, Pacific Islanders, or African Americans (Nadal, 2004). This next section will examine experiences of Filipino Americans, including history, culture, and demographics, that distinguish them from other Asian American groups. In learning about Filipino Americans, one can begin to understand how their unique background influences their mental health experiences on societal and individual levels.

Figure 1.2 A Filipino American couple who immigrated to the United States shortly after their wedding in the Philippines, circa 1969
Photo courtesy of Leo and Charity Nadal

EXPERIENCES OF FILIPINO AMERICANS

Filipino Americans are the second largest Asian American/Pacific Islander population in the United States (Barnes & Bennett, 2002; Reeves & Bennett, 2004) and are projected to become the largest Asian American population by 2010. With 1.37 million Filipino-born immigrants living in the United States (U.S. Census Bureau, 2000), Filipino Americans are the second largest immigrant population in the country (behind Mexican Americans), with over 2 million documented Filipino Americans in the United States and a possible 1 million undocumented individuals in the United States (Nadal, 2008c). The term "Filipino" will be used throughout this volume, as it is the most common spelling of the word. It is important to recognize that some Filipinos and Filipino Americans use the term "Pilipino" as a political identifier, signifying the lack of the letter "F" in indigenous and non-Spanish-influenced Pilipino languages (Nadal, 2004, 2008c; Revilla, 1997).

Filipino Americans are descendants of people from the Philippine Islands, a country made up of over 700 islands and 170 languages that is located southeast of mainland China and west of the Pacific Islands

11

(Posadas, 1999). Unlike other Asian nations, the Philippines has been influenced by several different countries and cultures due to Spanish and American colonization, Japanese occupation during World War II, and trade from China, the Pacific Islands, Portugal, and Australia (Posadas, 1999). Other Asian and Pacific Islander countries were colonized by Great Britain or the Netherlands; the Philippines was the only Asian or Pacific Islander country that was colonized by Spain. In fact, as with countries in Central and South America, the Philippines was colonized by Spain for almost 400 years. As a result, many Filipinos and Filipino Americans have Spanish last names, most are Roman Catholic, and many Filipino words are the same as or variations of Spanish words (Nadal, 2004). For example, *leche* means "milk" in both Tagalog (the first Filipino national language) and in Spanish; "meat" can be translated to *carne* in Spanish and *karne* in Tagalog.

Shortly after the Filipino people fought for their freedom from Spain in 1898, the United States invaded the Philippines, leading to almost 50 years of American colonization. As a result, the Philippines is one of the only Asian countries to have English as its second national language and teach most classes in institutions of higher education in English (Posadas, 1999). Given this fact, most Philippine educational systems have adopted American curricula, although it may not necessarily be culturally appropriate. For example, it is commonplace for Philippine elementary schools to teach that "A is for apple," even though apples do not grow in the Philippines. Moreover, in contemporary times, American television is widespread in the Philippines, leading many Filipinos to be aware of American trends, politics, events, fashions, and celebrities. So even though the Philippines is no longer a U.S. colony, American presence is still pervasive and dominant.

This colonial history has impacted the Filipino and Filipino American people in many ways. Chapter 2 explores how the intersections of indigenous Filipino cultural values with Spanish and American values may lead to identity conflict and societal tensions. Chapter 4 examines how Filipinos and Filipino Americans have developed a colonial mentality, in which many may internalize the values and beliefs of the colonizer (e.g., Spain and the United States) and view the mores of the colonizer as superior to those of the colonized (David, 2008, 2010; David & Okazaki, 2006a,b). Acknowledging that the Philippines has a distinctive history allows one to understand how its culture can be differentiated from other Asian countries and cultures.

FILIPINO AMERICAN HISTORY AND IMMIGRATION

Over the past 400 years, there have been four major immigration patterns or "waves" of Philippine immigration (Kitano & Daniels, 1995; Posadas, 1999). The first wave of Filipino immigrants was in the 16th century; these Filipinos are credited as being the first Asian Americans in the United States. During this time, Spanish galleon ships traveled among the Philippines, Mexico, and Spain, trading goods among the three. In 1587, some Filipino slaves and indentured servants jumped ship and landed in what is now Morro Bay, California (Kitano & Daniels, 1995; Posadas, 1999). Other Filipino slaves and servants abandoned their ships in Mexico and formed larger settlements in the bayous of Louisiana as early as 1763. These individuals consisted mainly of "Manilamen" who escaped the brutality of Spanish galleon ships (Kitano & Daniels, 1995; Posadas, 1999).

The second wave of Filipino immigrants included sponsored students, or *pensionados*. These young people were sponsored by the U.S. government to study in American colleges and universities in the early 1900s (Kitano & Daniels, 1995; Posadas, 1999). These students were recruited after the Philippine-American War in 1899. At the time, the U.S. government viewed the Philippines as its "little brown brother" and wanted to offer them an American education and "civilized" way of life. *Pensionados* were mainly Filipino men who studied at prestigious universities on the East Coast and in the Midwest. Many of these sponsored students succeeded in attaining their college degrees and moved back to the Philippines; however, others never completed their education; did not return to the Philippines for financial reasons, shame, or both; and worked in menial jobs in the United States for the remainder of their lives (Kitano & Daniels, 1995; Posadas, 1999).

The third wave of Filipino immigrants included Filipino laborers and nonsponsored students from the 1910s to 1940s (Kitano & Daniels, 1995; Posadas, 1999). Laborers immigrated to the United States in search of opportunities, in the same ways Chinese and Japanese immigrants did at the time. Nonsponsored students attempted to attain an

American education, as the government-sponsored students did; however, unlike the sponsored students, they came to the United States with their own resources. Many of these nonsponsored students were unable to succeed and instead joined the labor market. They lived primarily on the West Coast: in California (working as grape farmworkers), in Hawaii (working in the sugarcane plantations), or in Alaska (working as fish cannery workers). Most of these laborers and nonsponsored students were men who lived together in small ethnic enclaves. According to some authors, for every 10 to 15 Filipino American men, there was only 1 *Filipina* American woman (Cordova, 1983; Posadas, 1999).

In 1924, the Asian Exclusion Act was enacted, banning Asian laborers from immigrating to the United States. Many argue that anti-Asian sentiment during the time is what drove this act to be passed. During the Great Depression, Chinese, Japanese, and Filipino Americans were viewed as "stealing" jobs from Whites (Takaki, 1998). Consequently, Filipino (and other Asian) immigration was limited until 1952, when the Walter-McCarran Immigration and Naturalization Act repealed the Asian Exclusion Act of 1924 and allowed a token number of Asians to immigrate to the United States with right of citizenship (Kitano & Daniels, 1995; Posadas, 1999). Additionally, during this time many Filipino Americans were recruited by the U.S. government to serve in the U.S. Navy. Although laborers were not permitted, Filipino American naval officers were allowed to immigrate (Posadas, 1999).

In addition to this anti-Asian sentiment during the 1920s to the 1940s (which was further complicated because of the U.S. relationship with Japan and World War II), there existed a specific anti-Filipino sentiment as well. Because there were very few Filipina American women in the United States at this time, Filipino American men searched outside of their race for romantic relationships and companionship, dating White and Mexican women in particular. However, antimiscegenation laws prevented people of different races from marrying (Posadas, 1999; Takaki, 1998). Chapter 8 describes the history of antimiscegenation laws, particularly for Filipino Americans, in more detail.

Additionally, many White men viewed Filipino men as sexual competition and "sexual deviants" who were "stealing" White women away from them (Guevarra, 2008; Posadas, 1999; Takaki, 1998). This led to specific anti-Filipino racial discrimination in California, which ranged from the usage of the derogatory term "little brown monkeys" to describe Filipinos (Cordova, 1983) to the initiation of a "Positively No Filipinos Allowed" campaign. Signs with this phrase were displayed prominently on doors of hotels and businesses in California, and many Whites denied Filipino Americans civil rights, public accommodations, and property ownership (Cordova, 1983; Tiongson, Gutierrez, & Gutierrez, 2006).

The Immigration Act of 1965 completely repealed both the Asian Exclusion Act of 1924 and Walter-McCarran Immigration and Naturalization Act of 1952. This led to the final wave of Filipino immigrants, which consisted mainly of professionals. Most of these immigrants were educated in the Philippines and arrived in the United States with their college diplomas. Many were recruited to work as doctors and nurses in hospitals or as engineers in various manufacturing companies. As a result, many immigrants were able to succeed, unlike the previous generations of Filipino American laborers and nonsponsored students. Most of these post-1965 professionals settled on the West Coast (e.g., California and Washington) and Hawaii. However, because of an increased job market, many moved to other regions in the United States, including the East Coast (e.g., New York, New Jersey), the Midwest (e.g., Illinois, Michigan), and the South (e.g., Florida, Texas), settling mainly in suburban areas outside of major metropolitan cities. Chapter 5 describes the history of Filipino American communities in further detail.

Although the post-1965 professionals are viewed as the last official wave of Filipino immigration, other "nonprofessional" Filipino Americans continue to arrive in the United States on a regular basis. One group, which is often invisible in the Filipino American community, is the undocumented immigrants from the Philippines. Undocumented immigrants are often known as *TNTs* (*tago ng tago*), which can be translated as "to keep on hiding" (Montoya, 1997). Because of the poverty in the Philippines, many Filipino citizens search for better opportunities in the United States. Members of the TNTs may be educated or uneducated and have various immigration statuses, including those who enter the country with a legal visa and overstayed their welcome or those who violate the terms of their visa (Montoya, 1997). Many of these undocumented individuals work menial jobs (in which they are paid under

Figure 1.3 Three young Filipino American boys, circa 1982, who were born and raised in the United States
Photo courtesy of Leo and Charity Nadal

the table), even though they may have higher levels of education in the Philippines or advanced skill sets.

Contemporary Filipino American Experiences

Many recent contemporary events involving Filipino Americans have implications for mental health. Although the experience of racism may not be as relevant or pervasive as it may have been in the 1920s to 1940s, racism and racial discrimination still are present in some overt and mostly covert ways. For example, in 1999, Filipino American postal worker Joseph Ileto was killed as a result of a hate crime for "not being White" (Clinton, 2000). The number of hate crimes toward racial minority groups has decreased since the civil rights movement of the 1960s, but this event indicated that racism is still alive and still an issue for Filipino Americans in the United States. Racism also is present in more subtle ways. For instance, in 2007, Filipino Americans lobbied against ABC

16

Studios for airing an episode of the television series *Desperate Housewives* that made derogatory comments about Filipino medical schools (Vergara, 2008). Subtle forms of racism (on individual and societal levels) have been found to have a significant impact on the mental health of people of color, leading to an array of emotional reactions and potential psychological disparities (see Sue & Sue, 2008, for a review). Specifically, Filipino Americans experience an array of everyday discrimination (Alvarez & Juang, 2010; Nadal, 2008c, Nadal, Pituc, Johnston, & Esparrago, 2010) but tend to ignore such discrimination, which may negatively impact their mental health (Alvarez & Juang, 2010).

This history of blatant and subtle racism is important to understanding Filipino American mental health because studies suggest that race-related stress may impact other psychological problems (Harrell, 2000). In fact, it is essential to be familiar with the concept of "transgenerational transmission," which is defined as the historical contexts of racism or discrimination toward a group that are passed from generation to generation (Harrell, 2000). For example, African Americans may continue to feel distressed when thinking about slavery and Japanese Americans may continue to feel distressed when remembering Japanese internment camps during World War II. These feelings may exist despite the fact that both events occurred generations ago. Transgenerational transmission has been described as a type of trauma that is passed across generations and is related to psychological stressors, such as guilt and shame (de Mendelssohn, 2008). Transgenerational transmission may have varying impacts on one's racial/ethnic identity development (see Chapter 3), one's colonial mentality (see Chapter 4), and one's coping mechanisms and views of psychotherapy (see Chapter 9). Accordingly, acknowledging Filipino and Filipino American history with racism and discrimination is an important guide to examining the mental health and contemporary experiences of Filipino Americans. The next section reviews the current demographics of the Filipino American community, which will be helpful in further understanding their experiences in the United States.

FILIPINO AMERICAN DEMOGRAPHICS

There are currently 2.4 million Filipino Americans in the United States, with the majority identifying as "Filipino alone" (1.8 million) and the remainder identifying as "Filipino in combination with another race" (Barnes & Bennett, 2002; Reeves & Bennett, 2004). The Filipino American population has increased threefold between 1980 and 2000, and in the upcoming analyses of the 2010 Census, an even more significant increase will be reported.

Unlike any other Asian American group, Filipinos and Filipino Americans have been placed into several racial and ethnic categories (Nadal, 2004). According to the 2000 U.S. Census, Filipino Americans currently are classified as "Asian American" (Barnes & Bennett, 2002; Reeves & Bennett, 2004). However, according to the U.S. Department of Education, Filipino Americans have been categorized as "Pacific Islanders" (Horn, 1995), while some academics have classified Filipino Americans as "Hispanic" due to the Spanish colonization of the Philippines for 350 years (Trevino, 1987). Moreover, California Senate Bill 1813, which was passed in 1988, has required that all California state personnel surveys or statistical tabulations classify persons of Filipino ancestry as "Filipino" rather than as Asian, Pacific Islander, or Hispanic (Espiritu, 1992). Finally, because Filipino Americans may have a different phenotype, they often are mistaken as belonging to different racial/ethnic groups, including Latino, Pacific Islander, and Arab Americans (Nadal, 2004; Uba, 1994). These experiences (which may be positive, negative, or neutral) may also impact the ways Filipino Americans self-identify.

Being placed in various racial/ethnic categories has many implications for Filipino Americans. First, Filipino Americans may often feel torn regarding which group they belong to because various people identify these groups differently. For example, some may check boxes where they are identified as "Asian," "Pacific Islander," or specifically as "Filipino." Moreover, because of the hierarchies that occur within the Asian American community, many Filipino Americans may not identify with the Asian American racial group and choose to align themselves with Pacific Islanders, choose an "other" box, or identify specifically as "Filipinos" (Nadal, 2004). Finally, because of similar colonial histories and cultural values, some Filipino Americans may even identify as Latino before they identify as Asian or Asian American (Nadal, 2004). In California, some Filipino Americans have never had to identify themselves as anything other than "Filipino" because that state has a specific "Filipino" box. This distinctive conception of race is one that distinguishes Filipino Americans from most other Asian American racial groups, whose members may almost always consider themselves (and be considered by others) to be Asian and not of another racial group.

Although Filipino Americans are spread throughout the United States, more than half are located on the West Coast and Hawaii (U.S. Census Bureau, 2000). Over 25% of Filipino Americans live in Southern California, namely in Los Angeles and San Diego counties (U.S. Census Bureau, 2000), while about 13% of Filipino Americans live in the San Francisco Bay Area. Cities in Southern California with the most populous Filipino American populations include Carson, Cerritos, and West Covina in Los Angeles County; National City and Chula Vista in San Diego County; and San Francisco and Daly City in Northern California (U.S. Census Bureau, 2000). Filipino Americans also have a visible presence in Hawaii, making up 23% of the state population (U.S. Census Bureau, 2000). Other notable Filipino American settlements include Washington (Seattle and Tacoma), New York (Queens), New Jersey (Jersey City), and Illinois (Chicago and surrounding areas).

One may also acknowledge that the immigration and settlement patterns may vary significantly, based on geographic location. For example, individuals on the West Coast and Hawaii have immigrated in a number of ways—as laborers, post-1965 professionals, and students—while most Filipino Americans who immigrated to the East Coast, Midwest, and South arrived mostly as professionals. Although there were also large numbers of post-1965 professionals who immigrated to the West Coast and Hawaii, there have been settlements of Filipino Americans in California and Hawaii since the early 1900s. The differences in history between regions may have an influence on various experiences. For example, it was revealed that 84% of Filipino Americans in New York attained a college education (Asian American Federation of New York, 2004), in comparison to the 43% of Filipino Americans across the United States who attain a college degree (Reeves & Bennett, 2004). One must wonder why individuals in New York (and other regions) are attaining significantly higher levels of education than the general Filipino American population. Perhaps historical racism, immigration patterns, and identity may all have influences in regional differences (Nadal, 2008c).

Most Filipinos are Catholic or Christian, with about 85% being Catholic and an additional 5% to 10% being Protestant Christian (Gall,

1998). Because of this overwhelming Catholic/Christian presence, many Filipino and Catholic/Christian values, beliefs, and traditions are synonymous. A small percentage of Filipinos are Muslim; this group is predominantly from the southern regions of the Philippines (e.g., Mindanao) that are geographically close to other Southeast Asian countries with strong Muslim influences. Because of this majority Catholic culture, a religious hierarchy is created in the Philippines; Catholics are viewed as the norm; Protestant Christians (e.g., Methodists, Mormons, and members of Iglesia ni Cristo) are viewed as secondary; and all others are viewed as deviant or unacceptable. It is important to realize these statistics are based on Filipinos in the Philippines; statistics concerning religion with Filipino Americans are not known because of a lack of disaggregated data. Therefore, these numbers may be different for Filipino Americans in the United States, who may maintain Catholicism or Christianity, who may convert to different religions in the United States (e.g., Buddhism, Judaism, Wiccanism), or who may identify as nonreligious, agnostic, or atheist.

Demographic trends of Filipino Americans tend to be similar to those of other Asian American groups. Like most other Asian Americans, the majority of Filipinos are adults between the ages of 18 to 64 (69.1%), with a median age of 35.5 years (Reeves & Bennett, 2004). Filipino American immigration statuses are similar to those of the general Asian American population: 32.3% are native-born Americans, 41.6% are foreign-born citizens, and 26.1% are foreign-born noncitizens (Reeves & Bennett, 2004). Of the Filipino Americans who immigrated to the United States, there was a fairly equal distribution of the time frame of immigration: 31.3% immigrated prior to 1980, 33.0% immigrated between 1980 and 1990, and 35.6% immigrated after 1990 (Reeves & Bennett, 2004).

Filipino American marriage patterns are similar and dissimilar to those of both the general Asian American and the general American populations (Reeves & Bennett, 2004). Twenty-nine percent of Filipino Americans have never been married (which is similar to the 30% of Asian Americans and 27% of the general U.S. population); however, the Filipino American divorce rate (5.2%) is slightly higher than the general Asian American population (4.2%) but much lower than the general American population (9.7%). Similarly, Filipino American families (and most other Asian American families) are likely to have two parents as the heads of households. For Filipino Americans, 61.7% of families are two-parent households while 61.8% of the general Asian American population and 52.5% of the general American population have two-parent households. Although this smaller divorce rate might be viewed as a positive quality, one must also recognize that Filipino American couples may feel unable to divorce due to religious and cultural stigmas. Therefore, a lower divorce rate may not necessarily imply successful marriages or higher degrees of mental health.

Many other demographics must be identified in order to understand how the experiences of Filipino Americans may be similar or different from those of other Asian Americans. Filipino Americans are more likely than other Asian Americans to speak English very well; Filipino Americans have a rate of 75.9% of English proficiency, compared to the general Asian American population, which has a rate of 60.4% (Reeves & Bennett, 2004). This trend is likely due to the aforementioned prevalence of English in the Philippines, where English is a national language and taught in the school systems. This trait may be viewed as a positive one in that Filipino Americans are likely to be able to communicate effectively in workplaces and schools. However, it is important to notice how American colonialism has impacted Filipino Americans in negative ways, particularly for second-generation Filipino Americans who were never taught to speak Tagalog or other native Filipino languages by their parents.

Another statistic to consider is that Filipina American women are more likely to enter the labor force than Asian American women and the general American female population (Reeves & Bennett, 2004). According to the 2000 U.S. Census, 65% of Filipina American women were in the labor force, as compared to 56.4% of Asian American women and 57.5% of the general American female population. It is likely that these higher labor force rates for Filipina American women are influenced by gender roles and other cultural values. Unlike some other Asian American groups, in which women are not as encouraged as men in pursuing higher levels of education or traditional male fields, Filipina American women are equally encouraged as men to achieve. Chapters 2 and 7 explore gender roles and cultural values more in depth.

Additionally, Filipino Americans have the lowest poverty rate out of all Asian American groups and significantly lower than the general American population. Filipino Americans had a poverty rate of 6.3% as compared to the general Asian American poverty rate of 12.6% and the general American average poverty rate of 12.4% (Reeves & Bennett, 2004). One must recognize how cultural values may also prevent Filipino Americans from entering poverty or becoming homeless. Chapter 2 examines Filipino American cultural values and family structures that may partially explain why Filipino Americans have a significantly lower poverty level than other Asian American groups.

A few statistics from the U.S. Census are misleading and may need further analysis. It was discovered that 43.8% of Filipino Americans have attained a college degree, in comparison to 44.1% of the general Asian American population and 24.4% of the general American population. Although one may view this as a positive quality, one must recognize both that a majority of Filipino Americans are immigrants who arrived in the United States with a college degree from the Philippines and that second-generation Filipino Americans achieve a college degree at about half the rate as Filipino immigrants (U.S. Census Bureau, 1994). Additionally, while 22% of second-generation Filipino Americans attain college degrees, 51% of native-born Chinese Americans, 36.5% of native-born Korean Americans, and 34% of native-born Japanese Americans complete their degrees. Although all of these ethnic groups likely have parents who were post-1965 "professional" immigrants, second-generation Filipino Americans are not achieving at the same rates as East American groups.

Another statistic that is notable is that Filipino Americans have a higher median family income than other Asian American families and general American society. Filipino American families have a median income of $65,189, Asian American families have a median income of $59,324, and the general American family has a median income of $50,046 (Reeves & Bennett, 2004). Again, this statistic may appear to be a very positive quality, but it is misleading and needs to be scrutinized further. Although Filipino Americans have a higher median family income than other Asian American families and the general American public, it is necessary to recognize that in Filipino American families, an average of 3.41 family members are contributing to the household income, as opposed to the average of 2.59 family members in general American households and the average of 3.08 members in Asian American families. Given this, Filipino Americans average about $19,117 per person contributing to the family income, as compared to $19,322 per general American person and $19,266 per Asian American person. Moreover, further analysis reveals full-time Filipino American male workers make significantly less money than both Asian American male and general American male populations. Filipino American men who work full time earn an average of $35,560; the average American man earns an average of $37,057, and other Asian American men earn an average of $40,650. Chapter 6 discusses how racism and other factors may influence issues such as educational attainment, income, and socioeconomic status.

In examining these statistics, one can recognize that there are some positive and negative trends in the Filipino American community. In some regards, Filipino Americans may appear to fit the traits of the "model minority." They appear to have a higher family income, to have higher educational attainment, and to have more of a presence in the work-place. Women may enter the workplace more than other groups, Filipino Americans may have a lower poverty rate, and Filipino Americans may speak English more competently than members of other Asian American groups. However, looked at more deeply, Filipino Americans face several negative outcomes: For example, they may make less money than other Asian Americans and the general population, and second-generation Filipino Americans may have lower levels of education than East Asian Americans. Given these facts, one must wonder why Filipino Americans may not be achieving as well (financially or educationally) as their East Asian American counterparts. Additionally, one might wonder how experiences with race, differences in cultural values and histories, and issues concerning identity may impact mental health experiences.

MENTAL HEALTH EXPERIENCES OF FILIPINO AMERICANS

Very few studies focus on the mental health of Filipino Americans (David & Okazaki, 2006a; Nadal, 2004; Tompar-Tiu & Sustento-Seneriches, 1995). In fact, most studies on Filipino mental health involve Filipinos in the Philippines (Nadal, 2004). Moreover, many of the psychology studies regarding Filipino Americans involve eth-nic identity and may not include information about psychopathologies or psychological disorders. This section provides a brief overview of the small number of mental health studies involving Filipino Americans. Chapter 9 presents a complete review of Filipino American mental health and psychological disorders.

A few empirical studies examine depression in the Filipino American community. According to one study that investigated the prevalence of depression with Filipino Americans (both immigrants and second-generation individuals), 27% of the community sample had a major depressive episode or clinical depression of varying severity; this rate is significantly higher than that of the general U.S. population, which is usually reported at 10% to 20% (Tompar-Tiu & Sustento-Seneriches, 1995). Other studies found colonial mentality to be positively correlated with depression (David, 2008) and negatively correlated with self-esteem (David & Okazaki, 2006b). In other words, a Filipino American who internalizes Spanish and American values and beliefs as being the norm or superior is more likely to be depressed or feel low self-esteem (see Chapter 4 for a full review of colonial mentality and mental health). Finally, a study of Filipino American participants reveals racial/ethnic discrimination over a lifetime to be associated with increased levels of depressive symptoms (Mossakowski, 2003). This same study found that ethnic identity buffers the stress of racial/ethnic discrimination, suggesting that individuals with higher levels of ethnic identity will have the ability to manage their stress and overcome depressive symptoms.

Some authors have explored the prevalence of alcohol, tobacco, and substance use in the Filipino American community, purporting that Filipino Americans (particularly youth) may have higher incidences of use than other East Asian American groups (see Chapter 6 for a review). For example, one study found that Filipino American men smoke tobacco more than the general population (California Asian Pacific Islander Joint Legislative Caucus [CAPIJLC], 2009). Another study reported that Filipino Americans were the largest "abstainers" from alcohol among all Asian American groups; however, Filipino Americans drank for pathological reasons significantly more than any other group (Johnson, Schwitters, Wilson, Nagoshi, & McClearn, 1985). Given this, perhaps there may be a correlation between mental health and substance use among Filipino Americans. Although Filipino Americans may not be seeking help for their problems, they may be turning to substance use (e.g., drinking, tobacco, or other drugs) as a way of coping with their life stressors.

Additionally, while there are few studies that concentrate specifically on Filipino American mental health, there are some statistics on Filipino American physical health that may have implications for psychological well-being. For example, some studies have indicated Filipino American men and women have a higher prevalence of hypertension in comparison to White Americans (Ryan et al., 2000) and other Asian American sub-groups (Klatsky, Tekawa, & Armstrong, 1996). In fact, next to African Americans, Filipino Americans have been found to have the second highest prevalence of hypertension out of all ethnic groups (Stavig, Igra, & Leonard, 1988). Given that chronic stress and faulty coping reactions to stress are likely causes of high blood pressure (Sparrenberger et al., 2009), one must wonder if psychological distress (and inability to cope with such stress) may lead to health problems for Filipino Americans. Moreover, while there has been some research that indicates that racism may be a cause for cardiovascular problems in African Americans (see Wyatt, Williams, Henderson, Walker, & Winters, 2003), further research may be beneficial to understand the impacts of racism on the health disparities in the Filipino American community. For example, one study found that Filipino Americans' perceptions of unfair treatment may be associated with increased illness (Gee et al., 2006).

There are other health disparities that have been found to be most prevalent in the Filipino American community. For example, according to the recent State of Asian American, Native Hawaiian and Pacific Islander Health in California Report, among Asian Americans, Filipinos have the highest proportion (46%) of overweight or obese adults and 30% of Filipino American youth were listed as overweight (CAPIJLC, 2009). The same report also found that Filipino Americans have higher rates of diabetes than the general population, despite having a generally younger population. Other studies have also found that Filipino Americans have significantly higher rates of diabetes than Whites (Araneta, Wingard, & Barrett-Connor, 2002) and that Filipinas from lower socioeconomic statuses tend to be at risk for diabetes as well (Langenberg, Araneta, Bergstro, Marmot, & Barrett-Connor, 2007). Future research can examine whether discrimination and other stressors may influence other Filipino American health disparities (e.g., diabetes, cardiovascular disease, and obesity), but also other unhealthy behaviors, particularly alcohol and substance use.

Some studies compare Filipino American children with other White or Asian American children and suggest health disparities. A meta-analysis of scholarly articles through the medical database, *Medline* found that Filipino American children may experience a range of health problems including gestational diabetes, higher rates of neonatal mortality and low birth weight, and malnutrition in young children. Moreover, it was found that Filipino American children in general tend to be more overweight, physically inactive, and less physically fit, and tend to have higher rates of substance abuse (Javier, Huffman, & Mendoza, 2007). Again, future research may examine potential cultural and societal variables that may influence these disparities in order to prevent these health problems in children.

The lack of research on or knowledge about Filipino American mental health may be due to the underutilization of mental health services by Filipino Americans and other Asian American groups (Uba, 1994). As mentioned, Asian Americans may not seek mental health services due to cultural stigmas; therefore, underutilization of treatment may not indicate positive mental health. In fact, some authors have indicated that Filipino Americans may seek mental health services even less than other Asian American groups (see David, 2010, for a review). Thus, although there is a dearth of knowledge of Asian Americans' mental health help-seeking behaviors, even less is known about Filipino Americans' experiences with mental health treatment.

The lack of research may be due to the limited number of Filipino and Filipino American psychologists or academics or others who are interested in Filipino American issues. In fact, preliminary data from a national study of Filipino American academics found that there are fewer than 100 Filipino American tenured or tenure-track professors in the social sciences, education, or humanities (D. C. Maramba, personal communication, August 30, 2010). As noted, most research on Asian Americans tends to homogenize the group or focus specifically on East Asian Americans. Therefore, because few Filipino Americans (or other marginalized Asian Americans) are in academia, there may be few individuals who advocate for their mental health. Nonetheless, whatever the reason for the dearth of research, it is crucial for psychologists, educators, and other practitioners to provide ethical and multicultural services for their clients. Hence, this book aims to serve as a guide to working with Filipino American individuals.

FILIPINO PSYCHOLOGY

It is imperative to review the psychological literature on Filipinos in the Philippines in order to understand Filipino Americans in the United States. Extensive studies in the field of Filipino psychology, or *sikolohi-yang Pilipino*, examine how cultural values may influence Filipino psyche and personality development (e.g., Church, 1986; Church & Katigbak, 2002; Enriquez, 1982, 2004). Filipino psychology examines "traditional" Western psychology from a Filipino perspective. For example, Filipino psychology experts describe various personality patterns and development that exist in addition to those traditionally taught by Western psychologists, such as Freud, Erickson, and Wundt (Church, 1986). Therefore, when providing psychological services for Filipino individuals, psychologists and other practitioners may be able to incorporate cultural values into their case conceptualizations as a way of understanding clients' presenting problems and personality development from a cultural perspective.

Filipino psychology also incorporates Western psychological practices with indigenous healing and religious connotations (Enriquez, 2004). For example, although traditional Western psychology might view psychotherapy as the most effective form of treatment, Filipino psychology may regularly include spiritual and religious practices (e.g., praying, meditating) as well as indigenous methods (e.g., consulting with a shaman or "faith healer"). Religious, spiritual, and indigenous considerations, which might be viewed as pathological in Western practice, may be incorporated into treatment. For example, if Filipino individuals complain someone has "put a curse" on them, a Western counselor or clinician might view these individuals as delusional or schizophrenic; however, according to Filipino psychology, these individuals might be viewed as "normal" persons with spiritual beliefs.

Some of the major concepts of Filipino psychology will be provided when discussing Filipino American cultural values and family dynamics (Chapter 2), Filipino American group and community dynamics

(Chapter 5), and culturally competent counseling techniques for Filipino Americans (Chapter 9). Although these concepts can provide a context and can be applicable, the experiences of Filipino Americans are markedly different from Filipinos in the Philippines, in that they live in a country where they are the minority, they interact with individuals of other racial/ethnic groups in their everyday lives, they are exposed to and develop American cultural values more directly, and they experience racism and discrimination that Filipinos in the Philippines might not.

Similarly, concepts from Asian American psychology (see Tewari & Alvarez, 2008; Uba, 1994) might provide helpful insights into understanding Filipino Americans. However, the experiences of Filipino Americans are different in a number of ways. Because of differences in cultural values and colonial history, Filipino Americans may cope with problems differently and may have different presenting problems within their families and in groups. Moreover, because Filipino Americans have a distinctive experience with race (in that they are placed into several categories and mistaken as several racial groups), they may experience racial discrimination differently from other Asian American groups (Nadal, 2008c). Also, the varying experiences of Filipino Americans with educational achievement and socioeconomic status may also lead to various mental health experiences that may be dissimilar from those of other Asian American groups.

Because of the gaps in Filipino psychology and Asian American psychology, this book advocates for the creation and implementation of Filipino American psychology. Chapter 2 examines how Filipino Americans may possess cultural values that are different from those of Asian Americans in the United States. Chapter 3 reveals how Filipino Americans may experience a unique racial and ethnic identity development. Chapter 4 discusses how colonial mentality impacts Filipino Americans in unique ways. Chapter 5 discusses the distinctive dynamics that occur within Filipino American groups and communities, while Chapter 6 explains how Filipino Americans may experience difficulties with educational attainment, HIV/AIDS, and teen and out-of-wedlock pregnancy—all of which are not as pervasive in the Asian American community. Chapters 7 and 8 discuss subgroups of Filipino Americans and how the intersections of identities (e.g., gender, sexual orientation, multiracial/multiethnic identity) may have an impact on one's Filipino American experience. Finally, Chapter 9 shares culturally competent counseling techniques to be utilized when working with Filipino American individuals and groups.

DISCUSSION QUESTIONS

1. Why do you think that race is seen as a "Black or White" issue? How can race be more inclusive of other groups?
2. What are your cognitive and emotional reactions in learning about the history of racism with Asian Americans and Filipino Americans?
3. When you think about Filipino Americans, what are the first images or stereotypes that come to mind? Where did you learn about these images or stereotypes?
4. What racial group do you think that Filipino Americans belong to? Explain your answer.
5. In what ways are Filipino Americans similar to or different from Filipinos in the Philippines?
6. In what ways are Filipino Americans similar to or different from Asian Americans?

SUMMARY

This chapter introduced the history of race relations in the United States and how race is often viewed as a Black and White issue, which leads other racial/ethnic groups to become invisible or ignored. The chapter introduced the history and experiences of Asian Americans, discussing various immigration patterns, experiences with racism, and previous literature on mental health experiences. It also presents the history and experiences of Filipino Americans, explaining how Filipino Americans have a distinct history, cultural values, demographics, and contemporary experiences in the United States. Finally, the chapter explains the dearth of literature on mental health experiences of Filipino Americans in order to provide a context for the purpose of the book.

ACTIVITY 1: SELF-REFLECTION

The purpose of this activity is to learn more about Filipino American history and how it may impact individual mental health. Read the next poem regarding Filipino American historical and contemporary events. The poem's title, "Ikaw," is the Tagalog word for "you." The poem was originally performed in 2001. Appendix A includes historical events that correspond to each line of the poem.

Ikaw
You called me a *negrito* when you invaded my country.
You called me a savage when you enslaved my people.
You called me a monkey when I came to your country.
You called me a rapist and won an award.

You spat on my brothers for courting your women.
You beat on my sisters for not giving it up.
You lynched and you killed and you never said sorry.
You just put us on a ship and sent us back home.

You taught me Columbus discovered America.
You taught me Magellan discovered my land.
You taught me Cesar Chavez was the only farmworker.
You taught me MacArthur said he'd return.

You promised my *Lolo* you'd give him his benefits
for the war he fought for your damn country.
You forgot the hundreds of thousands of *pinoys* and
pinays that died in that war.
You forget the 5.5 pinoy vets that die each day.
Bataan won't be remembered, but the Alamo will.
Philip Vera Cruz won't be remembered, but Rosa Parks will.
Joseph Ileto won't be remembered, but Matthew Shepard will.

A hundred years ago
You kidnapped my people and took them to your country

You locked them in cages at the St. Louis Fair.
You put them on display with the rest of the animals.
"Come look at the Filipino monkeys"
That's what you said.

Eighty years ago
You killed my brother Fermin Tobera
to teach us a lesson that this was your country.
You burnt down our houses and tied us against trees.
You beat my brown ass and you left me for dead.
"Positively No Filipinos Allowed"
"Go home, monkey!"
That's what you said.
But you didn't mind paying me
one dollar
for fifteen hours
of work in the sun.

Sixty years ago
You put us to war, the second of the world.
You made my people fight in our native land,
while your people were safe at home.
Thousands of my people died in bloodshed
But you're the ones who get recognized.
You're the ones who won that war.
But what about my Lolo who lives no more?
Well, he got an American flag at his funeral
so what am I complaining for?

Forty years ago
You told my parents to come here
that they would have a better life.
But you didn't tell them they'd get spit on.
You didn't tell them they weren't allowed in your neigh-
borhoods or schools.
You didn't tell them that things weren't as they seemed.
America was just a dream.
"Life can be bright in America,
if you can fight in America.

31

Life is all right in American,
if you're a White in America."

Twenty years ago
you told me that life was better.
Better than they used to be.
But then you called me a dogeater.
Monkey.
Oriental.
Asian Nigger.
Chink.
Flip.
Fob.
You told me my skin was dirty and I'd never be like you.
You told that I was ugly because I didn't look like you.

Ten years ago
You killed my brother
Joseph Ileto
near the City of Angels
because he was brown.
You didn't make a movie, not even a television special.
Tomorrow, you won't even remember his name.

Today.
You tell me not to be angry.
You tell me that things are better than before.
You ask "Why can't we all just get along?"
But when I answer, you don't understand.
In fact, you weren't even listening.

You can't call me American because you know you'll never
mean it.
You can't tell me I'm foreign because I know I was
born here.
You can't tell me I'm yellow because I know that I'm
brown.
You can't tell me I'm ugly because I know that I'm
beautiful.

You can't tell me I'm different because I know I'm the
norm.
You can't tell me I'm invisible because I know that I am
not alone.

2.4 million
2.4 million
2.4 million *pinoys* and *pinays* in my barkada now.

Today
Tomorrow
You will remember my name.
Tomorrow
And tomorrow
You will say sorry.

Kevin Nadal

pinoys: a term used to describe Filipino Americans, usually as a term of
    endearment or a political identifier
pinays: the female counterpart to pinoy

QUESTIONS FOR DISCUSSION

1. Describe your cognitive and emotional reactions to the poem.
2. How do you feel about the historical events that are referred to in the poem?
3. Have you been educated about these historical events before? How do you feel about this?
4. For Filipino Americans: How does Filipino American history affect your life today?
5. For Filipinos and non-Filipinos: How do you think Filipino American history affects society today?

CHAPTER TWO

Filipino and Filipino American Cultural Values

Figure 2.1 *Three generations in a typical Filipino American family*
Photo Courtesy of Kristine Magat

CASE SYNOPSES

The Ramos family is a working-class Filipino American family that consists of Jorge (father), 52; Sheila (mother), 51; Ron (son), 20; and Annalisa (daughter), 18. Both children are currently living at home and are students at the local university. Lately the family has been having many problems because Jorge and Sheila claim that they "have no control" over their children. They feel that Ron has been performing poorly in school and getting into trouble with his *barkada* (group of friends), while Annalisa has been spending too much time with her boyfriend. The family has been arguing frequently with one another, leading to physical and emotional distance and a lack of communication among all of the family members.

Evelyn is a 34-year-old Filipina American woman who recently immigrated to the United States. She is a traveling nurse who was contracted to work at a pediatrics unit at a U.S. hospital. Although she enjoys her job and is having little difficulty with speaking English, she is having trouble making friends and relating to her American coworkers. She wants to stay in the United States because of her career and financial opportunities, but she is worried that she will never fully feel "at home."

INTRODUCTION

Because the Philippines had been colonized by Spain and the United States over a span of almost five centuries, there is a spectrum of cultural values that Filipinos and Filipino Americans maintain. These include:

- Indigenous Filipino cultural values that existed prior to colonial rule. These are the beliefs and traditions that were followed by Filipino societies before the Spanish invaded the Philippines in 1521.
- Influences that occurred as a result of Spanish colonialism. These are the consequences of 377 years of Spanish dominance and include the introduction of new gender role norms and the Catholic religion.
- Impacts of American colonialism, which were acquired during American colonization from 1899 to 1946 and continue today as a result of American globalization. Some of these values include an appreciation for U.S. education and an emphasis on competition and individualism instead of collectivism.

Because of all of these influences, present-day Filipino culture can be defined as a hybrid of indigenous and colonial values, beliefs, customs, and traditions.

The development of cultural values is even more complex for Filipino Americans (Filipinos who live in the United States). Filipinos who immigrate to the United States undergo many processes of negotiating their cultural identity. Through acculturation, assimilation, or biculturalism, individuals decide whether to adopt the cultural values, beliefs, and behaviors of the dominant group (American) or whether to maintain the cultural values of their own ethnic group (Filipino). For second-generation Filipino Americans (those born and raised in the United States), a similar process may occur, in which they learn to negotiate the culture that is taught in their families and communities (Filipino) with the culture that they experience in the dominant society (American).

This chapter discusses various Filipino American cultural values—those influenced by Spain and by the United States, and those that existed prior to colonial domination. This chapter considers how these values may align with each other and how they may conflict. This chapter also examines the processes by which Filipino Americans learn to balance various cultural identities in their everyday lives while also explaining why and how some Filipino Americans acculturate, assimilate, or become bicultural. By investigating all of these experiences, one will have the opportunity to learn about the influences of culture on personality development, self-esteem, mental health, and other Filipino American issues that are discussed in subsequent chapters.

FILIPINO CULTURAL VALUES

In order to fully comprehend the experiences of Filipino Americans, it is necessary to explore Philippine history and the values that existed prior to colonial dominance. Many authors have mentioned that indigenous Philippine society was much different than it is today. Although the indigenous population may not have considered themselves Filipinos hundreds of years ago (since it was not until they were colonized by King Philip of Spain that were labeled together as a united ethnic group), the populations of the various islands that are now the Philippines were similar in many ways.

For one thing, the culture of the indigenous population of the Philippines was very collectivistic, consisting of independent *barangays* (small villages) that managed their own political, social, and economic systems under the leadership of *datus* (tribal rulers; Constantino, 1975). These structures were significantly different from the Spanish-influenced centralized government system, in which a chief authoritative force held significant power over large regions. For another thing, precolonial Philippines was a very gender-neutral country, in which women and men were respected equally. Women were encouraged to be educated and to participate in politics, and they had power in family decision-making processes and economic management (Mananzan, 2003). This differs from the gender roles that were established during Spanish colonial rule, in which women were objectified, mistreated, disempowered, and given much less respect. Finally, the mentalities, worldviews, and value systems of precolonial Filipinos were significantly different from those of postcolonial Filipinos. Precolonial Filipinos were less likely to denigrate themselves, their culture, or their bodies, and were less likely to compare themselves negatively to outside cultures (whom they had limited contact). This concept conflicts with postcolonial culture, in which many Filipinos have developed a colonial mentality and denigrate themselves and their Filipino cultural values while accepting and glorifying the values of the colonizer (David & Okazaki, 2006a).

Despite these various influences of colonization, many indigenous Filipino values survived even after Spanish and American control. In the study of *Sikolohiyang Pilipino* (Filipino psychology), four main values are identified as fundamental to Filipino individuals, families, and society (Enriquez, 1982, 1997). These values include:

1. *Kapwa* (fellow being)
2. *Utang ng loob* (debt of reciprocity)
3. *Hiya* (shame)
4. *Pakikasama* (social acceptance)

Kapwa is defined as the core construct of Filipino psychology, in which all individuals feel a sense of togetherness or connectedness to each other. *Kapwa* is similar to the American definition of collectivism, which stresses human interdependence and the importance of the greater community. However, it is specific to Filipinos in that it implies a personal and emotional bond between individuals and groups (particularly between other Filipinos), regardless of previous relationships. *Kapwa* implies that Filipinos will feel intrinsically connected to each other interpersonally, spiritually, and emotionally; this connection may be with their family members, friends, acquaintances, or even

Filipino strangers whom they do not know. For example, many Filipino Americans will feel connected when meeting other Filipino Americans in public places; they may approach each other, ask "Are you Filipino?" and then enjoy a warm conversation with each other about their family history in the Philippines and personal lives. For second- and third-generation Filipino Americans, *kapwa* can be as simple as individuals trying to figure out how new friends are somehow related to them. For example, on social networking Web sites like Facebook or MySpace, many Filipino Americans may notice that they are connected in so many ways to so many different Filipino Americans.

Utang ng loob translates to debt (or norm) of reciprocity; this means that individuals are generous with each other and are expected to return favors or compensate their peers or neighbors in some way, whether it was asked or needed. For example, if a Filipino borrows money from another or babysits a neighbor's child, both parties expect that there will be remuneration for the act of kindness, even if there is not a verbal communication or agreement. This reciprocity demonstrates that Filipinos expect to rely on one another in any situation and hope that by being charitable to others, others will help them in their times of need. Additionally, because of *utang ng loob*, it is expected family members always will put other family members before themselves. Parents expect their children to be grateful and respectful toward them, while children realize that they should always care for, respect, and honor their parents' needs before their own. *Utang ng loob* can be exemplified by Filipino American domestic workers who send money back home to their families in the Philippines, even though they have barely enough for themselves in the United States.

Hiya can be defined as shame or a loss of propriety; it is governed by the notion that the goal of the individual is to represent oneself or one's family in the most honorable way. The individual wants to avoid shame, by acting respectably in the community, by being successful and making one's family proud, and by avoiding anything that would bring embarrassment to the family. This value can drive a Filipino American to success; she or he wants to (and knows she or he must) succeed, in order to please the family and represent the family well in the community. However, *hiya* often can lead to stigma and an inability to recognize and deal with problems in one's life or family. For example, an individual who is depressed or anxious may avoid going to therapy because of the fear of bringing *hiya* (shame) to the family. Another example may include a college student who is afraid to tell her family that she was placed on academic probation, for fear of disappointing or embarrassing them. It is common for these individuals to avoid telling their families and instead do everything possible to fix their problems, without their families ever finding out the truth.

Finally, the fourth major Filipino value, *pakikasama*, can be translated as social acceptance or conformity. With this value, Filipinos attempt to get along well with their peers, without making waves or causing conflict; the goal of Filipinos is to be socially accepted and celebrated, oftentimes without standing up for themselves or being different. For example, many Filipinos would rather remain in harmony with their peers than vocalize any disagreements or dissentions in a group. *Pakikasama* also means that Filipino Americans will more likely choose what is best for the collective than for the individual, in order to please everyone. For example, Filipino Americans often rearrange their schedules to accommodate other family members; if a family member was hosting a birthday party on the same day as a concert or sporting event someone wanted to attend, the individual might cancel the tickets in order to be with family and avoid conflict that may arise if she or he was absent from the family function.

Many other secondary Filipino values are important to understanding Filipino personality development. *Bahala na* (fatalistic passiveness) is best translated as "Leave it up to God." Individuals who subscribe to a *bahala na* attitude tend to live without worry, have a low *locus of control*, and accept things as they are. For example, some Filipinos will not go to the doctor because they believe if they were meant to get sick, that is "how God wanted it" (Nadal & Monzones, 2010). It is unclear whether this value was developed prior to Spanish colonization, but it is apparent that many Filipinos today can utilize the *bahala na* value in a Catholic context. *Lakas ng loob* (inner strength) is described as being courageous in the midst of problems and uncertainties. In these situations, these individuals may have a higher locus of control, in that they believe that by being resilient they can overcome struggle. *Lakas ng loob* can be best demonstrated through Filipino "People Power" protests in which groups found the strength to stand up for what they believed in (Macapagal, 2003). *Bahala na* and *lakas ng loob* represent opposite Filipino worldviews. On the one hand, Filipinos can be passive and defeatist, believing they have little control in their lives. On the other hand, Filipinos can be active and optimistic, believing that they can empower themselves and make changes in their lives.

Other Filipino cultural ways of being and beliefs that distinguish them from other ethnic groups. For example, Filipinos pride themselves on their close family ties. Because of *kapwa* (fellow being) and *utang ng loob* (debt of reciprocity), it is expected that Filipinos place their families first before anyone else. Unique to Filipinos is the fact that they usually consider their "immediate families" to consist of parents, siblings, grandparents, uncles, aunts, and cousins; many of these family members may live under the same roof and are never asked or persuaded to move out. Often it is expected that all these family members will be consulted for major decisions, regardless of the closeness of their blood relation (Nadal & Monzones, 2010). Additionally, Filipinos place emphasis on family relations, no matter how closely related individuals actually are. For example, a "third" or "fourth" cousin is still considered a "close" cousin in Filipino culture, whereas this may not be the case with other ethnic groups. Family friends who have no blood relations are also referred to as family members. For instance, it is expected for children to call their parents' friends, coworkers, neighbors, or former classmates *tito* (uncle) or *tita* (auntie), regardless of their actual lack of blood relationship. It is also common for Filipino Americans to have several *ninongs* (male godparents) and *ninangs* (female godparents). These individuals are expected to serve as second parents. Unlike other Catholic or Christian ethnic groups, Filipino Americans tend to have anywhere from 4 to 10 godparents each. Finally, in Filipino weddings, it is expected that as many family members will be involved as possible; thus, there are many roles that may be specific to Filipino weddings that are not included in a traditional American wedding. These include primary sponsors (i.e., "godparents" to the couple), second sponsors (e.g., people to light a unity candle or carry a veil and cord for the couple), junior bridesmaids and groomsmen (e.g., adolescents who are too old to be flower girls or ring bearers and too young to be bridesmaids or groomsmen), and a coin bearer (in addition to the numerous flower girls and ring bearers).

Filipinos hold an utmost respect for elders, both blood relatives and those in the community. Elders are considered revered family members, with vast wisdom and decision-making influence. Elders are encouraged to stay in the family homes indefinitely, and this practice is not to be seen as a burden. It is rare to find elderly Filipino Americans in retirement homes, as it is expected that someone in the family will take care of them. Additionally, elders are often encouraged to spend time with their grandchildren as a way to form bonds across generations while also imparting knowledge and affection. Often, third-generation Filipino Americans (i.e., children whose grandparents immigrated to the United States) are taught Tagalog or native languages from their grandparents, even if their own parents do not speak fluently themselves.

In general, Filipinos respect anyone who is older than they are. Within Filipino families, many terms of endearment are used to signify respect for anyone who is older. The word *"po"* is added at the end of sentences as a sign of respect for those who are older. For example, a child or teenager would say *"Salamat po"* (or "Thank you") to an adult but may only say *"Salamat"* to a peer. Additionally, many affectionate titles are given to people who are older. For example, depending on one's dialect, many Filipino families will use the words *kuya* (big brother), *ate* (big sister), *manong* (big brother), or *manang* (big sister) as a sign of respect. Such terms would be used not only for one's actual sibling but also with older cousins, siblings-in-law, or even older friends. Often, people utilize these terms along with the person's first name as a way of deciphering between the many "kuyas" or "ates" they have in their life (e.g., "Kuya Jay" or "Ate Gail").

Finally, another common trait of Filipinos is their hospitality. As a result of *utang ng loob* (debt of reciprocity) and *kapwa* (fellow being), Filipinos are known to be generous to others. When a family member or friend unexpectedly visits someone's home, it is likely that the host will cook a quick meal and offer the person something to eat. If an individual does not have a place to stay, it is commonplace for a Filipino to offer her or his home to that individual. Along with this hospitality, it is common for Filipinos to go out of their way for others (especially for other Filipinos), even when they are not asked. For example, if a Filipino meets a new Filipino coworker or classmate, it would be common for that individual to invite the new person to lunch and become her or his mentor or guide. For this reason, Filipinos and Filipino Americans often search for other Filipinos and Filipino Americans for mentorship and support in various academic and workplace settings (Nadal, Pituc, et al., 2010).

It is important to recognize that many of these Filipino values emphasize collectivism and a sense of community. In fact, *bayanihan* (community) is a word that is often used to describe the ability for Filipinos and Filipino Americans to work together for a common good. It is also evident that precolonial Filipinos had values that were similar to those of many non-Western societies (e.g., Buddhist teachings in China, Hindu traditions in India, indigenous customs in the Pacific Islands, or Native American traditions in North America), demonstrating how colonization by Europe and the United States has led to cultural shifts in many countries and societies. And while it is clear that Filipinos today hold many of these indigenous values that existed before Spanish rule, it is important to understand how years of colonialism may have impacted the current manifestation of these values. The next section examines the influences of Spain and Spanish colonization from 1521 to 1898.

INFLUENCES OF SPANISH CULTURAL VALUES

Colonization of the Philippines by the Spanish beginning in 1521 had three major influences on the Filipino people. The most prominent Spanish influence was the introduction of Roman Catholicism to the Philippines. This had a major impact on the country, as the Philippines became the only Asian country that to this day is predominantly Roman Catholic or Christian. In fact, recent reports indicate that 85% of the Philippine population is Catholic (Gall, 1998). Spanish colonization also had an influence on gender, with a greater emphasis being placed on gender role differences between men and women, when precolonial Philippines was a gender-neutral society. Last, Spanish rule has also led to the development of a colonial mentality, which is discussed at length in Chapter 4. Here we consider ways in which Spanish influences affect religion and gender roles as well as other values that have had a lasting impact on Filipino culture.

Religion

Prior to colonial rule, many Filipinos were Muslim, atheist, animistic, or polytheistic (Constantino, 1975). However, as a result of nearly 400 years of Spanish colonization, a majority of the Philippine people are now Catholics. As a result, there would be many influences and changes in Filipino culture, including a push for religious conservatism; an integration of church and state; and an influence on Filipino customs, behaviors, and traditions. For example, religious conservatism is pervasive in the Philippines, as demonstrated through the intense advocacy for abstinence instead of a push for safer sex practices. Although illegal sex work exists in the country, as well as an increase of HIV/AIDS, the government continues to ignore these facts and prevent the promotion of safe sex practices due to religious conservatism (Human Rights Watch, 2004). Because of the Spanish dominance, a symbolic integration of church and state has also occurred in the Philippines. Government and religious practices often have been interchangeable, as demonstrated in the facts that Spanish friars governed the Philippines during colonial rule and Catholic churches were constructed as the centerpieces of Filipino towns. Although separation of church and state was added to the Philippine constitution in 1987, religion still influences the nation today (e.g., divorce remains illegal).

Catholicism has had a major impact on Filipino customs, behaviors, and traditions. It is common for Filipinos (specifically those in smaller, provincial towns) to attend church every morning and to pray the rosary each night. Many Filipinos have patron saints that they model themselves after and pray to regularly. In fact, Filipino homes contain various statues of Jesus Christ, the Virgin Mary (Jesus' mother), and other saints. These altars might also include photographs of deceased loved ones as well as "offerings" to God (e.g., food, drinks, or flowers). Finally, Filipino festivals and community events may have a highly Catholic meaning, often honoring Jesus, Mary, and other saints. For example, in the province of Aklan, Philippines, an annual parade/festival called Ati-Atihan celebrates the Santo Niño (Baby Jesus).

Religion has also led to major divides in the Philippines and in Filipino American communities. Although the majority of Filipino Americans identify as Catholic, Filipinos may belong to many other religions, which may lead to religious tensions and hierarchies. Many Filipinos and Filipino Americans belong to other organized Christian religions, including Iglesia ni Cristo (Church of Christ), which is the largest indigenous Christian group that originated in the Philippines (Santiago, 1989). Many Filipinos and Filipino Americans belong to other Protestant religions, including the United Methodist Church, the Baptist Church, and the Presbyterian Church. Additionally, as mentioned in Chapter 1, many Filipinos and Filipino Americans (particularly those originally from the southern regions of the Philippines) are Muslim. Finally, many Filipinos and Filipino Americans may not identify with an organized religion but may be involved in various indigenous, spiritual practices.

Because the Philippines is predominantly Catholic, a hierarchy has arisen based on religion. Catholics are viewed as the dominant group, while Protestants (e.g., members of Iglesia ni Cristo, Methodists, and others) are viewed as secondary; Muslims, nonreligious, and other indigenous persons may be placed at the bottom of the hierarchy. Stereotypes may form about other groups, which may also lead to community divides and hostility. For example, Catholics often stereotype members of Iglesia ni Cristo as being religious radicals; Filipino Christians often stereotype Muslims and nonreligious persons as being uncivilized or unholy. Additionally, because Catholicism is the most dominant group, it is common for individuals to assume that Catholic and Filipino values are synonymous. As a result, counselors and clinicians must take care not to assume that all Filipino Americans are Catholic while recognizing the subtle ways in which religion—Catholic, Protestant, Muslim, or other—may influence values, beliefs, worldviews, family systems, coping mechanisms, and experiences within the Filipino American community.

Gender Roles

As mentioned, Filipino indigenous culture is egalitarian, and women are honored and respected as much as men. However, with the arrival of Spanish values, a *machismo* (male-dominant) culture emerged, and uneven gender roles began to influence Filipino culture. *Machismo*

45

can be defined as the belief in the superiority of males over females. It means men are expected to be strong, are the providers for the family, uphold rigid gender roles, and are likely to possess sexist attitudes toward women. *Machismo* began during Spanish colonial rule, when it was common for Filipina women to be raped and beaten by Spanish friars and government officials (e.g., Rizal, 1997). In contemporary times, *machismo* still may be evident in male attitudes yet may not necessarily reflect the inferiority of women. For example, present-day Filipina women are encouraged to be leaders and pursue academic and career opportunities as much as men (Nadal, 2004). However, Filipino men may still maintain *machismo* gender roles and expectations, in that they insist on being macho, hypermasculine, and prideful when it comes to asking for help or assistance.

In contrast to *machismo* is *marianismo* (female submissiveness), which is a Spanish term that can be defined as the expectation for women to be religious, pure, morally superior to, and spiritually stronger than men. The word is derived from the Virgin Mary (Jesus' mother) and is a major value in Latino and Catholic-influenced countries. *Marianismo* may lead to gender role inequalities in which men are allowed and encouraged to engage in a spectrum of "unholy" activities (e.g., premarital sex, drinking, smoking) while women would be discouraged from or condemned for engaging in such activities. *Marianismo* also implies that women are meant to be selfless and put their families' needs before their own, similar to how the Virgin Mary lived her life.

In examining Spanish gender roles, it is evident that they conflict with the gender expectations that existed in precolonial Filipino culture. In the contemporary Philippines, some indigenous values of gender neutrality have been maintained, in that women are encouraged to be community leaders and hold the "purse strings" in the family (Nadal, 2004). However, many self-images can be learned through gender role norms; for example, men may feel a need to see themselves as masculine providers, while women may feel pressure to be pure or religious. Moreover, certain rules and gender expectations are different for women and men. For example, it is common for adolescent Filipino Americans to be allowed to date earlier or have extended curfews; adolescent Filipina Americans are supervised more closely and are expected to be involved in all aspects of the family's life (Heras,

2007). Finally, dissonant feelings may arise in both individuals and families if a Filipino American does not fulfill gender role expectations. For example, if a Filipina woman becomes pregnant out of wedlock or if a Filipino man is not able to provide for his family, each may experience a guilt or shame that may lead to other mental health problems. The impact of gender roles on mental health is discussed further in Chapter 7.

Additional Spanish Values

Two other major Spanish values may have an influence on Filipino culture. First, there is the notion of *amor propio* (pride), which derives from the Spanish phrase "self-love." This concept involves a sense of self-esteem or self-respect that allows one to be self-congratulatory in times of prosperity and prevents a person from swallowing her or his pride in times of adversity. It might be argued that *amor propio* can negatively impact the previously mentioned Filipino values. For example, while *utang ng loob* (debt of reciprocity) maintains that Filipinos are always generous with each other, *amor propio* can hinder one's ability to ask for help. An example of *amor propio* negatively impacting *pakikasama* (social acceptance) might include an individual who wants to get along well with others but is ostentatious or acts in a superior fashion based on successes and wealth. Second, there is the concept of *personalismo*, a Spanish word for "interpersonal relationships," which is common in Latino and Spanish-influenced countries. This value directly correlates with the preexisting Filipino values of *kapwa* (fellow being), *utang ng loob*, and *pakikasama*. However, the Spanish influence of *personalismo* on Filipino culture is twofold. First, the Philippines is the only Asian culture where individuals prefer close, interpersonal warmness, even among strangers. This is demonstrated in the practice of kissing family, friends, and acquaintances on the cheek in greeting, a practice not common in other Asian cultures. Second, Filipinos are the only Asian people who tend to be more emotionally expressive. According to the literature, East Asian cultures (e.g., Chinese, Japanese, and Korean) are emotionally unexpressive and prefer logical ways of approaching problems; Filipinos, however, prefer emotional expression and closeness with others (Okamura & Agbayani, 1991).

Figure 2.2   A *lola* (grandmother) teaching her granddaughter how to play the piano
Photo courtesy of Julian Tamayo

INFLUENCES OF AMERICAN CULTURAL VALUES

When the United States helped the Philippines defeat Spain in 1898, the Filipinos initially believed the American people wanted to help the Philippines establish independence. However, shortly after the Philippine-American War, the United States colonized the Philippines, and it remained an American colony for almost 50 years. The three major cultural values the United States brought to the Philippines were an emphasis on education, an emphasis on individualism and competition, and a division between those who are Americanized and those who are not. American teachings pervaded Philippine education systems, and English was taught as a prominent language in many secondary schools and in almost all institutions of higher education. In fact, the Philippines is one of the only Asian countries to have English as a second national language, which explains the high English proficiency Filipinos have prior to immigrating to the United States (Nadal & Monzones, 2010). With the influence of American culture

48

came American value sets, such as individualism and competition. As mentioned, the indigenous Philippines was a completely collectivistic culture, but the Americanized Philippines had new hierarchy structures, in which individuals strived to be more successful in order to exceed or surpass their peers. Competition in the community can manifest through vocational or educational attainment, socioeconomic status, property ownership, or prestige in leadership. Finally, American colonization added to the already present colonial mentality that was created by the Spanish prior to 1898. The American contributions to the colonial mentality of Filipinos are discussed in depth in Chapter 4. The next sections focus on the American values of education, individualism, and competition.

Education

It may be well known that many Asian and Asian American families value educational attainment. However, the need for formal educational attainment was not a priority for Filipinos until the U.S. invasion in 1899. Prior to that invasion, the Philippines had its own educational systems, where individuals became skilled at various practical crafts and trades. After the U.S. arrival, there was an increase in educational systems in the Philippines, with education focusing on reading, writing, and mathematics. Many of these schools utilized American teaching techniques, even when they may not have applied to the Philippines. For example, as mentioned, Filipino students to this day may learn that "A is for apple," even though apples cannot be grown in the Philippines due to the climate. However, with the American influences, school enrollment multiplied fivefold, and many Filipinos were encouraged to study abroad in the United States and even Europe. Literacy rates increased to 50% in the 1930s; present-day literacy rates are up to 92% (Central Intelligence Agency, 2008).

Education has also led to several types of discrimination within the Filipino and Filipino American communities. Filipinos who speak the most eloquent English without a Filipino accent commonly are seen as the most prestigious and educated, while others who speak with a Filipino accent are viewed as inferior or uneducated. This fact may lead to a hierarchy in the Filipino and Filipino American communities in which uneducated Filipinos may be resentful of those with education, while those who are educated may feel superior to the uneducated. Additionally, educational attainment may influence cultural identity, in that highly educated Filipinos may attempt to assimilate to American culture and speak without an accent. Although some may view this as a positive—in that the individual is adjusting well into the dominant culture—others may view it as a negative because the individual may possess internalized racism and self-hate about her or his own culture. Because of many immigrants' desires to assimilate, it is common for second-generation Filipino Americans to not speak Tagalog (or their parents' native languages) because their parents wanted them to assimilate to American society and avoid speaking with a Filipino accent.

Individualism and Competition

The American dream can be defined as the opportunity for immigrants to achieve greater financial and material prosperity in the United States. It assumes that such would not have been possible if they stayed in their countries of heritage. Achieving the American dream can be measured by material wealth, financial wealth, career prestige, and education. With the introduction of the American dream to the Philippines during American colonization, Filipinos were taught that they could succeed if they attained higher education. However, with this dream came American values of individualism and competition, where Filipinos were taught (either directly or indirectly) that, in order to succeed, they needed to become self-sufficient and independent from their families. They also learned American ways of competition; in order to be individually successful, they may have to be competitive with others, a value that is not inherently Filipino.

Although present-day Filipino and Filipino American communities are still noticeably collectivistic, there are many ways in which individualism and competition have been integrated into the culture. For example, many Filipinos have become competitive with and hurtful toward each other. This competition can be demonstrated through the common practice of tsismis (gossip) in both the Filipino and Filipino American communities, which has been cited to be a normal part of Filipino communication (Nadal, 2004). Although Filipinos yearn to be socially accepted and to get along well with others, *tsismis* is used as a way of belittling their peers (e.g., if one gossips about others or talks about them negatively behind their backs, it brings others down and makes one feel good about oneself). *Tsismis* is widespread regardless of relationships, in that *tsismis* transpires between family members, between friends, and within the community. It is unclear when *tsismis* first began to be a noticeable trend in the community—it is apparent that it exists in contemporary times, leading to many divisions within Filipino society and the Filipino American community.

An element of competition also is common within Filipino American communities. In the United States, members of many Filipino American organizations often fight for power and authority; sometimes members form break-away organizations if they lose an organizational election. In Filipino American college student organizations, often competition arises among students who want to be the "stars" of Pilipino Cultural Nights or PCNs (Gonzalves, 1997). Finally, in many Filipino American beauty pageants, there are intense competitions to ensure that certain

Figure 2.3 Two Filipino American men of two different generations at a family gathering
Photo courtesy of Ken Paprocki

families win the coveted prize of "queen" or "princess." Although these are seemingly innocuous organizations and situations, they represent impediments to community building that may occur among Filipino Americans. They also speak to the divides that prevent Filipino Americans from community organizing or activism. For example, there are very few Filipino American politicians in the United States; perhaps if Filipinos fully supported Filipino American candidates in the ways other racial or ethnic groups do, there would be more Filipino American representation in the U.S. government. Chapter 5 provides an in-depth look at Filipino American communities and how participating in these communities may lead to psychological stress. The next section reveals ways in which Filipino Americans deal with various cultural values and the processes through which they form their cultural identities.

ACCULTURATION, ASSIMILATION, AND BICULTURALISM

"Acculturation" can be defined as the systematic process where one cultural group comes into contact with another group and experiences changes in attitudes, values, and beliefs as the group adheres to the values of the dominant society (Nadal & Sue, 2009), whereas "assimilation" refers to a process in which members of one cultural group abandon their beliefs, values, and behaviors and fully adopt those of a new host group (Nadal, 2004). For Filipino Americans, the processes of acculturation and assimilation are unique to their individual immigration status and experiences. Filipino American individuals who immigrate to the United States (e.g., first generation and 1.5 generation) experience a change in cultural values, beliefs, habits, and language upon arrival. Although they have learned certain cultural norms and standards in the Philippines, they may adjust to dominant cultural norms and standards in the United States (acculturate), or they may reject their heritage and accept the norms of the dominant group (assimilate). For example, when a first-generation 25-year-old Filipino American immigrates to the United States, she or he can make the decision to fully accept and observe all American practices while rejecting Filipino traditions (assimilation) or can learn to utilize both value sets depending on the situation (acculturation).

Meanwhile, second-generation Filipino Americans (those born and raised in the United States) may experience these processes of assimilating or acculturating differently (Nadal & Sue, 2009). Although second-generation individuals are, by definition, born in the United States, they may be taught by their foreign-born parents certain cultural values, beliefs, and behaviors that are preserved in their homes during childhood. When Filipino American children attend school for the first time, they can adjust to the dominant American cultural norms and standards at school while still practicing Filipino customs and traditions at home (acculturation). They can also choose to accept dominant cultural norms at school and make an effort to stop practicing any cultural heritage behaviors at home (assimilation). For example, an 8-year-old second-generation Filipino American girl might enter school and not participate in class, because her parents taught her to be passive and quiet around authority figures and adults in general. Being compliant with authority figures is something that may be viewed positively in the home, but the child may need to acculturate and be more vocal in school in order to be most successful. Conversely, the child may learn that this American way of actively engaging with adults is a positive behavior and may become more active or loud around all adults, even at home. Many Filipino and Filipino Americans parents may view this behavior as disrespectful and culturally inappropriate.

Because of the conflicting processes of negotiating between acculturation and assimilation, many Filipino Americans experience what is known as "acculturative stress" (Nadal & Sue, 2009). For example, although a Filipino American may be taught Filipino values of being respectful and compliant with all adults regardless of the situation, American values might teach a person to be individualistic, argumentative, verbal, and to always speak one's mind. This is an example of a conflict of wanting to please one's family and cultural group while also wanting to satisfy one's individual needs. In order to balance the two conflicting cultural value sets, many Filipino Americans may learn to be "bicultural," which can be defined as the ability for a member of two cultural groups to maintain beliefs, values, and behaviors of both groups. Although Filipino American family members may pressure individuals to maintain their strong Filipino cultural values over American values, bicultural individuals discover ways to please both parts of their identities. Bicultural Filipino Americans learn to acquire and practice the cultural values and behaviors of the dominant American society while preserving a strong connection with their Filipino identity, family, and community. For example, a bicultural Filipino American individual may learn to be competitive, vocal, and argumentative at work while being respectful, passive, and collectivistic at home.

DISCUSSION QUESTIONS

1. Which values do you think conflict the most with each other? How do you think individuals deal with these conflicting values?
2. Which values do you view as the most positive? Which values do you view as the most negative?
3. Do you think it is better to acculturate, to assimilate, or to be bicultural? Explain your choice.
4. In what ways are Filipino American cultural values similar to those of other Asian groups? To those of other communities of color? To those of White Americans?
5. For Filipino Americans: Of the three influences (indigenous Filipino, Spanish, and American), which values (e.g., *kapwa*, *machismo*) do you practice the most? Which values do you practice the least?

SUMMARY

This chapter discussed the various cultural values that Filipino and Filipino Americans may experience. By examining the cultural norms and values that existed prior to colonial rule, the chapter considered how Filipino Americans were significantly impacted by Spanish and American colonization. Additionally, by exploring these influences, individuals may be able to acknowledge that many of these cultural values conflict and clash with one another. This may lead to different types of stressors, identities, and personality traits for Filipino American individuals. Finally, by reviewing the processes through which Filipino and Filipino Americans learn to negotiate these various cultural values and identities (e.g., acculturation, assimilation, or biculturalism), the chapter introduced various types of stressors and conflicts impacting Filipino

American mental health. This chapter next presents two case studies that demonstrate how cultural values may affect Filipino Americans' lives and psychological stressors. These examples also demonstrate ways that these cultural values may have an impact on psychotherapy.

Case Studies

Case 1: The Ramos Family and Its Cultural Clashes

The Ramos family is a working-class Filipino American family that lives in Seattle, Washington. Jorge, 52, the father of the family, immigrated to the United States 22 years ago with his wife, Sheila, 51. Both parents are originally from Cebu, a major province in the Philippines. After arriving in the United States, they had two children and lived together in a predominantly Filipino American neighborhood. Both parents speak English fluently and are thriving at their jobs; Jorge's job as a mechanic is profitable, and Sheila has been promoted twice at her job in a local government office. Their children (Ron, 20, and Annalisa, 18) are currently living at home and attend the local university. Both Ron and Annalisa claim that they were pressured to live at home and that their parents would not pay for their tuition if they attended a college far away.

Lately, the family has been having many problems because Jorge and Sheila claim they "have no control" over their children. They feel Ron has been performing poorly in school and has been getting into trouble with his *barkada* (group of friends), who happen to all be Filipino. Ron has been staying out late on school nights and hardly ever spends time at home with his family. He likes being with his friends because he relates to them as American-born Filipinos; they always have a good time with each other, and Ron feels special and accepted when he is around them. Annalisa has been in relationship with her Irish American boyfriend, Tony, for the past three years, and she spends all of her time at his house or talking on the phone with him. Although she loves Tony, she likes the idea of being in a relationship as a way to "escape" from feeling "trapped" in her parents' home.

For the past six months, Jorge and Sheila have been feeling very frustrated and disheartened about their family situation. They yell at the

(Continued)

children almost every night, with the topics primarily focusing on Ron and Annalisa's "disrespect" and "lack of consideration" for their parents. Jorge and Sheila constantly remind them what they as parents have "sacrificed" for their children to come to the United States and that if they were still in the Philippines, they as parents would never be treated with disregard. Ron is more passive in these arguments; he tends to listen silently and then walk away when his parents are finished yelling. However, Annalisa has been more vocal with her parents; she argues back and consistently yells, "We live in America now! You need to stop being so strict and controlling!" with her parents yelling back, "Walang hiya!" ("Have you no shame!")

As a result of these arguments, the family members have stopped talking with each other. Jorge and Sheila have also become distant in their marriage because they are both so frustrated with their children and have different approaches for dealing with stress. Sheila has attempted to be a "peacemaker" but cannot manage to keep everyone calm and in the same room at the same time. One of Sheila's coworkers suggested that the entire family seek family counseling, which would be covered by their health insurance. However, when Sheila mentions this prospect to her husband, Jorge, he angrily responds with "Bahala na!" ("Leave it up to God!") and refuses to consider the option.

Case 2: Evelyn and Her Difficulty Adjusting to American Life

Evelyn is a 34-year-old Filipina American woman who immigrated to the United States three years ago. She had been a nurse for the past eight years in Manila, but she wanted to move to the United States for more career and financial opportunities. Her family lives in poverty in a province outside of Manila. Evelyn wants to be able to make enough money to send home, so her family can live comfortably. She joined a traveling nurse program, where she was contracted to work at a pediatrics unit at a hospital in Detroit, Michigan, a city where she knew no one. Although she enjoys her job and is having little difficulty with speaking English, she is having trouble making friends and relating to her American coworkers. She believes her coworkers are too "direct" and "forward" in their communication, as demonstrated through a supervisor scolding her when she did not follow correct procedures when filling out paperwork. She also feels that her coworkers are sometimes too "liberal," in that they talk freely about sex and other nonreligious topics. She does not have any relatives in the nearby area, so she often goes home after work feeling depressed and alone. She wants to stay in the United States because of her career opportunities, but she is worried she will never fully feel "at home."

While at work, Evelyn becomes frustrated easily and cannot perform her duties. For instance, there have been times when she could not perform a simple task like taking patients' blood or administering blood pressure tests (both tasks that she was very skilled at in the Philippines). After these incidents, she often goes into the restroom and cries. Her supervisor has recognized this behavior and has pulled Evelyn aside to find out what is wrong. Evelyn told her supervisor about her homesickness and her difficulty in making friends; her supervisor suggested that she seek therapy with the hospital psychologist. Evelyn reluctantly agrees and attends her first session with a White American female psychologist named Dr. Herbert. She is very quiet during her first session and barely maintains eye contact. When Dr. Herbert asks her questions, Evelyn responds with a simple head nod or "no." Evelyn continues to attend counseling for several sessions and repeats these same types of behaviors, leaving Dr. Herbert confused regarding how best to help her.

Case Study Discussion

In reviewing these two cases, one may notice how cultural values may impact the psychological stressors of Filipino Americans in a myriad of ways. For example, one might perceive how the process of negotiating culture is different for each individual, which leads to various ways of dealing with one's own problems. In the case of the Ramos family, one might detect that the parents (Jorge and Sheila) may be more acculturated than assimilated. Although it is clear that they are able to operate in American society (e.g., they are successful in their careers and are able to sustain a home), they appear to uphold many of their traditional Filipino family values at home (e.g., they expect their children to stay close to home and they want to be an integral part of their children's lives even through adulthood). Meanwhile, based on the information presented, it appears that the children may straddle between assimilation and biculturalism. Annalisa may appear to be more

(Continued)

assimilated, in that she is very outspoken and argumentative with her parents; because Filipinos highly value respect for authority figures, children in the Philippines would never argue with their parents (even when they are legally adults). Ron may appear to be more bicultural, in that he may respond to his parents in ways that would be considered culturally acceptable by Filipinos; he listens to his parents when they are upset and does not challenge them as authority figures. However, he is also American in that he does not change his behaviors to appease them; he would rather be individualistic and behave in ways that he enjoys without worrying about the impact he is having on his parents.

In the case of Evelyn, it appears she is having difficulty acculturating to American ways of life. Not only does she feel homesick, but she also feels unable to connect with her coworkers on personal levels. She believes their ways of communicating are too "direct" or too "forward," which is different from Filipino ways of communicating. Indirect communication is the primary form of communicating interpersonally in Filipino culture, both within families and within the community (Nadal, 2004). For example, individuals may speak in general terms around the dinner table to express feelings about a family member's behaviors, instead of confronting the person directly. Evelyn may be more accustomed to this type of communication and not American direct communication. This acculturative stress may have led to her inability to function fully at work, even though her abilities were superior in the Philippines (her culture of origin).

Nevertheless, by Evelyn's willingness to go to therapy, she shows signs that she may be adjusting to some American cultural norms. In Filipino culture (and in many other Asian countries), there is a stigma to seeking therapy, a topic discussed thoroughly in Chapter 9. It is possible that Evelyn overcame this stigma because she felt hopeless and had nowhere else to turn. Yet her inability to acculturate is apparent in the therapy sessions themselves, when she does not know what to say and does not feel comfortable discussing her problems, particularly with someone who is culturally different from her.

In both cases, Filipino cultural values are fully present and have manifested in the ways that conflicts manifest and the ways people react to them. In the Ramos family, the parents may preserve several cultural values. Both parents may feel a sense of kapwa (fellow being), in that they feel connected to their children and worry about them in the same way as they worry about their own lives. Both parents believe in *utang ng loob* (debt of reciprocity), in that they wish that their children would recognize the sacrifices they as parents have made for them. Their yearning is for their children to be respectful, obedient, and grateful for everything that they gave to them. This issue may also address the topic of *hiya* (shame) within the family. In Filipino families, it is a goal to avoid *hiya* at all costs by always thinking about the family's reputation with every decision or action an individual takes. In this case, Jorge and Sheila may be frustrated because Annalisa is bringing *hiya* to the family. By always spending time with her boyfriend, it may be possible that Annalisa is sexually active, which would contradict the *marianismo* value of women being sexually pure. Additionally, Annalisa may bring *hiya* to the family by being disrespectful to them as parents, a definite taboo for Filipino American families.

The men in the Ramos family may be experiencing two other values. Ron may feel a sense of *pakikasama* (social acceptance) with his friends, which may prevent him from following his parents' desires. It appears that he may be spending so much time with these friends because he wants them to like him and because he wants to feel special. By telling his friends that he has to spend time with his parents, he may worry that they will laugh at him, not include him in future events, and not accept him (when in reality they actually may be sympathetic to his family obligations and relate to his conflicts because they are Filipino American themselves). Finally, it appears that Jorge may maintain *amor propio* (pride), *machismo* (male dominance), and *bahala na* (fatalistic passiveness). Although it is clear that there are problems within the family that are causing everyone stress, Jorge's sense of pride (particularly his pride as a man) prohibits him from seeking help. As a result, he chooses to do nothing about his problem and leaves his problems to God.

In the case of Evelyn, there are several ways in which Filipino cultural values are being enacted. First, it is clear that Evelyn is devoted to her family; she moves to the United States because she wants to be able to provide for her impoverished family in the Philippines. In doing so, she is demonstrating the values of *kapwa* (fellow being) because she is selflessly thinking about her family's needs before her own. She is also

(Continued)

executing *utang ng loob* (debt of reciprocity) because she realizes her family members have given her so much and she wants to be able to repay them, even if they will not be able to repay her financially. Even though she may be unhappy in the United States, she is more concerned about her family's happiness than her own. Evelyn also demonstrates the value of *marianismo* (female submissiveness). One of her complaints about not relating to her coworkers is that she does not like how they talk so openly about sex and other nonreligious topics. In the Philippines, it would be considered improper for a woman to discuss such issues. At the same time, Evelyn would not feel comfortable directly telling her coworkers about her discomfort, which leads to the continuation of upsetting and unwanted conversations for her. Finally, the notion of *hiya* (shame) also is prevalent in Evelyn's case. She is trying to avoid *hiya* in four ways:

1. She does not want to tell her family that she is unhappy in the United States because it may worry them or make them embarrassed regarding her inability to succeed in the United States.
2. She does not want any of her American coworkers to know that she is having a difficult time adjusting or making friends.
3. She does not want to tell her psychologist any of her problems for fear of bringing shame to the family.
4. Because the psychologist is American and an authority figure, Evelyn is very embarrassed and does not want to show weakness in front of this person, whom she is supposed to impress or appear proper.

Therefore, it is important for the psychologist to be aware of culturally competent counseling techniques that could be used in working with a client like Evelyn. These techniques are fully discussed in Chapter 9.

Case Study Discussion Questions

For undergraduate students and general readers, please consider these questions:

1. What are your initial reactions to these two case examples?
2. How do you feel about the ways that cultural values impact the Ramoses problems? Do you agree or disagree with how the Ramoses handle their situation? Explain your answer.

3. How do you feel about the ways that cultural values impact Evelyn's problems? Do you agree or disagree with how Evelyn handles her situation?

4. How might the experiences of these case examples relate to your own experiences?

For helping professionals and graduate students of psychology, please consider these questions:

1. Who in the Ramos family do you believe you would have the most difficult time working with? Who in the Ramos family do you believe you would have the easiest time working with? Explain your answer.

2. What would be the most difficult part of working with Evelyn?

3. What might be some of your transference or countertransference issues with Jorge? With Sheila? With Ron? With Annalisa? With Evelyn?

4. Do you believe that the counselor's or clinician's race, ethnicity, or gender would make a difference in working with the Ramos family? With Evelyn? Why or why not?

CHAPTER THREE

Racial and Ethnic Identity Development for Filipino Americans

Figure 3.1 A Filipina American woman with her daughter
Photo courtesy of Julian Tamayo

CASE SYNOPSES

Glenn is a 32-year-old Filipino American man who works for a major corporation in a large metropolitan city. He went to college at a renowned university, where he joined a Greek fraternity, had mostly White friends, and dated White women exclusively. For the past few years, he has been trying to "climb the ladder" in his company but realizes it is difficult for him to do so. Although he believes his work is superior to that of his peers, he notices that many of them have been promoted while he has always been overlooked. One of his coworkers, a Puerto Rican man, tells him: "You know you're not getting promoted because you're brown, right?" Glenn is conflicted by this statement and starts to feel extremely anxious when he goes to work.

Cheryl is a 24-year-old second-generation Filipina American graduate student. She grew up in a middle-class neighborhood in California that consisted mainly of Filipino and Mexican Americans. When she first arrived at her graduate school in the Northeast, she noticed she was the only Filipino at the entire university. She spoke with her academic advisor about this problem, and she was referred to the Asian American student group on campus. Cheryl attended a meeting for this organization, where she felt isolated, different, and alone. Weeks passed, and she started to feel depressed. This began to negatively impact her schoolwork, her sleeping, and her eating habits. She decided to go to the college counseling center as a last resort because she felt like she "had no one else she could talk to."

INTRODUCTION

Filipino Americans may experience a unique process of racial and ethnic identity development that is different from that of other racial and ethnic groups in a variety of ways. For example, Chapter 2 reviewed how the Philippines had been colonized by Spain for over 370 years, which is the period similar to the length of Spanish colonization of most Latin American countries. Because of this experience, the Philippines is the only Asian country that would identify itself with Spain, and Filipinos are the only Asian American ethnic group that could possibly be considered "Hispanic" (Trevino, 1987). Additionally, while many East Asian and Southeast Asian individuals may clearly identify themselves as "Asian," Filipinos may fluctuate in identifying themselves as "Asian," "Pacific Islander," or exclusively "Filipino/Pilipino" (Nadal, 2004). In fact, Filipinos are the only ethnic group to lobby to be separated from the Asian American category, as demonstrated by the California Senate

Bill 1813. Passed in 1988, it requires all California state personnel surveys or statistical tabulations to classify persons of Filipino ancestry as "Filipino" rather than as Asian, Pacific Islander, or Hispanic (Espiritu, 1992).

This chapter investigates how Filipino Americans may develop a unique racial and ethnic identity that is different from that of other Asian Americans and other people of color. Previous racial identity development models have revealed various statuses that people of color develop throughout their lifetimes, including:

- Wanting to assimilate to White society.
- Questioning their racial realities, usually after experiencing racism or learning about racism.
- Choosing to isolate themselves from White society and immersing themselves into their racial group.
- Accepting themselves as racial beings and learning how to integrate themselves into White society and their own racial groups (Helms, 1995).

However, some authors have noted that "race" and "ethnicity" often are used interchangeably with Asian Americans and that many researchers and scholars neglect to notice the differences between various Asian ethnic groups (Alvarez & Yeh, 1999; Kohatsu, 1993; Lee, 2002). For example, when Filipino American individuals are asked about their "racial group," it is unclear whether they think first about other Filipinos, other Asian ethnic groups (e.g., Chinese, Vietnamese, Thai), or both.

Accordingly, this chapter examines how many Filipino American individuals may follow a similar identity development outlined in these models and how they may undergo unique experiences because of their race (Asian) and because of their ethnicity (Filipino). Additionally, because of historical and cultural differences from other Asian Americans, many Filipino Americans may reject an Asian American identity and may adopt an ethnocentric Filipino American identity (Nadal, 2004). Finally, because Filipino Americans may have a physical appearance that varies from that of other Asian Americans (and they often are called Latino, Pacific Islander, Arab, or multiracial), they will experience racism differently from their Asian American counterparts.

DEFINITIONS OF RACE AND ETHNICITY

Before understanding the differences between racial identity and ethnic identity, one must first be familiar with the difference between race and ethnicity. "Race" can be defined as a classification of humans, based on a combination of various physical characteristics, including skin color, facial form, and eye shape (Jones, 1991). Race has many psychological impacts, including the ways in which one is responded to by others on the basis of visible racial characteristics as well as in the implications of such responses for one's life opportunities and sense of identity (Phinney, 1996). "Ethnicity" can be defined as the membership in a particular national or cultural group and observance of that group's customs, beliefs, and language that are often transmitted across generations (Phinney, 1996).

Given these definitions, it is important to become familiar with where Filipinos fit in terms of race and ethnicity. The U.S. Census categorizes Filipinos under the Asian racial umbrella (U.S. Census Bureau, 2000). However, in the past, the U.S. Department of Education has categorized Filipinos as Pacific Islanders (e.g., Horn, 1995). Some have argued that because Filipinos have a darker skin color and a larger eye shape than East Asians (e.g., Chinese, Japanese, Koreans), they may not fit in the same racial category as Asians (Nadal, 2004, 2008c). For example, during the civil rights movement, Filipino Americans did not join the Asian "Yellow Power Movement" because they (and other Filipinos today) identify with the color "brown" (Ignacio, 1976). Moreover, Filipinos often are mistaken for members of other racial/cultural groups, namely Latinos or Pacific Islanders, or multiracial individuals (Nadal, 2004; Rumbaut, 1995; Uba, 1994), which may lead to differential race-based treatment for Filipinos than for other East Asian groups (Nadal, 2008c). Given all of this, if race is based solely on physical characteristics (specifically skin color, facial features, and eye shape), it appears that Filipinos do not fit seamlessly into any one racial category. And while it is widely accepted that Filipinos are classified as Asian, the racial classification of Asian is likely due to geography of the Philippines, some historical similarities, and similar immigration experiences (see Chapter 1 for a review).

In terms of ethnicity, Filipinos are considered to be their own ethnic group because they are a cultural group with a unique set of customs, beliefs, and languages that are distinguishable from those of other Asian groups. However, previous literature in psychology often categorized Asian Americans as an ethnic group, not as a racial group (Alvarez & Yeh, 1999; Lee, 2002), pointing out that similar cultural values are held across Asian ethnicities. Yet there are clear, fundamental differences in cultural value orientations between Filipino Americans and East Asian American groups (Kim, Yang, Atkinson, Wolfe, & Hong, 2001). For example, Filipino Americans indicated lower scores of emotional self-control, family recognition through achievement, familial piety, conformity to norms, and collectivism than East Asian Americans.

With the definitions of race and ethnicity clarified, it is necessary to establish how Filipino Americans will be referred to in terms of their racial and ethnic groups. First, in terms of race, this textbook defines Filipinos as Asian, due to their classification in the U.S. Census, their social construction in U.S. society as Asian, and their personal and community histories of identifying as Asian. Although Filipinos may not fit perfectly into the Asian racial category, race is a social construct in which many labels may not feel completely appropriate or fitting. For example, South Asians (e.g., Indians, Pakistanis, and Bangladeshis) are also considered Asian, even though their physical characteristics may be completely different from those of East Asians. Similarly, many Latinos do not identify with their racial classifications as "White" or "Black," offering more evidence that current racial classifications are flawed and often irrelevant. Additionally, this chapter discusses the history of Filipinos in the Asian racial category, including this conflict of identifying as Asian, the history of marginalization of Filipinos in the Asian diaspora, and the impacts these experiences may have on their racial identity.

Second, in terms of ethnicity, the textbook defines Filipinos and Filipino Americans in the United States as Filipino American, with unique cultural values, beliefs, and traditions that are different from those of other Asian American groups. The term "American" is included to signify how Filipinos living in the United States adopt American values, beliefs, traditions, and worldviews that are different from those of Filipinos who are living in the Philippines. Additionally, it is necessary to recognize that cultural differences may emerge between first-, second-, and third-generation Filipino Americans, while many similar values and traditions are transmitted across generations. This chapter examines the varying ways Filipino Americans may identify with their ethnic group, the ways they may accept or reject their groups, and the impacts these experiences have on their ethnic identity.

RACIAL IDENTITY

A plethora of research in psychology discusses racial identity theory, or the extent to which a person of color perceives him- or herself to share a common racial heritage with his or her respective socioracial group (Helms, 1990). Within racial identity theory, there exist numerous racial identity development models that explain the various stages or statuses a person of color encounters as he or she identifies with a racial group. One of the first models to be published is Cross's (1971) Nigrescence Model for Black Americans, which originally cited five unique stages of racial identity development through which a Black individual passes. The model has since been translated into new models for other racial groups and for people of color in general, eventually resulting in the People of Color Racial Identity Attitudes Scale (POCRIAS; Helms, 1995), one of the most widely used identity models and racial identity measures in psychology today.

According to the POCRIAS model, individuals undergo four major statuses in identifying themselves as racial beings. The first status is *Conformity*, in which individuals do not recognize the salience of race in their lives. The individuals are oblivious to race; want to be accepted by the dominant, White society; and fail to recognize they are people of color. The second status is *Dissonance*, in which individuals acknowledge the impact of race in their lives for the first time. They may have experienced discrimination for the first time, which may allow them to question race, experience feelings of conflict, and feel uncertain about the world that they live in. The third status is *Immersion*, in which individuals idealize their own racial group, exclude themselves from the White world, and associate only with others of their same racial group. Individuals may experience feelings of anger or resentment toward Whites, may distance themselves from former White friends or colleagues, and may associate exclusively with others who think about race in similar ways. The fourth status is *Internalization*, in which individuals may commit themselves to combating racism while integrating with members of their own racial group and the dominant White group. Individuals may learn that not all White persons are malicious or hurtful and may discover how to incorporate themselves as racially aware and knowledgeable persons into the real world.

In the POCRIAS model and other models measuring racial identity development, individuals are discussed in terms of how they identify with their own race and the dominant race, but not with any other race or ethnic subgroup. For example, a Black individual is measured in terms of how she or he identifies with other Black individuals and Whites, without understanding how she or he identifies with other racial groups (e.g., Asians) or with subgroups within the Black race (e.g., Caribbean Americans, Black Latinos, and African immigrants). Similarly, for Asians, racial identity refers to how an individual identifies with the larger Asian or Asian American collective, including all of the various Asian ethnic groups (Ancheta, 1998; Espiritu, 1992). However, previous Asian racial identity development models (e.g., Kim, 1981; S. Sue & Sue, 1971) fail to focus on within-group differences and ways that Asian Americans may or may not identify with other Asian ethnic groups.

Some authors (e.g., Alvarez, 1996; Alvarez & Kimura, 2001; Sodowsky, Kwan, & Pannu, 1995) have argued that Asian identity development models put emphasis on ethnic identity development and not racial identity development. These Asian identity development models measure how individuals retain and identify with the cultural values, norms, languages, and beliefs of their ethnic group without understanding how Asian individuals respond to and internalize their experiences with race or their reactions to racial oppression (Nadal, 2008c). In addition, while Asian identity models include how Asian American individuals feel about themselves, their ethnic group, other people of color, and Whites, they fail to recognize how Asian Americans self-identify with other racial group members of different Asian ethnic groups (Nadal, 2008c). For example, when measuring the Immersion status, it is unclear whether individuals are idealizing or associating with the entire Asian group, their specific Asian ethnic group (e.g., Vietnamese, Thai, Pakistani), or a combination of both. Finally, these identity models do not examine how Asian Americans are involved in racial practices (e.g., customs or behaviors across the pan-Asian racial category), how Asian

Americans view their Asian racial group, or how Asian Americans have a cultural commitment to their racial group (Espiritu, 1992).

One author maintains that Asian Americans struggle with the processes of acculturation, racial identity, and ethnic identity simultaneously (Alvarez, 1996). For Asian Americans, racism may lead to the development of (a) a racial consciousness apart from ethnic identity, (b) an ethnic identity apart from a panracial identity, or (c) both identities concomitantly (Alvarez, 1996). Simply stated, depending on individuals' experiences with race, individuals may identify more with their racial identity over their ethnic identity; they may identify with their ethnic identity over their racial identity; or they may identify with both concurrently. For example, if a person of Indian heritage is discriminated against or stereotyped as being a terrorist, he or she might choose not to associate with East Asian Americans who do not have similar experiences with race. However, if a person of Japanese heritage is discriminated against or stereotyped as being a foreigner, he or she might choose to associate with other Asian Americans who may also have similar experiences.

One reason why these models do not examine Asian racial identity is because many Asian ethnic group members may not view themselves in terms of race but rather in terms of ethnicity (Nadal, 2008c). Additionally, Asian and non-Asian individuals often think of "Asian" as equivalent to "East Asian," without recognizing other subgroups that are included in this category (Nadal, 2008c). The Asian subgroups that tend not to identify themselves as Asian include South Asians (e.g., Indians, Pakistanis, and Bangladeshis), Southeast Asians (e.g., Vietnamese, Cambodians, and Laotians), Filipino Americans, and Pacific Islanders (e.g., Native Hawaiians, Samoans, and Chamorros; Nadal, 2008c).

This experience takes place in other racial groups as well; certain ethnic groups and other subgroups may be more likely to identify with their ethnicity or culture of origin than with their racial group. This fact can be demonstrated with Black Caribbeans who are more prone to identify with their country of origin (e.g., Jamaica, Haiti, or Trinidad) instead of their Black racial group (Waters, 2001). However, research has established that there is a significant positive relationship between racial identity and ethnic identity for second-generation Caribbean Americans (Hall & Carter, 2006). This means that if Caribbean Americans raised in the United States identify highly with their racial group, they also will identify highly with their ethnic group. Conversely, if they do not identify with their ethnic group, they also will not identify with their racial group.

For Asian Americans, it is unclear whether this phenomenon would be similar because no known studies measure the differences between an Asian American's racial identity and ethnic identity. Moreover, no studies have focused on how Asian Americans self-identify with other Asian racial group members (of different Asian ethnic groups), how Asian Americans are involved in racial practices (which would include practices across the pan-Asian racial category), or how proudly Asian Americans view their racial group or have a cultural commitment to one's Asian racial group (Nadal, 2008c). Furthermore, when Asian Americans complete instruments that ask about race, they may answer questions thinking about their race and ethnicity interchangeably (Liu, Pope-Davis, Nevitt, & Toporek, 1999). This may be considered a problem with the instrument, in that the instrument is not culturally sensitive enough to recognize that some people do not know the true definitions of race and ethnicity. For example, when taking the POCRIAS, a Hmong American may read an item that asks about views of one's own racial group (Asian). However, if individuals answer the question while thinking specifically of their ethnic group (Hmong) because they think of ethnicity as race, then racial identity is not being measured.

ETHNIC IDENTITY

Earlier psychological literature often used the term "racial identity" interchangeably with "ethnic identity" and even "acculturation" when discussing Asian Americans (Kohatsu, 1993). For example, J. Kim's (1981) model of Asian American identity development uses the terms "race," "ethnicity," and "culture" interchangeably and discusses acculturation processes instead of racial or ethnic identity development. This phenomenon is reflective of most of the literature on Asian ethnic identity, making it unclear as to whether the literature focuses on Asian Americans as a racial or an ethnic group (Alvarez & Yeh, 1999; Lee, 2002). In order to examine the differences between racial identity and ethnic identity, first it is crucial to define what "ethnic identity" means.

Originally the term "ethnic identity" was used to refer to one's membership in an ethnic group, with subcategories including self-identification, sense of belonging or commitment to an ethnic group, attitudes toward one's ethnic group, and ethnic involvement (Phinney, 1990). "Self-identification" refers to the ethnic label that one uses for oneself (i.e., whether one refers to oneself as Filipino, as American, or as Filipino American). "Sense of belonging" or "commitment" refers to the degree to which one feels connected or bonded to one's ethnic group (i.e., whether an individual feels a bond with other Filipino Americans). "Attitudes toward one's ethnic group" include both positive and negative beliefs or feelings individuals have about their ethnic group (i.e., whether a Filipino American holds positive or negative stereotypes about other Filipinos). "Ethnic involvement" includes social participation and cultural practices with one's ethnic group. Some of these behaviors may include language (i.e., whether the individual speaks the same language as others in the ethnic group); friendship (i.e., whether the individual has friends of the same ethnic group); religious affiliation and participation (i.e., whether the individual belongs to the same religious organizations or practices similar religious behaviors as other ethnic group members); structured social ethnic groups (i.e., whether the individual is a member of ethnic-specific organizations); political ideology and activity (i.e., whether the individual has similar political views as other ethnic group members); area of residence (i.e., whether the individual lives in an ethnic enclave or near other members of her or his ethnicity); and miscellaneous ethnic or cultural activities and attitudes (i.e., whether the individual listens to ethnic-specific music or participates in ethnic-specific celebrations).

In addition to these components of ethnic identity, one author states that the experiences associated with minority status, including powerlessness, discrimination, and prejudice, may have an impact on one's ethnic identity (Phinney, 1996). Although experiences with discrimination may appear to be specific to race and have impact on racial identity, it is important to decipher the different ways that discrimination or prejudice may influence ethnic identity. When an Asian American experiences discrimination, she or he may feel culturally different from members of the dominant White group. Not only does the person feel like a racial minority (in that she or he is physically different from the dominant race and discriminated against accordingly), but she or he is also an ethnic minority (in which she or he may have different values, beliefs, traditions, or worldviews from members of the dominant ethnicity/culture).

Additionally, experiences with discrimination may influence a Filipino American's ethnic identity. As aforementioned, previous literature stated that Filipino Americans often are mistaken for members of other racial/ethnic groups, namely Latinos, Pacific Islanders, and multiracial persons (Nadal, 2004; Rumbaut, 1995; Uba, 1994) because Filipino Americans may have a different phenotype from other East Asian Americans (Nadal, 2008c). A recent study found that 99% of a Filipino American sample reported experiencing at least one event of everyday racism in the past year (Alvarez & Juang, 2010). Another study found that Filipino Americans may have higher frequencies of experiences with both vicarious racism and racial microaggressions than other Asian Americans (Alvarez, Juang, & Liang, 2006), and still another study discovered that Filipino Americans were more likely than Chinese Americans to experience similar types of discrimination that is stereotypically more common for African Americans and Latinos (Nadal, 2008c). For example, Filipino Americans were more likely to be assumed to be criminals and be treated as intellectually inferior to Chinese Americans. However, it was found that both groups experience similar discrimination of being treated as perpetual foreigners, which suggests that Filipinos may experience a spectrum of occurrences of racial discrimination, while Chinese Americans may experience discrimination that is specific only to Asians. Because of this, Filipinos may feel different from other Asian ethnic groups and may even align themselves with groups that have similar experiences of discrimination. This finding can be demonstrated in the strong historical alliances between Filipino and Mexican Americans during the United Farm Workers Movement in the 1930s and the allegiance between Filipino Americans and African Americans in contemporary hip-hop culture (Nadal, 2004, 2008c). Moreover, because of colonialism, Filipino Americans may feel more connected to Latino ethnic groups, who share matching colonial histories, religions, customs, cultural values, and surnames and similarities in language.

In understanding ethnic identity for Asian Americans and Filipino Americans, it is also important to comprehend the cross-ethnic inter-actions that occur across Asian ethnic groups. A hierarchy within the Asian diaspora has been well documented, in which brown Asians (e.g., Filipinos, Southeast Asians, and South Asians) often feel marginal-ized or discriminated against for not being "Asian enough" (Espiritu, 1992; Nadal, 2004; Okamura, 1998). Additionally, Filipinos are often the targets of ethnic jokes within the Asian American community, with stereotypes of being inferior, criminal, or uncultured (Okamura, 1998). Because of this fact, resentment often may occur between Filipinos and other Asians, particularly East Asian American groups (Espiritu, 1992; Nadal, 2004), which may lead Filipinos to separate themselves from the Asian American group (Nadal, 2004; Okamura, 1998). This finding is exemplified by California Senate Bill 1813, whose passage resulted from Filipinos lobbying to be separated from the Asian American category in census data, as well as various Filipino American college student organ-izations in California that have broken away from Asian American col-lege umbrella groups (Nadal, 2004).

Figure 3.2   Three Filipino American young professionals enjoy a day at the park
Photo courtesy of Kevin Nadal

FILIPINO AMERICAN IDENTITY DEVELOPMENT MODEL

Given this understanding of the differences between "racial identity" and "ethnic identity," this section examines the ways a Filipino American may develop a racial and an ethnic identity simultaneously. According to Nadal (2004), Filipino Americans may experience racial and ethnic identity development that is different from that of other Asian American groups. The model includes six stages (or statuses) that are nonsequential and nonlinear (meaning that the statuses are independent from each other and individuals may fluctuate between the statuses). The model is based on Atkinson, Morten, and Sue's (1998) Racial/Cultural Identity Development Model, S. Sue and Sue's (1971) Asian American Identity Model, and Kim's (1981) Asian American Identity Model. The model also reflects statuses of other racial identity development models (e.g., Cross, 1971; Helms, 1990). Finally, the model includes newly developed statuses that can be applied specifically to racial and ethnic identity development of Filipino Americans.

The six statuses of the Filipino American Identity Development Model include:

1. Ethnic awareness
2. Assimilation to dominant culture
3. Social political awakening
4. Panethnic Asian American consciousness
5. Ethnocentric realization
6. Introspection (See Table 3.1).

Status 1: Ethnic Awareness (which typically occurs during early childhood), describes when individuals understand they are Filipino based on the people to whom they are exposed, the languages and accents they hear, and other factors, such as food and music.

Status 2: Assimilation to Dominant Culture occurs when Filipino Americans realize they are different from dominant cultural norms. This may result from meeting school and neighborhood friends of different ethnic backgrounds or watching television shows where Filipinos are not represented. In this stage, individuals may attempt to assimilate into the dominant culture and reject being Filipino.

Status 3: Social Political Awakening is when individuals become actively aware of racial and cultural differences from the dominant group. Usually this status is triggered by something negative (e.g., being discriminated against) or even something positive (e.g., learning about one's history or culture through a college class).

Status 4: Panethnic Asian American Consciousness is a stage in which Filipino Americans adopt an Asian American identity. Individuals may associate with other Asian Americans and feel a sense of community with them, due to similar experiences with acculturation or discrimination.

Status 5: Ethnocentric Realization is a stage in which Filipino Americans may reject an Asian American identity and may be accepting of a Filipino ethnocentric identity. This status may be triggered by an ethnic slur or discrimination by an East Asian American or by learning of the historically marginalized experience of Filipino Americans in the Asian American community.

Status 6: Introspection is a stage in which Filipino Americans have learned to accept their role as Asian Americans while still maintaining a strong sense of ethnic identity. Individuals in this stage realize how wearisome it is to remain angry and instead utilize their energy toward proactive positivism.

One can notice how this model integrates both racial and ethnic identity and how there are implications for both race and ethnicity in each status. For example, in Status 3: Social Political Awakening, individuals may become aware of race, in that they experience racial discrimination, but they also may become aware of ethnicity, by learning the history of oppression of Filipinos and Filipino Americans. One can also notice that Status 4: Panethnic Consciousness and Status 5: Ethnocentric Realization represents the conflict in racial and ethnic identity. For example, persons who are panethnic may have a high sense of racial identity and feel a sense of belonging across Asian American ethnic groups. However, those who are ethnocentric may have a low sense of Asian racial identity and a high sense of Filipino American ethnic identity, and may feel disconnected from or unaffiliated with other Asian American ethnic groups.

The statuses of the model can be categorized based on the ways in which Filipino American individuals view themselves in relation to others, specifically other Filipino Americans, Asian Americans, other persons of color, and Whites. In Status 1: Ethnic Awareness, Filipino

Americans may view themselves and other Filipino Americans positively, because Filipinos are the only persons to whom they are exposed. Both Asian Americans and other people of color may be viewed as neutral, while viewing Whites positively, as a result of their exposure to Whites on television and other forms of media. In Status 2: Assimilation to Dominant Culture, individuals will view Whites positively and have negative perceptions of themselves and other Filipino Americans. Filipino Americans in this stage may view Asian Americans and other people of color in a negative or discriminatory fashion, as a way of feeling superior to them. In Status 3: Social Political Awakening, individuals initially may feel conflicted but then may view themselves and all people of color very positively while viewing White people negatively. In Status 4: Panethnic Asian American Consciousness, individuals may continue to view all people of color positively but may lean toward a greater appreciation for Asian Americans as a racial group. In Status 5: Ethnocentric Realization, Filipino Americans may view themselves and other Filipino Americans as empowering while also feeling connections to other marginalized communities of color, particularly African Americans, Latinos, and Pacific Islanders. Depending on the shift into the Ethnocentric Realization status, individuals may have neutral or negative feelings toward Asian Americans and still may feel anger or frustration toward Whites. Finally, in Status 6: Introspection, individuals may appreciate themselves as Filipino Americans and persons of color while accepting their role as Asian Americans. The individuals may learn to become accepting of Whites and gain a selective appreciation of them; the individuals will not exert exhaustive anger toward anyone, as it may feel time consuming and unproductive.

Psychologists, counselors, clinicians, and other helping professionals must be aware of Filipino American identity because all individuals are unique in their racial and ethnic identity development and may need to be approached differently. For example, if a Filipina American woman in psychotherapy is assimilated, she may not maintain any Filipino cultural values and may not view race or ethnicity as a salient part of her life. Accordingly, it may not be as important for a clinician to discuss issues of race or ethnicity in a psychotherapy session, as the client may not be interested. Conversely, if a psychotherapy client identifies as ethnocentric, she or he will likely think about race and ethnicity often,

Table 3.1 Filipino American Identity Development Model

Stage of Filipino American identity	Attitudes toward self	Attitudes toward Filipinos	Attitudes toward Asians	Attitudes toward other minority groups	Attitudes toward Whites
Ethnic Awareness	P/Neutral	P/Neutral	Neutral	Neutral	P/Neutral
Assimilation to Dominant Culture	N/SD	N/GD	N/D	N/D	P/GA
Social/political Awakening	P/SE	P/GE	P/GA	P/A	N/D
Panethnic Consciousness	P/SA	P/A	P/GA	P/A	N/D
Ethnocentric Consciousness	P/SE	P/GE	N/GD	P/GE	N
Introspection	P/SA	P/GA	P/A	P/A	A

Source: Nadal, 2004

Note: P = Positive, N = Negative, SD = Self-Deprecating, GD = Group-Deprecating, D = Discriminatory, GA = Group Appreciating, SE = Self-Empowering, GE = Group-Empowering, A = Accepting, SA = Self-Appreciating

which will make discussions of race and ethnicity an important part of the therapeutic relationship. Therefore, it is important for clinicians to be able to conceptualize clients' racial and ethnic identity statuses, in order to provide the most culturally competent services for them.

As a final point, people's status of racial and ethnic identity may influence their worldview, their interpersonal relationships, and their ability to cope with problems. For example, individuals who are assimilated may associate only with Whites, which means that they may not be aware of how race or ethnicity impacts their lives. It also may mean that they may not have opportunities to talk about race or ethnicity if they experience racism or ethnic discrimination. Individuals who are panethnic may associate primarily with other Asians and Asian Americans and maintain Asian cultural values (e.g., shame, collectivism, emotional control). Consequently, these individuals may have difficulty expressing emotions to their families or peers and may feel a stigma in attending counseling because it brings dishonor to the family. Individuals who are introspective may associate with members of their own racial or ethnic groups as well as members of other groups; these persons may understand the positive and negative values and beliefs of their racial group, their ethnic group, and the dominant group. Accordingly, these individuals may be able to express emotions, may be able to examine how race and ethnicity has an impact on all aspects of their lives, and may be open to discussing how race and ethnicity can impact their relationships with a counselor or clinician.

DISCUSSION QUESTIONS

1. What are your first memories of race? What are your first memories of ethnicity? How do these memories influence your racial identity and ethnic identity today?
2. In what ways do you identify with your race? In what ways do you identify with your ethnicity?
3. How have experiences with discrimination influenced your racial identity? How have experiences with discrimination influenced your ethnic identity?
4. Of the six statuses of Filipino American identity development, which status do you think is the most mentally healthy? Which status do you think is the least mentally healthy? Explain your answer.
5. For Filipino Americans: Which status of Filipino American identity development do you identify with the most? Have you identified with other statuses in the past? If so, which ones?

SUMMARY

This chapter discussed the ways race and ethnicity may impact Filipino Americans' lives. In defining race and ethnicity, the chapter explained the ways in which individuals develop distinct racial identities and ethnic identities. By examining how Filipino Americans have been classified in various racial and ethnic categories (e.g., Asian, Pacific Islander, and Hispanic), the chapter shared how Filipinos often have been mistaken for members of other racial/ethnic groups, how they may experience forms of racial discrimination different from other Asian Americans, and how these experiences may influence some Filipinos to reject an Asian American identity. The chapter explored how Filipino Americans may develop unique racial and ethnic identities that are different from those of other Asian American groups. This chapter next presents two case studies that demonstrate how racial and ethnic identity may influence Filipino Americans' mental health. Through exploring the individuals' experiences, their statuses of racial and ethnic identity, and other factors that contribute to mental health, one can gain a sense of how race/ethnicity may impact the lives of all Filipino Americans in diverse ways.

Case Studies

Case 1: Glenn

Glenn is a 32-year-old Filipino American man who works for a major corporation in New York City. His parents immigrated to the United States before he was born, and he was raised as the only child in his family within a predominantly White neighborhood (where he was the only Filipino). As a child and adolescent, his parents tried to teach him about Filipino cultural values and traditions at home, but because he only had White friends, Glenn tried his hardest to "be like the other kids." Glenn went to college at a renowned university, where he joined a Greek fraternity, continued to have mostly White friends, and dated White women exclusively. He maintained a satisfactory relationship with his parents while he was in college, but he had very little exposure to other family members during his adult years. After college, he pursued his master's in business administration from a prestigious Ivy League institution, where he was the only Filipino American and one of the only students of color. If asked about race, Glenn would say "race wasn't important" and he wanted to live in a "color-blind" world. However, based on his friendships and romantic relationships, it was clear he was associating almost entirely with Whites.

While a graduate student, Glenn met a woman named Julie, a White American, with whom he fell in love. After he received his MBA, he married Julie, and he was hired at a Fortune 500 company. For the past few years, he has been trying to "climb up the ladder" in his company but recognizes that it has been difficult for him to do so. Although he believes his work is superior to that of his peers, he notices that many of them have been promoted while he has not been. One of his coworkers, José, a Puerto Rican man, tells him, "You know you're not getting promoted because you're brown, right?" Initially Glenn is offended by José's statement, but eventually he begins to realize that there may be truth to what José is suggesting. Everyone on the board of directors is White, and his coworkers who have been promoted are all White too. Glenn is disgusted by this realization but does not have anyone to talk to. He starts to feel uneasy around his coworkers (who are almost all White) and eventually begins to feel anxious every morning before he goes to work. He has difficulty breathing and heart palpitations before he enters his office, and he sometimes wakes up crying in the middle of the night. When Julie asks him what is wrong, Glenn feels uncomfortable and begins to withdraw from their relationship. Julie suggests couples counseling, and Glenn agrees unenthusiastically. In their first session, Glenn does not mention anything about how his recent realizations may be causing his anxiety.

Case 2: Cheryl

Cheryl is a 24-year-old second-generation Filipina American graduate student. She grew up in a middle-class neighborhood in California that consisted mainly of Filipino and Mexican Americans. She is the older of two daughters, but she had many aunts, uncles, and cousins who lived in the neighborhood, leading Cheryl to feel like she had "5 moms, 5 dads, and 20 brothers and sisters." She attended a college close to home, where she commuted. As an undergraduate student, she maintained contact with all of her friends and family while establishing other friendships through her Filipino American college student organization. In her senior year, she was elected president of this organization, and she did her best to balance her club responsibilities while applying for graduate school. Cheryl was accepted into a small, liberal arts graduate university in the Northeast, where she was offered a full scholarship. Although she suspected that she would be the only Filipino at the college (and potentially in the small town where it was located), she accepted the offer and moved away from her family and friends for the first time.

(Continued)

When she first arrived at her graduate school, she noticed that she was the only Filipino at the entire university. She spoke with her academic advisor about this problem, and he referred her to the Asian American student group on campus. Because there were no Filipino American organizations on campus, she reluctantly attended a meeting for the Asian American organization, where she did not feel she could fit in because she had never had any non-Filipino or non-Mexican friends. At the meeting, Cheryl was the only Filipino; all of the other club members were either Chinese or Korean American. She felt she could not relate to anyone and vowed never to attend a club meeting again.

Cheryl tried to talk to her family and friends in California about how she was feeling, but she believed they could not fully relate to her. She did not want to move home because she liked her academic program and wanted to finish, but she also felt very homesick, lonely, and misunderstood. She started to feel depressed, having intense feelings of sadness, hopelessness, and loneliness. This began to negatively impact her schoolwork, her sleeping, and her eating habits. She decided to go to the college counseling center as a last resort because she felt like she "had no one else she could talk to." She wanted to see a Filipino American counselor, but because that was not possible, she asked if she could meet with a Latino or African American counselor.

Figure 3.3 Many Filipino Americans, like the ones in this picture, often consider their relationships with their cousins to be as close as relationships with their siblings
Photo courtesy of Kevin Nadal

Summary

Case Study Discussion

In reviewing these two cases, one can notice how racial identity and ethnic identity may impact the mental health problems of Filipino Americans. For both cases, one may observe how racial identity and ethnic identity may have impacts on one's worldviews, on one's ability to cope with problems, and one's ability to relate with others interpersonally. One also may notice that sometimes racial identity may be more salient than ethnic identity, sometimes ethnic identity may be more salient than racial identity, and sometimes both are relevant or unimportant at the same time. Finally, applying the statuses of the Filipino American Identity Development Model to each case will be helpful, to reflect the person's racial and ethnic identity and how statuses of identity development may manifest in therapy.

First, in reviewing the case of Glenn, one can recognize that while he attempts to live in a color-blind society, he has chosen to associate mainly with Whites. Based on his friendships and history of romantic relationships, it appears that Glenn exemplifies a transition between Status 2: Assimilation to Dominant Culture and Status 3: Social Political Awakening. Glenn has lived his life trying to assimilate to be like Whites; he has turned a blind eye to ways in which race and ethnicity may have affected his life. And now he has been awakened to a situation where race may be interfering with his career. As a result, Glenn begins to develop anxiety and other psychological problems.

Because Glenn has approached life in an assimilated status, he has developed a worldview in which he may believe he has a high internal locus of control or the belief he has the ability to be in command of his life. It appears that he has had no difficulty in attending a prestigious college and graduate school, and he was able to get a job at a good company. However, when he recognizes how race may hinder his success, he feels dissonance because it contradicts his worldview. Additionally, Glenn's assimilated status has an impact on his relationships and coping mechanisms. Because he has associated only with White friends and married a White woman, he may not feel comfortable discussing issues of race or ethnicity with them. It also appears that he has a limited relationship with his family, which limits his opportunities to talk about his problems with people of the same race or ethnicity. Accordingly, he

(Continued)

may repress his emotions, which leads him to feel even more isolated, anxious, and distressed.

Cheryl is a 24-year-old graduate student who grew up in a large Filipino American family within a large Filipino American neighborhood and who moved to a predominantly White graduate school far away from her family. Based on her close family relationships and her strong ties to Filipino American friends and organizations, it appears that Cheryl has advanced past the assimilation and social/political awakening statuses. She prefers to affiliate herself with other Filipino Americans and does not choose to connect with other Asian Americans, which means that it is likely that Cheryl would identify in the ethnocentric status. Because of this, Cheryl has a difficult time connecting with others, namely Asian Americans and Whites, which leads to depression, loneliness, and other emotional issues.

In holding an ethnocentric status, Cheryl may have developed a world-view in which it is important for her to be surrounded by family and friends of her same cultural group. She may have learned that the values of her ethnic group are the norm, and she has become accustomed to living in an ethnocentric environment. Although Cheryl appears to have only Filipino American friends, she also maintains some Mexican American friends who grew up in her neighborhood. Perhaps she feels a bond with these friends because they have similar social class backgrounds, their parents have similar immigration experiences, they may have similar experiences with race and racial discrimination, and they have similar cultural values due to colonialism. Cheryl may feel a distance from the Chinese and Korean American students she meets at the Asian American organization because she may feel that they have different experiences with race and racial discrimination, different cultural values, and perhaps even different social class backgrounds. As a result, Cheryl may feel isolated and may have difficulty establishing relationships with others.

Cheryl's ethnocentric status also may influence her ability to cope with problems. Although she may have a strong support system in theory, she feels that her family and friends have no idea what she is undergoing because they live in a very different world from hers. She wishes she could have Filipino American friends in her new environment who would know firsthand about the issues she faces. Additionally, because of her ethnocentric status, it is likely that she highly endorses Filipino American values, which she feels may not be supported or understood in her new environment. Cheryl may feel *hiya* (shame) for feeling that she cannot handle her own problems. She may feel isolated and alone, which is in direct conflict with her value of *kapwa* (fellow being), in which she thrives on being with her loved ones and feeling connected with them. As a result of this culture shock, it almost seems inevitable that Cheryl feels some sadness and seclusion. In fact, her inability to deal with her emotions has led her to become depressed.

Both cases represent varying levels of racial and ethnic identity. Glenn is assimilated in both his racial and ethnic identities. In terms of race, he tries to live in a color-blind world where he convinces himself that his race does not affect him in any negative way. In terms of ethnicity, he tries to adopt White cultural values, beliefs, and traditions by establishing only White friendships, dating only White women, and marrying a White woman. He rejects his Filipino ethnicity by distancing himself from his family, by being individualistic, and by refusing any of the Filipino cultural values, such as *kapwa* (fellow being) or *utang ng loob* (debt of reciprocity) his parents may have tried to teach him. Cheryl's ethnic identity is salient for her, in that she prefers to be around members of her same Filipino American ethnic group. However, it appears that prior to moving to her new environment, Cheryl had never thought of herself as an Asian or Asian American. In fact, it appears that she would be more comfortable in relating with other people of color, namely Latinos and African Americans, than she would be with East Asian Americans. So although she is not assimilated in any way, she may be considered to be maintaining a low racial identity because she does not relate to members of the entire Asian racial group.

Given these individuals' racial and ethnic identities, there are several implications for counseling or psychotherapy. It appears that Glenn is most comfortable with Whites in his everyday life, but he is not secure in discussing issues of race or ethnicity with them. Therefore, it would be important for a counselor or clinician of any racial group to create an environment where Glenn does feel comfortable discussing these issues. This environment may be attained in a variety of ways (e.g., asking about his family history and his childhood or inquiring about his parents' cultural values and how they raised him). It appears that Cheryl is most comfortable primarily with Filipino Americans. Accordingly, it would be

(Continued)

important for a counselor or clinician of any race to validate her ethnocentric identity and demonstrate competence in working with Filipino Americans. For example, a counselor or clinician might share with Cheryl her or his knowledge about the history of Filipino Americans and disclose how it is difficult for many people to talk with someone outside of their ethnic group. This counselor or clinician might also convey how she or he is someone who hopes to gain Cheryl's trust and who genuinely cares about her well-being.

Case Study Discussion Questions

For undergraduate students and general readers, please consider these questions:

1. What are your initial reactions to these two case examples?
2. How do you feel about the ways that racial identity and ethnic identity impact Glenn's problems? Do you agree or disagree with how Glenn handles his situation? Please explain.
3. How do you feel about the ways that racial identity and ethnic identity impact Cheryl's problems? Do you agree or disagree with how Cheryl handles her situation?
4. How might the experiences of these case examples relate to your own experiences?

For helping professionals and graduate students of psychology, please consider these questions:

1. What would be the most difficult part of working with Glenn? What would be the most difficult part of working with Cheryl?
2. What might be some of your transference or countertransference issues with Glenn? With Cheryl?
3. How would your race, ethnicity, or gender impact your work with Glenn or Cheryl? How do you think they would react to you based on your race, ethnicity, or gender?
4. What would be helpful to create a therapeutic alliance with Glenn? What would be helpful to create a therapeutic alliance with Cheryl?

ACTIVITY 2: SELF-REFLECTION

The purpose of this activity is to examine how racial and ethnic identity may manifest in popular media forms. For example, many Filipino American comedians, hip-hop artists, performance artists, poets, and spoken word artists speak about Filipino American issues. (See Appendix B for a suggested list of Filipino American artists.)

1. Review the work of Filipino American artists on www.youtube.com.
2. In particular, search for the music video "Deep Foundation— Children of the Sun Remix" (featuring Hydroponikz, Nomi, Koba, Kiwi, and Encite).
3. Reflect on your cognitive and emotional reactions.
4. How do you believe the presence of Filipino American artists in the media impact the racial and ethnic identity of Filipino American individuals?

CHAPTER FOUR

Colonial Mentality of Filipino Americans

Figure 4.1 Filipino American college students performing a Spanish-influenced dance at a Pilipino Cultural Night (PCN)
Photo courtesy of Ernie Peña

CASE SYNOPSES

Agnes is a 14-year-old second-generation Filipina American and is the youngest of three daughters. Agnes always felt like she had to compare herself to her two older sisters, Marjorie, 21, and Bernadette, 18, who were both popular in high school, maintained good grades, and were winners of their Filipino association's beauty pageants. Agnes's mother consistently berates Agnes for "spending too much time in the sun" or for "being fat," even though Agnes has typical Filipino brown skin and an average body type. Agnes begins to develop low self-esteem and starts to restrict her eating.

Roderick is a 30-year-old Filipino man who recently immigrated to the United States. He was a teacher in his hometown in the Philippines and wanted to search for more career opportunities in the United States. He moved in with his aunt and uncle, who have lived in the United States for the past 30 years, with their two American-born sons: Steven, 27, and Matthew, 24. Roderick is having difficulty getting along with his cousins, who often make fun of his "fobby" ways and force him to act more "Americanized." He starts to feel self-conscious about his accent and feels anxious whenever he socializes with his cousins and their Filipino American friends.

INTRODUCTION

The Philippines is the only country in Asia that has been colonized by both Spain and the United States. In total, the Philippines have been colonized for about 420 years, with approximately 370 years of Spanish colonization and almost 50 years of American colonization. Although the Philippines have been free from colonial rule for about 60 years, the impressions of colonialism still have an impact on Philippine society, particularly through religion, educational systems, culture, language, values, and standards of beauty. Additionally, colonialism continues to have a lasting impact on the mental health of Filipinos and Filipino Americans, particularly their self-esteem, worldviews, and interpersonal relationships.

Previous authors have stated that Filipinos and Filipino Americans may develop a "colonial mentality," which is defined as a form of internalized oppression, in which the colonizer's values and beliefs are accepted by the colonized as beliefs and truths of their own; the colonized come to believe that the mores of the colonizer are superior to their own (David & Okazaki, 2006a). Research has also found that Filipinos and Filipino Americans often denigrate themselves and their culture, discriminate against those that are less acculturated, and are tolerant and accepting of contemporary oppression of their ethnic group (David, 2008, 2010; David & Okazaki, 2006a). This chapter examines specific ways in which colonialism has impacted mental health, including perceptions of standards of beauty, education, language, and self-efficacy. Finally, this chapter delves into ways that colonial mentality has led to divisions and tensions within Filipino American families and communities.

History of Colonialism

The colonization of Asian countries by European empires began as early as 1511 and was initiated mainly for economic reasons (Nadal, 2008a). European countries searched for raw materials that were unavailable in their home countries but were plentiful elsewhere, including Asian countries. For example, many Asian countries possessed precious metals and spices that were not available in Europe. As a result, colonizers conquered many Asian countries by force and stripped the countries of their natural resources, which would be used for trade. These resources were taken for free or little reimbursement, and colonizers would gain more wealth for their home countries. Accordingly, the economy of the colonizing country would grow, with little attention paid to the economics of the colonized countries (Nadal, 2008a). Concurrently, many of these European countries aimed to expand their empires in the Far East and sought to conquer as many "uncivilized" lands as possible, in order to increase dominance and prestige. For example, Great Britain and France established colonies in Africa, North America, and Southeast Asia, while Spain conquered most of South America and the Philippines. Whichever European empire had the most land was viewed as the most superior and powerful.

Some colonizing empires were more interested in cultural and religious expansion than in economic expansion. Some colonizers, for example, believed it was their duty and responsibility to ensure that "uncivilized" persons of the world were introduced to European ways of life. This topic was first introduced in Rudyard Kipling's *White Man's Burden* (1899), which describes the belief of many colonizers that their Western way of life was better than that of the colonized and that, therefore, Europeans were morally obliged to enforce a Western culture. Because Europeans viewed members of these indigenous cultures as "savages," they felt it was their duty to civilize and educate them about religion, culture, language, and etiquette. They believed that in order to be good, moral Christians, it was their responsibility to "save" indigenous people (Nadal, 2008a).

Although it is clear that there were economic and expansion reasons for the colonization of the Philippines, the conversion to Catholicism (and Christianity) was the most important reason for the Spanish colonization. This can be shown in the excessive and brutal force used by Spanish friars to convert native Filipinos. Jose Rizal, the national hero of the Philippines, has written about several incidents of Spanish friars who physically beat and harmed indigenous Filipinos who did not follow Catholicism or refused to be taught (e.g., Rizal, 1997). This tactic of using force did have an impact on the Philippines, in that many Filipinos converted. Today, 85% of the Filipino population is Catholic (Gall, 1998).

When the United States colonized the Philippines in 1899 (shortly after the Philippines gained independence from Spain), there were clear political and cultural reasons in doing so. Politically, the United States would use the Philippines as a "shield" to protect it from Japan and other Asian forces it viewed as enemies or threats. In fact, during World War I and World War II, when the Philippines was under U.S. rule, it was used as a battleground, although no major battles were fought in the continental United States. The U.S. government also may have wanted to colonize the Philippines to expand its empire and to compete with the already established European empires. In fact, the United States had conquered Hawaii as well as the newly independent Guam and Puerto Rico, which shows that the nation was interested in acquiring territories elsewhere. During this time, Filipinos (as well as Hawaiians, Guamanians, and Puerto Ricans) were encouraged to replace their native identities with American identities, through changing their indigenous names, speaking English, and pledging to the U.S. flag (Strobel, 2001). The United States also referred to Filipinos as America's "little brown brothers," in that the Philippines was an ally to the United States, and it was the responsibility of the American people to educate Filipinos and to encourage them to become more Americanized (Miller, 1982).

SOCIETAL INFLUENCES OF COLONIALISM

Spanish and American colonialism has impacted the Philippines and the Filipino and Filipino American people in numerous ways. Chapters 1 and 2 presented the history of how Spanish and American dominance influenced Filipino cultural values and worldview, specifically how Catholicism influenced Filipinos' beliefs, values, and traditions and how Spanish culture introduced new male-dominant gender roles. Additionally, those chapters discussed how almost 50 years of American rule led to the increased appreciation for American education systems and a shift toward individualism and competition. While religion and education are arguably the most notable effects of colonialism in the Philippines, this chapter concentrates specifically on the impact of colonialism on Filipino economics, government, language, arts, food, and societal standards of beauty. The chapter also discusses the concept of colonial mentality, and its effects on the mental health of Filipino and Filipino American individuals.

Economics

The Philippines has seen economic growth as a result of both Spanish and American colonization. During Spanish rule, the Philippine economy grew primarily because of trade in Manila–Acapulco galleons, the Spanish trading ships that sailed annually or semiannually between Manila and Acapulco, Mexico (Williams, 1999). During American rule, the Philippines became an agricultural export economy, producing sugar, abaca (sometimes referred to as Manila Hemp), copra, and tobacco for the U.S. market (Steinberg, 2000). However, after American colonialism ended in 1946, the Philippine economy plummeted for about a decade. Nationalistic policies that were implemented in the Philippines so that Filipino people could be in control of their economy without the help of other governments. For this reason, trade with foreign countries decreased.

In the late 1960s, new leadership in the Philippines led to increased trade with the United States and other foreign countries, leading to an increase in economic growth (Steinberg, 2000). However, due to political problems from the 1970s to the present day (including Ferdinand Marcos's implementation of martial law and corruption of subsequent presidents), the Philippine economy has not grown significantly. Additionally, while technological advancement occurred in the Philippines from the 1970s and beyond, the government has not kept up significantly with the technological advances of other modern countries (Steinberg, 2000). Finally, it is important to recognize that today, almost half of the citizens of the Philippines live in poverty (Balisacan, 1994).

Government

When the Philippines was granted independence from the United States in 1946, it was the first time in almost 400 years that the nation had sustained an independent and united democratic government. In fact, in the precolonial period, inhabitants viewed the Philippines as independent islands with their own governing systems and cultures. In establishing a central government, the Philippines was merely mimicking the government of the United States. When Ferdinand Marcos was elected president in the 1960s, he encouraged the islands of the Philippines to come together as a nation to attempt to rebuild their failed economy and government (Steinberg, 2000). However, in 1972, he declared martial law under the guise of political instability and communist threat; his true intent, however, was to cover up political corruption and block his political adversaries (Steinberg, 2000). Since then, the Philippine government has suffered from varying levels of corruption and instability.

One must also recognize how Spanish and American colonialism has influenced the Philippine government. Prior to colonialism, there was limited war and combat between the Filipino people. The *barangays*, or villages, with their individual governing systems maintained peace with each other and with any other countries they were exposed to (Constantino, 1975). However, after colonization, the Filipino people were introduced to power struggles, corruption, and fighting that had not been documented in indigenous or precolonial times. Accordingly, when forming a centralized government after 1946, Filipinos modeled their leadership on corrupt Spanish friars and the expansion-seeking American empire.

Language, Arts, and Food

Colonialism also introduced new languages to the Philippines. Although many Filipinos never adopted Spanish, English was commonly taught during American rule as a way for Filipinos to become "citizens of the world" (Steinberg, 2000). In fact, as noted in Chapter 2, English has been utilized in Philippine public school systems as a way of promoting the American educational system to the Filipino people. Additionally, for Filipinos of higher social classes, it was much more common to speak the English language (Nadal, 2008a), as Filipinos in poorer provinces may not have had exposure to teachers who spoke English. As a result, a division has been created in Philippine society, in which individuals who speak English are viewed as more "civilized" or educated while those who do not speak English are viewed as uncultured or uneducated.

In terms of arts, food, and other cultural practices, colonialism also has had an impact on Filipino culture and society. Traditional Filipino folk music consists of influences from Spain, Asia, and Middle Eastern countries. Contemporary Filipino music in the Philippines is performed in Taglish, or a combination of the two national languages of the Philippines: Tagalog and English. Filipino foods are influenced heavily by Spanish cooking, with some almost identical to delicacies eaten in Spain or Latin American countries (e.g., flan, menudo, jamon, and paella). Spanish, Latino, and Filipino people celebrate religious holidays almost identically. For example, Filipinos celebrate Christmas, Holy Week (before Easter), All Saints Day, and All Souls Day in similar ways that Catholics in Spain and Latin American countries might. Finally, American colonization and globalization has led Filipinos to have opportunities to be informed of the newest trends and happenings in American fashion, music, television, movies, and popular culture.

Societal Standards of Beauty

Spanish and American colonialism in the Philippines also has influenced societal standards of beauty among the Filipino people. First, although it is unclear whether precolonial Filipinos placed importance on skin color or skin tone, it is evident that skin color and skin tone has become an issue for postcolonial Filipinos (David & Okazaki,

2006a; Nadal, 2008a). Lighter-skinned Filipino and Filipino Americans often are referred to as *mestizo* or *mestiza*, which literally translates to someone who is part Spanish or multiracial Filipino and White (Root, 1997a). However, today *mestizo* is used to refer to anyone who is light-skinned or who appears to have Spanish features (e.g., lighter skin and smaller noses). Being a *mestizo/a* is highly valued in Filipino and Filipino American communities. Historically and contemporaneously, numerous light-skinned celebrities (e.g., musicians, actors, etc.) have been the most popular in Philippine entertainment and media, with biracial actors (mixed with White/European) receiving the highest salaries in the Philippines (Nadal, 2008a). Because of this fact, Filipinos and Filipino Americans commonly try to achieve a *mestizo/a* look by investing in skin-bleaching creams or even by pinching their noses to make them smaller, less flat, or somehow attain a bridge in their noses.

COLONIAL MENTALITY

Some authors assert that, as a result of both Spanish and American colonization, Filipinos and Filipino Americans may develop a "colonial mentality" (David & Okazaki, 2006a,b). As mentioned, "colonial mentality" is defined as a form of internalized oppression, in which the colonizer's values and beliefs are accepted by the colonized as beliefs and truths of their own; the colonized come to believe that the mores of the colonizer are superior to their own (David & Okazaki, 2006a). Filipinos with colonial mentality may glorify both Spanish and American values, such as lighter skin tone, Spanish cultural or religious traditions, or American education, over their darker brown skin or indigenous Filipino traditions and education (David & Okazaki, 2006a,b; Nadal, 2008a). It is also argued that colonial mentality includes an "uncritical rejection of anything Filipino" and an "uncritical preference for anything American" (David & Okazaki, 2006b, p. 241). Colonial mentality can affect both Filipino nationals (those born in the Philippines) and Filipino Americans (those born in the United States) on various levels. Some studies have found colonial mentality to be negatively related to enculturation, personal self-esteem, and collective self-esteem (David & Okazaki, 2006b) and positively correlated with depression (David, 2008; David & Okazaki, 2006b). In other words, people who have higher levels of colonial mentality are likely to be less enculturated, to have low self-esteem, and to have low collective self-esteem; concurrently, they are more likely to be depressed.

Previous authors have cited the four levels in which colonial mentality can impact an individual, including (1) denigration of oneself, (2) denigration of one's culture, (3) discrimination against those who are less acculturated, and (4) tolerance and acceptance of contemporary oppression of one's ethnic group (David & Okazaki, 2006a). Denigration of oneself may include the ways an individual may acquire low self-esteem because she or he does not match the physical or cultural characteristics of the colonizer. For example, a darker-skinned Filipino may believe that she or he is inferior to one who has lighter skin. Denigration of one's culture includes the ways individuals develop negative feelings toward their cultural group because the group's cultural values and traditions do not match those of the colonizer. For example, an individual may believe Filipino music, arts, or cooking is inferior to American or Spanish music, arts, or cooking. Discrimination against those who are less acculturated includes how individuals judge others who are less acculturated to colonizer values. For example, a second-generation Filipino American may insult a recent immigrant who speaks with a heavy accent or who is not aware of current American fashion trends. Finally, tolerance and acceptance of contemporary oppression of one's ethnic group includes how an individual may be forgiving of colonialism because she or he learned to be indebted to and appreciative of the colonizer. For example, a Filipino might claim Spanish and American colonizers are "civilizing, freedom-giving, or unsanctified heroes" (Nadal, 2008a) and deny any negative impacts of colonialism.

A Colonial Mentality Scale (CMS) was created to measure ways individuals of colonized cultures have internalized colonialism in their worldviews, attitudes, and behaviors (David & Okazaki, 2006b). The CMS includes five subscales:

1. Within-group discrimination
2. Physical characteristics
3. Colonial debt
4. Cultural shame and embarrassment
5. Internalized cultural/ethnic inferiority

Items measuring within-group discrimination focus on feelings toward new immigrants, or "fobs" (those who are *fresh off* the *b*oat). Items measuring physical characteristics involve feelings about one's physical features, such as skin color or nose width. Items measuring colonial debt include feelings about how Spain and the United States have been positive influences on the Philippines. Items measuring cultural shame and embarrassment involve feelings about belonging to the Filipino culture or group. Items measuring internalized cultural/ethnic inferiority include feelings about whether to be a member of the dominant or colonizer group.

In the Filipino and Filipino American community, it is common for individuals to completely deny their Filipino ethnicity or claim that they are "mixed" (Nadal, 2008a). In fact, many Filipino Americans state that they are part Spanish, part Latino or part Hawaiian; some even deny their Filipino heritage altogether by stating that they are full Spanish, full Latino, or full Hawaiian. Many Filipino Americans may state that they are "mixed" or only a certain percentage Filipino in order to gain perceived status in the community. Individuals who are *mestizo* are often viewed as ideal, beautiful, and prized (Root, 1997a). Accordingly, some Filipinos and Filipino Americans may state that they are mixed in order to feel valued or superior to others. In fact, in Hawaiian culture, where being *hapa,* or multiracial, is celebrated and where Filipinos are denigrated (Okamura, 1998), Filipino Americans may feel embarrassed of their ethnicity and claim to be *hapa.* Finally, denying one's Filipino heritage has been a common trend for Filipino American celebrities in the media. For example, actress Tia Carrere, *American Idol* finalist Jasmine Trias, and professional baseball player Benny Agbayani have claimed in the past to be Spanish, Hawaiian, or Chinese instead of Filipino (Jorge, 2004; Nadal, 2008a). This phenomenon has been referred to in the Filipino American community as the IMSCF syndrome, otherwise known as the I-am-Spanish-Chinese-Filipino syndrome.

Finally, colonial mentality also may create a hierarchy between Filipinos and Filipino Americans, leading to tensions between persons of the same ethnic group. Hierarchies are created based on physical appearance, educational levels, religion, language abilities, and region. For example, there are hierarchies based on phenotype, in which light-skinned persons who are *mestizo* or appear to be Spanish are considered the most beautiful or most talented or as making the best leaders. In educational hierarchies, individuals who are educated in American institutions are more valued than those who are educated in the Philippines. In hierarchies based on religion, Filipino Christians (e.g., Catholics and Protestants) are viewed as superior to Filipino Muslims or Filipino Buddhists. Language hierarchies are also present in which Filipinos who speak English without a Filipino accent will be viewed as the most eloquent, educated, or respectable. In regional hierarchies, individuals who live in (or are originally from) certain areas in the Philippines are viewed as superior to others. For example, Manila is a major metropolitan city in the Philippines with many Spanish and American influences and a breadth of technological advances. Based on regional hierarchies, people from Manila would be viewed as more important or cherished than those who live in the provinces.

Figure 4.2 Filipina American immigrant women enjoying themselves at a fancy event
Photo courtesy of Ken Paprocki

DECOLONIZATION FRAMEWORKS

Because colonial mentality has been demonstrated to impact self-esteem and depressive symptoms, many scholarly works have focused on decolonization as a theoretical framework. "Decolonization" can be defined as the process of humanizing the dehumanized by promoting positive mental health and identity for persons of colonized backgrounds (Strobel, 2001). The purpose of decolonization is to reject colonial mentalities that have been passed on through generations of colonized peoples. By teaching people to "decolonize" themselves, it is expected that individuals can increase their self-esteem and develop positive images of themselves and their ethnic group (Halagao, 2004b).

A few decolonization models have been used with various colonized people. For example, one framework was developed for Native Hawaiians, a group that had been colonized by both Great Britain and the United States (Laenui, 2000). According to this model, one must pass through five stages in order to decolonize oneself:

1. Rediscovery/recovery
2. Mourning
3. Dreaming
4. Commitment
5. Action

Rediscovering/recovery means that individuals first have to learn and recognize that their ethnic group has been colonized. They can do this by learning about colonialism in history classes, by talking with community members about the impacts of colonialism in their own lives, or by recognizing the ways in which colonial mentality has led to discrimination in the community. People become more aware of their colonial mentality and make efforts to try to dispel it. For example, a Filipino or Filipino American may attempt to reject *machismo* gender roles (Spanish cultural values) and promote matriarchy or gender-neutral roles, which are considered indigenous Filipino cultural values. In the *mourning* stage, individuals from a colonized group recognize and grieve for the culture that was taken away. For example, Filipinos or Filipino Americans might have feelings of sadness or loss when recognizing they have lived their lives with colonial mentalities; they also may feel sorrow for the ways that their group has been treated throughout history. In the *dreaming* stage, people from the colonized group are able to imagine living in a world free of self-denigration. For example, Filipinos or Filipino Americans might envision ways in which their family and community could be free of discrimination based on racism or colonialism. The *commitment* stage is when individuals learn to commit their lives to decolonizing themselves. This can be depicted by Filipino Americans who are always cognizant of their own colonial mentality while also promoting decolonization among the people around them. Finally, the *action* stage is where individuals commit to the next level and promote decolonization on greater societal levels.

One author offers a concise model of decolonization that is founded specifically on the post-1965 Filipino American immigrant experience (Strobel, 2001). The model has three simple stages: (1) naming, (2) reflecting, and (3) acting. The *naming* stage occurs when Filipino American individuals are able to recognize the colonial oppression and understand its impact on their identity. The *reflection* stage is when Filipino Americans are able to think critically about how colonialism has impacted their lives as well as those of others. Finally, the *acting* stage is where Filipino Americans are able to "give back" to the Filipino American community by becoming leaders and role models and encouraging others to decolonize themselves.

Many authors suggest that decolonization is not just an individual process for Filipino Americans but rather a process in which several members of the community need to be involved (Halagao, 2004b; Strobel, 2001). For example, one author believes that teachers and counselors (both Filipino American and those of other racial/ethnic backgrounds) need to assist their Filipino and Filipino American students in decolonizing their mind-sets (Halagao, 2004b). This can be done by teaching the history of the Philippines prior to Spanish and American rule, emphasizing the positive traits of the precolonial culture. It also can be accomplished by working directly with parents to teach children about the negative impacts of colonialism. If a child's family is not combating the colonial mentality at home, decolonization may be difficult in the classroom. Finally, providing positive Filipino and Filipino American role models can be helpful in decolonizing mind-sets. In becoming decolonized, Filipino and Filipino American youth can learn to be proud of their own cultural group instead of the White American role models to whom they are accustomed.

DISCUSSION QUESTIONS

1. Do you believe that colonialism in the Philippines was positive, negative, or both? Explain your answer.
2. Do you believe that Spanish colonialism was better or worse than American colonialism? Were they both equally good? Were they both equally bad?
3. In what ways has colonialism affected you and your everyday life personally (e.g., your values, your worldview, and your perception of body image or beauty)?
4. In what ways has colonial mentality affected your community (e.g., how people interact with each other, how people perceive others)?

SUMMARY

This chapter discussed the ways colonialism and colonial mentality may impact Filipino Americans on societal and individual levels. The chapter reviewed how 420 years of Spanish and American colonialism has influenced the Philippines through religion, educational systems, culture, language, values, and standards of beauty. This chapter also examined how colonialism has led Filipino Americans to develop a colonial mentality, which has been demonstrated to have a direct effect on their worldviews, personal self-esteem, collective self-esteem, ethnic identity, and interpersonal relationships. Finally, ways in which colonial mentality could lead to psychological stress, depression, and hierarchies in the Filipino American community were discussed, leading many individuals to advocate for the decolonization of Filipino Americans. This chapter now presents two case studies that show how colonialism and colonial mentality may impact a Filipino American's mental health. Additionally, these case studies reveal how colonial mentality may influence one's ability to seek mental health treatment and impact psychotherapeutic relationships.

Case Studies

Case 1: Agnes and Her Body Image Issues

Agnes is a 14-year-old second-generation Filipina American and is the youngest of three daughters. Her parents immigrated to Hawaii over 20 years ago from a small province in the Visayan region of the Philippines. She has two older sisters—Marjorie, 21, and Bernadette, 18—both of whom are attending college away from home. Agnes always felt that she had to compare herself to her two older sisters, who were both popular in high school, maintained good grades, and were winners of their Filipino association's beauty pageants. One major reason why Agnes may compare herself to her sisters is her relationship with her mother. Agnes's mother consistently berates Agnes for "spending too much time in the sun" or for "being fat." Her mother often refers to Agnes as her "dark daughter" or her "fat daughter" (while referring to Marjorie and Bernadette as her "light-skinned daughters" or "skinny daughters"), which is perplexing since Agnes has typical Filipino brown skin and an average body type.

Agnes begins to develop low self-esteem and feels disgusted about what she sees in the mirror every morning. She thinks she is fat, ugly, and dark. She believes boys will not like her because she is unattractive and disgusting. She buys makeup that makes her skin appear lighter in tone. She even starts to restrict her eating, to the point where she is eating one meal a day, which consists of two slices of turkey and half an orange. When her parents ask her to eat breakfast, she says she will "catch something to eat at school." When her parents ask her to eat dinner, Agnes says she "already ate" and goes directly to her room. This behavior continues for two months before Agnes's mother finally recognizes her daughter's weight loss. She confronts Agnes and attempts to force her to eat; however, when Agnes refuses, her mother takes her to her pediatrician.

Case 2: Roderick and His "Fobby" Accent

Roderick is a 30-year-old Filipino who recently immigrated to the United States. He is the eldest son of five children, and the rest of his family still lives in the Philippines. He was educated in the Philippines (majoring

(Continued)

Figure 4.3 A second-generation Filipino American father holding his third-generation Filipina American daughter
Photo courtesy of Kevin Nadal

in education), and he became a teacher in his hometown. However, because he wanted to search for more career opportunities in the United States and had always wanted to move there, he decided to move in with his aunt and uncle, who have lived in Texas for the past 30 years. He met his two Filipino American cousins—Steven, 27, and Matthew, 24—who both have successful jobs in business and higher education respectively. In fact, Matthew even helped Roderick to find a job working as an administrator at his local university.

Steven and Matthew are very proud of their Filipino American ethnicity, and most of their friends are second-generation Filipino Americans. However, when Roderick moved in with them, they often made fun of him because of his "fobby" accent and behaviors. They told him that he needs to become more "Americanized" by losing his Filipino accent, learning American slang terms and American ways of dressing, and developing American mannerisms and an American sense of humor. Their friends often joined in the mocking, repeating words that Roderick spoke with a Filipino accent and laughing hysterically afterward. Sometimes Roderick's aunt and uncle would notice these interactions between their sons and their nephew. However, they never reprimanded their sons or talked to Roderick about their sons' behaviors.

Roderick starts to feel self-conscious about his accent. He makes an effort to watch more American television and tries to mimic their accents and slang terms. However, when he hangs out with his cousins and their Filipino American friends, he begins to feel extremely socially anxious, to the point where he finds himself having difficulty speaking and starts to stutter, tremble, or breathe rapidly. As a result, he begins to avoid his cousins and their friends altogether because of his fear of being scrutinized, judged, or embarrassed by them. He even moves out of their home and finds his own place in a completely different neighborhood. He has difficulty making new friends because he worries that they too will judge him on his accent and/or mannerisms. This situation becomes very difficult for Roderick because he does not like feeling as if he is being disrespectful or distant from his family, especially since they took him in when he first arrived in the United States. However, he would rather feel isolated than feel inferior when he is around his cousins.

Case Study Discussion

Colonial mentality may impact the mental health problems of these two Filipino Americans in several ways. In both cases, one can see how an individual's colonial mentality may have been influenced by the colonial mentality of those around them. For example, Agnes may have been negatively affected by her mother, while Roderick may be deeply pressured by his cousins. One also can observe how colonial mentality influences various mental health issues and coping mechanisms. For Agnes, colonial mentality has affected her self-esteem and her perceptions of her body image, while colonial mentality affects Roderick's self-esteem and his ability to form social relationships. Finally, in both cases, it is important to recognize how colonial mentality passes down from generation to generation in overt and covert ways. In the case of Agnes, colonial mentality is blatantly transferred from mother to daughter, whereas in the case of Roderick, colonial mentality is indirectly taught to be tolerated or acceptable by Roderick's aunt and uncle.

(Continued)

People's concept of colonial mentality is heavily influenced by the messages of those around them. For Agnes, her mother's colonial mentality directly impacts her own mind-set and self-esteem. Perhaps Agnes's mother has her own self-hatred about her own skin color or body type and she is merely projecting this low self-esteem onto her daughter. Her mother is even creating a hierarchy between her daughters by referring to Agnes as a "dark" or "fat" daughter, subtly communicating that her "light" daughters are more valued or beautiful. So while Agnes may love and respect her sisters, her mother's colonial mentality (and Agnes's subsequent colonial mentality) may create tension or resentment between Agnes and her sisters. Roderick receives many direct and subtle messages from his cousins that may shape his own colonial concept. Much like Agnes's mother, Steven and Matthew, Roderick's cousins, may be combating their own colonial mentality or internalized racism, in which they feel insecure about who they are as Filipino Americans or as people of color. Accordingly, they establish a hierarchy between themselves and their new immigrant cousin as a way of feeling superior or higher in social status.

As a result of receiving these negative colonial messages, it appears that both Agnes and Roderick have developed mental health disorders. It is obvious that Agnes displays symptoms of an eating disorder, while Roderick appears to be exhibiting symptoms of a social phobia. Both disorders are influenced directly by colonial mentality. Agnes's eating disorder may have been triggered by the negative messages about her body image that she has been receiving from her mother. In precolonial Philippines, body image was not much of an issue; Filipinos came in all shapes and sizes, and there was little tension based on skin tone or color. However, after Spanish colonialism, it became evident that light or White skin was valued in the Philippines, and after American colonialism, it became obvious that Filipinos were encouraged to have body types like Hollywood celebrities and movie stars.

Roderick's social phobia may be triggered specifically by his cousins and cousins' friends who consistently make fun of him for his accent, mannerisms, and fashion. While he may not have experienced these feelings of anxiety prior to moving to the United States, he starts to suffer classic symptoms of social phobia: He worries intensely about being teased or criticized, he has difficulty speaking in social groups, and he stutters, trembles, and breathes heavily whenever he socializes with his cousins. Roderick's social phobia even causes him to have cultural distress, in which he must be individualistic and separate himself from his family. Although Roderick may want to honor the Filipino cultural values of *kapwa* (fellow being) or *utang ng loob* (debt of reciprocity), doing so only causes him more psychological distress. As a result, he isolates himself altogether and continues to feel culturally conflicted.

Finally, both cases display how colonial mentality transmits across generations in direct and indirect ways. Colonial mentality can be direct in the ways Agnes's mother has communicated messages about skin color and body size to her daughters. Previous authors have asserted that Filipino American children are often the recipients of criticism from their parents, which often leads to psychological stressors and self-esteem issues (Heras, 2007). While all children may be subjected to such criticism, Filipino children may be criticized as a result of their parents' colonial mentalities. Although Agnes's mother may feel that her criticisms of her daughter are innocuous or nonthreatening, the disparaging comments have negative effects on Agnes's mental health. This is similar to the implied acceptance of colonial mentality conveyed by Roderick's aunt and uncle when they allow their sons to tease their cousin. In many ways, indirect acceptance or tolerance of colonial mentality may be just as damaging or powerful as direct messages are. For example, if a Filipino American tells someone that she or he is handsome or pretty because she or he looks "Spanish" and that person says "thank you," the messages being transmitted to both parties (and any observers) is that appearing to be Spanish equates beauty. Similarly, if a Filipino American insults another person for being fobby and no one says anything about the interaction, the messages being transmitted are that it is acceptable to insult persons who are less Americanized and that Filipinos or Filipino immigrants are inferior to Filipino Americans who were born and raised in the United States.

Case Study Discussion Questions

For undergraduate students and general readers, please consider these questions:

1. What are your initial reactions to these two case examples?
2. What are the ways that colonial mentality impacts Agnes's mental health?

(Continued)

3. What are the ways that colonial mentality impacts Roderick's mental health?

4. How might the experiences of Agnes or Roderick relate to your own experiences or those of someone you know?

For helping professionals and graduate students of psychology, please consider these questions:

1. What would be the most difficult part of working with Agnes? What would be the most difficult part of working with Roderick?

2. What might be some of your transference or countertransference issues with Agnes? Roderick? Agnes's mother? Roderick's cousins?

3. What is your theoretical orientation? Which theoretical orientation(s) do you think would be most effective in working with Agnes or Roderick?

4. Do you believe that the counselor or clinician's race, ethnicity, or gender would make a difference in working with Agnes or Roderick? Why or why not?

ACTIVITY 3: SELF-REFLECTION

The purpose of this activity is to understand how colonial mentality may impact Filipino Americans on individual and societal levels. As mentioned, Filipino and Filipino American media sources may promote colonial mentality, both subtly and directly, in a variety of ways. For this activity, watch any form of Filipino television programming (e.g., comedies, dramas, or variety shows on The Filipino Channel) for one hour, or watch a Filipino or Filipino American movie (see Appendix B for examples).

1. While watching the television show or movie:
   a. Count the number of dark-skinned Filipino individuals that you see.
   b. Count the number of light-skinned Filipino individuals that you see.
   c. Pay attention to other ways that colonial mentality may manifest in these programs or media.
2. Discuss these findings with your peers, examining your cognitive and emotional reactions.

CHAPTER FIVE

Filipino American Groups and Communities

Figure 5.1 *Two young Filipino professionals enjoying each others' company at a Filipino dinner party*
Photo courtesy of Kevin Nadal

CASE SYNOPSES

Ben is a 22-year-old second-generation Filipino American college student who was referred to the counseling center by his psychology professor. Recently, Ben failed his midterm exam and shared with his professor how he had been extremely stressed out with balancing school and his extracurricular activities. He is currently the president of his Filipino American student organization, works 20 hours a week for a nonprofit organization, and is taking a full course load for the semester. Upon meeting with a counselor for the first time, Ben explained his situation and said that he "absolutely could not" give up his job or presidency, and he did not want to drop any of his classes. He revealed that he needed his job to help pay for school and that he needed to fulfill his duties to the organization because he did not want to appear to be a failure or let anyone down.

Maritess is a 50-year-old first-generation Filipina American who has served as the executive director of the Filipino American Community Center (FACC) for the past 10 years. FACC is a nonprofit organization that services a Filipino American community in a major metropolitan area; it offers youth empowerment programs, promotes community service projects, and hosts many social events in the neighborhood. Over the past five years, Maritess noticed that there has been a decline in support of the organization. Donations have been decreasing, and there has been less participation in and attendance at all of the programs. She hires an organizational psychologist to conduct a program evaluation of the community center and discovers that there is serious tension among several groups in the organization, namely immigrants versus American-born Filipinos, youth versus adults, and Ilocanos versus Tagalogs (two Filipino regional/ethnic subgroups). It is also discovered that *tsismis* (gossip) is very prevalent within the community and has led several formerly active members to distance themselves from the FACC.

INTRODUCTION

This chapter examines the history and experiences of various Filipino American communities in the United States. Previous literature has discussed how politics and colonial mentality in the Filipino American community often leads to separation and competition between various subgroups (Nadal, 2008a). Other authors have found that distinct generational differences lead to conflicts in the Filipino American community, namely between post-1965 immigrant parents and their

American-born children (Espiritu & Wolf, 2001). Moreover, different types of Filipino American organizations and events, including pageantry participation, membership in college student organizations and youth groups, and involvement in activist groups may have an impact on mental health, self-esteem, and ethnic identity. Finally, social class and immigration differences have led to divisions in Filipino American communities, where often the wealthy and educated are separate from the poor and uneducated, as well as tensions between American citizens and undocumented immigrants. This chapter considers the impacts of community dynamics on mental health Filipino American individuals and groups.

History of Filipino American Groups and Communities

In order to understand the current state of Filipino American groups and communities, it is important to review the history of Filipino Americans in the United States. As discussed in Chapter 1, Filipino American communities began forming as early as the 1700s, when the first Filipino immigrants formed small settlements along the bayous of Louisiana (Posadas, 1999). Most of these Filipinos escaped Spanish slave ships en route from Manila to Acapulco to Spain. These communities consisted mostly of immigrant men; there were few Filipina women. Thus for these immigrants began the gradual disconnection from the Philippines and intermarriage with other racial groups. The people's lessening identification as "Filipinos" or "Filipino Americans" led the community to dwindle over generations.

The second and third waves of Filipino American communities occurred in the early 1900s, when many Filipinos immigrated to the United States, mostly to the West Coast and Hawaii, as sponsored and nonsponsored students (Kitano & Daniels, 1995; Posadas, 1999). Many of these individuals were in search of a better life away from the Philippines but were met with institutional and interpersonal racism. Some students succeeded in their educational pursuits, but others who did not have resources resorted to enter into menial labor (e.g., farmworkers or fish cannery workers). These communities were also predominantly male, with an estimated 10 to 1 ratio of Filipino men to women. (Some authors cite this ratio as 15 to 1.) Accordingly, many men married outside of their race, leading to a new generation of multiracial and multiethnic Filipino Americans (see Chapter 8). Many of these Filipino Americans were involved in community organizing, fighting and advocating for workers' rights (e.g., the United Farm Workers in California in the 1960s). Because these Filipino Americans worked in similar fields, had similar interests, and made similar amounts of money, many lived in comparable neighborhoods and homes, forming ethnic enclaves in various metropolitan areas along the West Coast (e.g., Historic Pilipinotown in Los Angeles, the Tenderloin District in San Francisco, and downtown Seattle, Washington). Most of these Filipino Americans were working class or lower middle class, and many of their children were raised in these ethnic enclaves.

The last major wave of Filipino American immigration took place after the Immigration Act of 1965, which allowed Filipinos (and those from other countries) to immigrate in mass numbers to the United States. Many of these individuals were professionals who were educated in the Philippines as doctors, nurses, and engineers (Kitano & Daniels, 1995; Posadas, 1999), and many moved to different areas of the United States, where their professional services were needed. Although a majority of Filipinos may have immigrated to the West Coast or Hawaii (where they may have had other family members), others settled elsewhere in the United States, including the East Coast, Midwest, and South. Because many in this new wave of immigrants had professional careers and were highly educated, they earned more money than working-class Filipinos. Thus, they moved to suburban areas instead of the Filipino ethnic enclaves in metropolitan cities. Over time, many of these "Filipino neighborhoods" slowly disappeared as the existing Filipinos moved to different neighborhoods or the suburbs themselves. In present day, many communities in various metropolitan areas attempt to preserve these neighborhoods for historical significances; however, gentrification and difficult economic situations make some of these efforts more difficult.

The history of these Filipino American communities has many implications for contemporary Filipino American groups. One can notice how social class may unite Filipino Americans. For example, working-class Filipinos may have had similar jobs, lived in similar neighborhoods, and may have had similar political interests; thus, they sought to live in close proximity in order to remain cohesive and maintain the values of *kapwa* (fellow being) and *pakikama* (togetherness). Conversely, social class also may divide Filipino Americans. When the professional immigrants came to the United States, they chose to separate themselves from the working-class Filipino Americans who lived in less affluent metropolitan neighborhoods. Thus, these professionals chose to live apart from other Filipino Americans. Given these experiences, social class can be viewed in both positive and negative ways, in that it has been a source of connecting and disconnecting the Filipino American community.

CONTEMPORARY FILIPINO AMERICAN COMMUNITIES

This section examines various types of Filipino American organizations in order to understand how community and group dynamics might form. As with many other ethnic groups, among Filipino Americans, subcommunities and organizations may exist in a variety of forms, including youth and college student organizations; Filipino cultural and regional associations; Filipino American community, political activist, and other interest groups; and online communities. In reading about these types of Filipino American groups and communities, one may examine the specific values, norms, and culture of these types of networks, which consequently may lead to unique psychological stressors.

Youth and Student Organizations

Although many Filipino American youth initially were encouraged to assimilate into American dominant mainstream society, many members of the second generation have learned to reclaim and revitalize their Filipino American ethnic identity through youth organizing and empowerment (Strobel, 2001). As a result, Filipino American student organizations first began forming in the mid-1960s (around the civil rights movement), primarily in California. These organizations evolved predominantly at major universities, such as San Francisco State University and the University of California at Los Angeles, Berkeley, and Irvine, where there was a small but noticeable number of Filipino American students (Tiongson, 2006). Today, most major colleges and universities across the United States have well-established Filipino or Filipino American organizations (in addition to umbrella Asian American organizations), with a variety of social and cultural activities and established alumni networks (Okamura & Agbayani, 1997). In fact, there are an array of regional conferences in the East Coast, Southwest, and Northwest, in which hundreds of Filipino Americans come together to socialize, learn about their culture and history, and show pride in their specific college organizations. Some of these annual conferences include the Filipino Intercollegiate Networking Dialogue (FIND) in the East Coast and the Filipino Americans Coming Together (FACT) conference, held annually at the University of Illinois.

Some authors state that Filipino Americans seek these types of organizations in order to learn more about their culture, to resolve issues of ethnic identity, and to serve as a source of social support. This fact can be demonstrated in a statement by one Filipino American graduate student who asserts: "I turned to the Filipino student organization. . . . They were *so* crucial in helping me vent and hear me out. I was able to also have great friendships that have continued to this day" (Nadal, Pituc, et al., 2010, p. 7).

Within these organizations, many Filipino Americans become involved in various political issues while many express themselves and their ethnic identities through performance arts and dance (Gonzalves, 1997). Filipino American and Pilipino Cultural Nights (PCNs) have emerged as regular staples on college campuses across the United States. Filipino American students perform traditional dances from different regions of the Philippines and contemporary American culture. For example, students perform festive Spanish waltzes, native Igorot tribal rituals, and Muslim-influenced dancing, plus modern and hip-hop dance. These PCNs have included dramatic or comedic theatrical plays highlighting present-day Filipino American issues. Such performances have been essential for Filipino American college students to learn about their culture and identity while also educating their audience members. However, many of these cultural displays have become such elaborate productions that they have interfered with and sometimes injured participants' academic and personal well-being (Gonzalves, 1997). Although these cultural nights may have positive intentions, they also may lead to detrimental mental health consequences.

Filipino Cultural and Regional Associations

When Filipino immigrants first arrived in the United States, many formed organizations as a way of staying connected to others from their regions or hometowns in the Philippines (Espiritu, 2003; Okamura, 1983). In any given part of the United States, organizations may bring together members from specific regions in the Philippines. For example, the Aklan Association of the Eastern Seaboard is an organization based in New York and New Jersey whose members originally lived in the province of Aklan. Other organizations bring together former residents of a particular town. For example, the Malinao Brotherhood Improvement Society of the San Francisco Bay Area consists of members from Malinao, a small town in the Visayan Islands.

Because of this spectrum of Filipino American organizations, there may be a divide or competition between many regional and hometown groups. Some have argued that there is disunity in the Filipino American community as a result of the many regional associations that exist (Espiritu, 2004; Pido, 1986; Posadas & Guyotte, 1990). According to an earlier study, the island of Oahu, Hawaii (which has a land area of about 600 square miles), had about 62 Filipino American regional and hometown groups (Okamura, 1983). More recently, it has been reported that in San Diego County, California, which has a landmass of 4,500 square miles, there are between 150 and 175 Filipino American organizations (Espiritu, 2003). Competition may arise between these various groups, leading to regional pride (e.g., Ilocanos or Visayans) and hometown pride (e.g., Cavite or Boracay) versus ethnic or national pride as Filipinos or Filipino Americans.

Previous authors also have discussed numerous interorganizational disputes within these various associations, along with disputes that often are publicly fought. Such conflicts might involve leadership or politics, financial mismanagement, "discourteous" interpersonal behavior, and differences in organizational goals (Espiritu, 2003, 2004; Pido, 1986; Posadas & Guyotte, 1990). In these associations, members often compete for status, which is received through attaining leadership positions (e.g., becoming the association president) or through boasting about family accomplishments (Espiritu, 2003). Additionally, these regional or hometown associations also may host elaborate events, such as officer installation galas or beauty pageants, as ways of showcasing a family's social standing and socioeconomic status. These events may be featured prominently in local and ethnic newspapers, leading to further competition and division (Espiritu, 2003).

Finally, previous literature has noted how *tsismis* (gossip) is prevalent in the Filipino American community and how it is acceptable and common-place to gossip about one's own friends and relatives while at the same time yearning to be socially accepted and celebrated by those same people (Nadal, 2004). So although these organizations may be formed to pro-mote *bayanihan* (community) and collectivism—considered core Filipino values—they also may foster competition and individualism—considered American colonial values. Because of this conflict, Filipino American regional and hometown associations can be described as both cohesive and fragmented (Espiritu, 2003). They are cohesive in that they bring Filipino Americans together, but they are fragmented in that they often lead to struggles within and between various organizations.

Filipino American Community, Political Activist, and Other Interest Groups

Many Filipino Americans have created cultural organizations or com-munity centers that promote a united Filipino or Filipino American identity and members may be from various regions of the Philippines. Many such organizations exist in California, Washington, Hawaii, Virginia, Michigan, Illinois, New York, and New Jersey, housing numer-ous programs that endorse Filipino and Filipino American culture, education, and empowerment. For example, the Search for Involving Pilipino Youth (SIPA) in Los Angeles, Filipino Youth Activities (FYA) in Seattle, and the Filipino American Human Services, Inc. (FAHSI) in New York have well-established youth groups where Filipino American teens have group discussions, participate in art and cul-tural dance, and learn about Filipino and Filipino American history. Other educational programs, such as Pinoy Teach (a curriculum that has been taught in Washington and Hawaii) and Pin@y Educational Partnership (taught in San Francisco), combine instruction with politi-cal activism and service learning (Halagao, 2004a; Tintiangco-Cuballes, 2007). Participants learn about political issues in the Philippines and the

United States while becoming empowered to participate in rallies, protests, marches, educational forums, and other forms of community organizing (Halagao, 2004a).

There also exist numerous Filipino American organizations aimed at members of specific career fields or those who hold common interests. For instance, there are national and regional associations for Filipino doctors or nurses as well as regional Filipino American youth basketball leagues. Many community dance and performance groups give Filipino Americans, especially youth, opportunities to express and learn about their ethnic identity. These groups may include various art forms, including dance (both traditional Philippine folk dance and contemporary American hip-hop), spoken word, poetry, community-based theater, stand-up comedy, studio art, music, and fashion. The sense of community that is felt by many of these group members can be exemplified by one Filipina American woman who was part of a cultural dance group:

> *In high school and in college, all I could think of was Philippine dance . . . I focused all my energy on [our Filipino dance group]. . . . I enjoyed the camaraderie—being with a bunch of people. . . . It was like being in a gang; those people were like family to you. (Cabato, 1995, pp. 146–147)*

This quote demonstrates how many Filipino Americans may search for a community in order to feel a sense of belonging and self-worth. Joining organizations may be especially salient for younger persons, who may be searching for their ethnic identity and hope to gain more cultural awareness and friendship from others who share their same cultural values and struggles.

Online Groups and Communities

A final way that Filipino American communities form is through online groups. Virtual communities have increased since the mid-1990s, and many Filipino Americans have used these cybercommunities to strengthen a sense of national, ethnic, and racial identity with others while developing meaningful and personal relationships (Ignacio, 2005). These online communities, which are specific to the Filipino and Filipino American issues, can occur through newsgroup debates, list serves, blogs, and Web site postings where individuals can discuss various Filipino and Filipino American issues, such as gender, mail-order brides, or identity (Ignacio, 2005). More recently, online communities have been established on Facebook and MySpace, where individuals can network and connect with others (e.g., long-lost friends or new "Facebook friends") while sharing photographs and videos and participating in political and social groups. Individuals who utilize online communities appear to have higher levels of social capital; usage of such sites suggests increasing self-esteem and life satisfaction (Ellison, Steinfeld, & Lampe, 2007). Through online interactions, Filipino and Filipino Americans can feel a sense of community with others and bridge the Filipino diaspora, despite the geographic distance that may separate them (Ignacio, 2005).

Tensions within Filipino American Groups and Communities

Given the variety of Filipino American groups and communities, it is important to examine the different tensions that might exist between subgroups. First, generational and age issues may impact Filipino American organizations. Within any given Filipino American group or community, there probably are immigrant and American-born members. Accordingly, there is the prospect of a number of issues, based on whether or not the organization should follow more American norms or Filipino norms. Members may have differing communication styles, acculturation levels, and views of leadership and authority. For example, if staff members of a Filipino American community center are older immigrants and young American-born professionals, there may exist an unspoken hierarchy and power, regardless of actual leadership positions. Members of the older immigrant generations may expect younger members to adhere to their opinions and ideas. Concurrently, members of the younger American-born generations may have difficulty voicing dissenting opinions or critical concerns. This may be especially prevalent in regional and hometown organizations, where many of the members are related (through heredity or through family kinship).

Second, previous literature has noted how social class may cause a divide in many Filipino regional and hometown associations (Espiritu, 2003). Because the culture of these associations includes individuals boasting of accomplishments, many members from higher social classes (e.g., those with higher income or levels of education) may discriminate against those from lower social classes (e.g., those with lower income or levels of education). This phenomenon is evident when members plan lavish events with high-priced tickets that only those from the upper middle class can afford (Espiritu, 2003). Such experiences are not limited to regional and hometown associations; it may occur in college student organizations (e.g., a group that plans costly semiformal events and group vacation trips) and community centers (e.g., a center that coordinates expensive annual galas and dinner dances).

Third, citizenship and immigration status also may cause divisions among different Filipino American groups. Chapter 1 introduced the concept of undocumented immigrants from the Philippines, or *TNTs* (*tago ng tago*), which translates as "to keep on hiding." Most undocumented Filipino TNTs enter the country with a legal visa but overstay their welcome, or they enter the country legally but violate the terms of their visa (Montoya, 1997). TNTs may be marginalized within the Filipino American community, particularly when legal immigrants and citizens view or treat them as inferior. Because of this phenomena, many TNTs hesitate to join organizations in order to avoid mistreatment by others or because of the fear that others may discover their undocumented status.

Religious tensions also may cause rifts in Filipino American groups and communities. Because 90% of Filipinos and Filipino Americans are Catholic or Christian, religious practice often is assumed to be an acceptable part of community events. For example, many groups with non-religious purposes or missions begin major events with an invocation; sometimes the group may even invite a priest or Christian religious official to lead the prayer. Additionally, many Filipino American community centers host annual Christmas parties, in which members freely wish each other *"Maligayang Pasko!"* ("Merry Christmas!") and assume that everyone would be Catholic or Christian. These types of religious practices may be examples of "religious microaggressions," or subtle forms of discrimination toward members of oppressed religious groups (Nadal, 2008d; Nadal, Issa, Griffin, Hamit, & Lyons, 2010). When these religious microaggressions occur in various organizational meetings, those who are non-Christian (e.g., Muslim, Hindu, Jewish) or nonreligious (e.g., atheist, agnostic, spiritual) may feel marginalized, which may affect their participation, comfort, or attitudes in such groups.

Finally, many other cultural identities and subgroups might cause tension within Filipino American communities or groups and will be discussed in other chapters. For example, gender may lead to different group dynamics on organizational levels and interpersonal interactions (see Chapter 7). Individuals who identify as biracial or multiracial may feel marginalized in Filipino American organizations where a majority of members are monoracial (see Chapter 8). Lesbian, gay, bisexual, and transgender (LGBT) Filipino Americans often may feel unaccepted in Filipino American groups or communities where heterosexuality is assumed to be the norm and where they may not be able to express their sexual identities freely (see Chapter 7). Last, colonial mentality may play a huge role in group dynamics, in that members may judge others based on skin color, language and accents, educational levels, or regions of the Philippines (see Chapter 4). The competition issues and political struggles within Filipino American organizations, as well as the need to promote social status, may be considered a direct effect of colonial mentality. Filipinos and Filipino Americans may view those with power as being "superior" or "better"—the same message that was taught by the Spanish and Americans who encouraged Filipinos to emulate their ways.

Impacts of Groups and Community

Given these various types of Filipino American communities, one might wonder what influence that community might have on Filipino American mental health. One study examined predictors of ethnic identity (pride in one's ethnic background and community) and social identity (an individual's ability to relate well interpersonally with others of all backgrounds) among Filipino Americans participants (Fabella, 2002). Results indicated that the more exposure an individual has to Filipino American family members, friends, culture, and community, the higher one's ethnic identity will be. This finding suggests that Filipino Americans with large support networks of other Filipino Americans will have higher levels of both ethnic and social identity, perhaps because they are surrounded by others who are culturally and physically similar to themselves. Therefore, they are presented with positive messages, which can be validating or normalizing.

These findings may explain why many Filipino Americans search for groups or communities. They want to be able to feel a sense of belonging and acceptance; they want to be around others who are like them and have similar cultural and personal experiences; and they want to have opportunities to celebrate and learn about their racial, ethnic, and cultural identities. However, as mentioned, several factors may lead to psychological stressors within Filipino American groups and communities. These include power struggles, cultural value conflicts, *tsismis* (gossip), and inter- and intra-organizational tensions. Those who feel marginalized within groups (e.g., persons of lower social classes, religious minorities, or undocumented immigrants) may experience a range of emotions, including shame, guilt, embarrassment, frustration, or

Figure 5.2 *Group of Filipino Americans singing at a Philippine Independence Day Parade*
Photo courtesy of Kevin Nadal

anger. The next section reviews theories from social and organizational psychology and discusses their implications for Filipino Americans.

CULTURAL IMPLICATIONS FOR SOCIAL AND ORGANIZATIONAL PSYCHOLOGY

Given this spectrum of Filipino American communities and groups, as well as the types of problems that may occur within each, it may be important to examine basic theories of social psychology and organizational psychology, in order to understand how the cultural nuances affect Filipino Americans differently than other ethnic groups. Social psychology, in the most basic terms, is the study of how people and groups interact. Organizational psychology studies the well-being of individuals within a specific context (e.g., workplaces, companies, and institutions). It is important to study both disciplines of psychology because both can be useful in understanding Filipino American groups and systems more effectively. In studying social psychology, one can understand how Filipino Americans interact with each other generally (e.g., in their families and communities). In studying organizational psychology, one can recognize how Filipino Americans interact in organized groups (e.g., regional and hometown associations or community centers). This section reviews some basic theories and concepts utilized in both social and organizational psychology that may apply to Filipino American groups and communities.

Review and Application of Social and Organizational Psychology Theories

Power can be defined as the ability to change, influence others, and receive what one desires. In social psychology, power is divided into five major forms:

1. *Coercive power.* The power to force someone to do something against their will
2. *Reward power.* The power to give other people what they want in exchange for other favors
3. *Legitimate power.* The power that comes from holding a specific authority role (e.g., police officer, professor)

4. *Referent power.* The power that comes from another person liking you or wanting to be like you
5. *Expert power.* The power that comes when an individual has knowledge and skills that someone else requires (French & Raven, 1960)

For Filipino American groups (e.g., family systems and friendship networks), all of these types of power may come into play. Coercive power may take forms of parents forcing their children to do things that they do not want to do, ranging from household chores to choosing particular career paths. Reward power may be similar to *utang ng loob* (debt of reciprocity), which, as described in Chapter 2, is where individuals may assume that others will do things for them out of reciprocity and respect. Legitimate power may occur through generational dynamics, in which Filipinos and Filipino Americans are taught to respect and unthinkingly give control to authority figures, particularly elders, regardless of actual relationship. Referent power is relevant to Filipino Americans because of *pakikasama* (social acceptance), which also is described in Chapter 2, wherein individuals yearn to be accepted by their peers and family members and are compliant to avoid disharmony. Finally, expert power is also related to *utang ng loob*, in that individuals who have particular skills (e.g., doctors, mechanics) know that others within the system may need them; thus, they may perform duties knowing there will be reciprocity in the future.

For Filipino American organizations (e.g., community centers or regional and hometown associations), power also may manifest in these five forms. Coercive power might not be as apparent as it would be in family systems, but as mentioned, generational and age differences may intimidate younger Filipino Americans to follow and be obedient to elders. Reward power may take place in political interactions, with members of organizations doing things in return for other favors (e.g., "I will vote for you for president if you vote for me for vice president"). Legitimate power and referent power appear to be what members of these organizations may be striving for; many Filipino Americans desire to gain leadership roles in their community in order to garner automatic respect and become popular in their communities (Espiritu, 2003). Finally, expert power in Filipino American organizations can be exemplified by the boasting and glorifying of one's accomplishments. Individuals who do so hope to distinguish themselves from others, not only to gain respect and adoration but also unconsciously so that they are viewed as unique and considered necessary for the community.

The concept of "social influence" is similar to the concept of "power;" social influence is defined as a change in one's behavior usually caused by another person's intentional or unintentional power (Milgram, 1983). Social influence occurs in three areas: conformity, compliance, and obedience. Conformity is changing how one behaves in order to be more like others; people conform in order to feel a sense of belonging to groups and to seek the approval of others. For example, if everyone in a group chooses to wear a new trend in clothing, a person might follow the trend, simply to fit in or be accepted. Compliance occurs when a person does something when someone else asks them to. People have a choice when they comply, but sometimes they may agree only to avoid repercussions or conflict. For instance, when someone asks another person to go to a movie, the person is compliant when she or he agrees and attends the movie. She or he may not necessarily want to go to the movies (or may want to watch a different movie), but she or he agrees to avoid appearing impolite, rejecting, or demanding. Obedience is the act of doing something that an accepted authority figure tells one to do. The compliant person still has a choice; the individual who is obedient, however, does not believe there are any alternatives. For example, younger children are obedient to their parents because they know their parents provide for their basic needs, such as food, shelter, transportation, and money.

These concepts of social influence may manifest themselves in many ways in Filipino American groups and communities. Conformity to cultural values and social norms is commonplace for Filipino Americans and other racial/ethnic minority groups. Social norms are defined as the explicit or implicit rules that a group uses as a guide for appropriate or inappropriate values, beliefs, attitudes, and behaviors. Because of *hiya* (shame), which is described in Chapter 2, many Filipino Americans conform to societal and community norms in order to avoid bringing shame to the family. Such conformity can occur in Filipino American groups as well (e.g., family systems and friendship networks). For example, individuals may believe they are expected to go to college and get married like everyone else, even if they have no interest in education or monogamy. Conformity also can occur in Filipino American organizations (e.g., community centers or associations), with individuals attempting to conform to group norms to avoid feeling different or facing discrimination. For example, a Filipino American couple in a troubled or failed marriage may attempt to save face and pretend to be happily married, so they can conform and appear to be like everyone else.

Compliance also may impact Filipino American groups and organizations. In Filipino American families, individuals may comply with their family members, even though they may not fully agree. For example, many Filipino American individuals are expected to go to church when they are with their families (particularly during the holidays), even when they may not be practicing Catholics in their everyday lives. In these cases, the individuals technically have a choice whether to go, but they choose to attend in order to avoid family conflict or social consequences. Similar situations occur in Filipino American organizations, when members are asked to pay membership dues or provide money for certain projects and events. Again, individuals may not want to participate, but they may comply in order to avoid social ramifications, which may include becoming ostracized or the target of *tsismis* (gossip).

Obedience within Filipino American groups and organizations may have several cultural implications. In traditional Western social psychology, obedience implies the individual does *not* have a choice. For example, many Nazi soldiers who followed orders to carry out the Holocaust claimed they did not agree with the orders but felt that they would be punished (perhaps even killed) if they did not obey their superiors. For Filipino Americans, not obeying likely would not lead to physical punishment but instead severe psychological punishment. For example, some studies on LGBT Filipino Americans have revealed how many individuals refuse to come out of the closet because they feared their parents and families would disown or ostracize them (Nadal & Corpus, in press). Many of these LGBT Filipino Americans might be obedient and pretend to be heterosexual to avoid the severe psychological costs that might occur. In Filipino American organizations, this trend of obedience may occur between generations; younger, American-born individuals may not voice dissent toward older immigrants because they fear the psychological distress that would occur if they spoke out against them.

"Social impact theory" describes how people will respond to social influences—whether they will conform, comply, or obey—based on three factors: (1) strength, or how important the influencing group of people are to the individual; (2) immediacy, or how close the group is to the individual (in space and time) during the influence attempt; and (3) number, or how many people there are in the group (Tanford & Penrod, 1984). For example, if a parent asks a child to do something, there may be more pressure to carry out the behavior than if the child was asked by a stranger (strength). Someone who is asked for something over the phone may find it easier to reject than if she or he was asked in person (immediacy). Finally, if five people ask a person to do something, it may be harder for that person to reject than if she or he was asked by only one person (number).

Many cultural implications for social impact theory are specific for Filipino Americans. The notions of guilt (e.g., "Filipino guilt" or "Catholic guilt") have been described in other literature as impediments to ideal mental health as well as modes of preventing individuals from living their independent lives away from their families (Espiritu, 2003; Nadal & Corpus, in press). Filipino or Catholic guilt can be defined as the feeling of remorse, self-doubt, or personal responsibility that results when a Filipino or Catholic engages in sinful or inappropriate acts. This guilt may be directly correlated with *hiya* (shame), with Filipinos and Filipino Americans behaving in ways that would avoid bringing shame to the family at all costs. Given this fact, Filipino Americans may attempt to conform, comply, or obey in order to avoid shame and to relieve their Filipino and Catholic guilt.

Because of Filipino cultural values such as *utang ng loob* (debt of reciprocity) and *pakikasama* (social acceptance), Filipino Americans may conform, comply, or obey because they expect that others will return the favor or because they want to be socially accepted by others. Because of these values, the concepts of strength, immediacy, and number still may have an impact on social influencing, but it also is likely Filipino Americans will conform, comply, and obey due to cultural values, norms, and expectations.

Previous literature has cited indirect communication as a primary form of communicating for Filipino Americans (Nadal, 2004). In many instances, Filipinos and Filipino Americans will not express themselves directly to others; rather they are passive or passive-aggressive in their behaviors, facial expressions, and/or body language. For example, although someone might not directly ask a person to do something, indirect communication might be both a powerful and a subtle expression of what is desired. Filipino Americans may pick up on these subtle cues as additional social influences, which in turn may impact their conformity, compliance, or obedience.

The phrase "social desirability bias" describes how individuals may behave in a way that they believe is socially acceptable and desirable, specifically when they know others are watching (Fisher, 1993). This bias may be relevant for Filipino Americans who may act or behave a certain way in groups (e.g., an individual who pretends to be happy and have high self-esteem when in reality she or he is depressed and has low self-esteem) or organizations (e.g., a leader of a community organization who appears to be friendly and caring when she or he really is manipulative or fake). Social desirability is related to *hiya* (shame); individuals are trying to prevent feeling dishonorable and embarrassing to themselves and their families, as well as *pakikasama* (social acceptance), in that Filipino American individuals always yearn to be recognized and liked by their peers.

Finally, "pluralistic ignorance" describes how a majority of individuals in a group assume that most of their peers are different in some way while the truth is they are more similar than they realize (Prentice & Miller, 1993). For example, one study discovered that college students may have participated in binge-drinking activities and parties, even when they did not want to, simply because they thought everyone else was doing so. The study revealed that many of these students actually did not want to binge drink but participated out of fear of social ramifications (Prentice & Miller, 1993). This concept may be relevant for Filipino American groups and organizations in a few ways. First, Filipino Americans may assume that everyone else is doing well in their professional and personal lives (and therefore may want to paint a facade that everything is going well for themselves), when in reality, a majority of individuals may be struggling personally, financially, or professionally. For example, a Filipino American in a college student organization may

Figure 5.3 A mixed group of Filipino Americans in a large metropolitan neighborhood
Photo courtesy of JoAnn Garcia

pretend to be succeeding academically while actually failing the classes. If others have similar experiences but do not say anything, the group continues to believe that everyone is succeeding. A culture where others cannot admit to difficulties is created, as a result. Second, because of *hiya* (shame) and *pakikasama* (social acceptance), individuals may not want to admit that they do not agree with others' opinions, values, or belief systems. For example, in an organizational meeting, if someone presents an idea and the majority of individuals do not speak up, it may be assumed that others agree with the speaker. So even if the majority of people do not agree, no one will know because of pluralistic ignorance.

FILIPINO CRAB MENTALITY

The final concept that is important to be aware of when discussing Filipino American communities and groups is the Filipino crab mentality. "Crab mentality" can be defined as the desire to outdo, outshine, or surpass another (often of one's same ethnic group) at the other's expense

(Tan-Alora & Lumitao, 2001). Although very little academic research describes this concept, it is an idea well-known in the Filipino American community. According to one Filipino news reporter, the origins of the term can be described in this way:

> *As a familiar story goes, one can leave a basket full of crabs and not worry that a single one of them can ever climb out of it and escape the cooking pan. The moment one succeeds in pulling itself up an inch, there will be a dozen claws that will make sure it doesn't make it to the top. (Mejorada, 1996)*

The metaphor is used within the Filipino American community because individuals often compete with each other and attempt to pull each other down so that no one will succeed. The belief includes the idea that "if I can't succeed, then you can't," which is why the metaphor of crabs preventing each other from escaping is relevant and applicable. Instead of allowing one crab to escape and be free from the boiling water, the others want it to suffer like them.

This crab mentality can be exemplified in a few different ways. As mentioned, some literature has concentrated on regional and hometown Filipino American associations in which individuals may be competitive with each other, may be boastful with each other, and may publicly struggle for power and leadership positions. When individuals from organizations have irreconcilable political differences, it is common for them to break away and create their own, new organizations. This situation can be especially problematic when both organizations have the same missions, objectives, and target populations. For example, in many metropolitan areas, there may be more than one Filipino American center, more than one Filipino American youth program, and more than one association of persons from the same region or hometown (e.g., more than one Ilocano association). As a result, these organizations end up fighting one another for membership, resources, and event participation. Instead of forming one organization, the crab mentality of these individuals, consciously or unconsciously, prevents any of them from succeeding. This concept is similar to the *sari-sari* stores (convenience stores) of the Philippines; often Filipinos build the same type of stores (often next door to each other), thus preventing either business from profiting.

In the fields of entertainment and sports, the crab mentality has presented itself in a few forms. In the mid-1990s, a Filipina American singer named Jocelyn Enriquez emerged from the San Francisco Bay Area and had several hits, including "Do You Miss Me?" and "A Little Bit of Ecstasy." Despite her successes, many members of the Filipino American community were publicly skeptical and doubtful of her racial authenticity and loyalty (Pisares, 2006). Although Pisares did not label this action the crab mentality, any Filipino American who gains a bit of public visibility may be subject to *tsismis* (gossip) and doubt. World-champion boxer Manny Pacquiao has claimed to be the victim of crab mentality, stating that other Filipinos are trying to bring him down by questioning or wanting to investigate some of the boxing matches he has won (Quismundo, 2008). Again, instead of being happy for an accomplished Filipino athlete, some may be uncomfortable with another Filipino's success and would rather see him fail. This concept can be applied to Filipino American politics as well; Filipino Americans often scrutinize Filipino American political candidates more than they scrutinize candidates of other racial groups. Instead of being happy for another Filipino American who could hold political office (and, it is hoped, advocate for the needs of the Filipino American people), crab mentality encourages individuals to bring each other down.

DISCUSSION QUESTIONS

1. What types of community and groups have you been exposed to? Do you see any similarities or differences with the groups that are presented in this chapter?
2. In what ways does your culture influence the ways that you behave in social groups or organizations?
3. What types of power do you have? What types of power do others have over you?
4. What are the social norms in your family? With your friends? In your school or workplace?
5. In what ways are you conforming, obedient, or compliant? In what situations might you act differently?
6. How do you feel about Filipino crab mentality?

SUMMARY

This chapter described and discussed the various types of Filipino American groups and communities that have existed when Filipinos first started immigrating to the United States and the ones that thrive today. Some contemporary groups include college student groups, regional and hometown organizations, political activist and community organizations, and online communities. By examining the diverse ways Filipino and American cultural values can impact group and community dynamics, some key concepts from social and organizational psychology were applied to Filipino Americans. Finally, the concept of Filipino crab mentality was introduced as a common way of thinking that divides the community. Two case studies are presented next to exemplify how Filipino American communities can impact the psychological health of individuals and groups. One case deals with a person who seeks individual counseling; the other involves a community center whose director sought assistance from an organizational psychologist. Readers should pay attention to the various cultural values that play a part in each scenario while brainstorming how different coping mechanisms and group dynamics may be culture-specific for Filipino Americans.

Case Studies

Case 1: Ben and His Attempts to Balance a Leadership Position and School

Ben is a 22-year-old second-generation Filipino American college student who is majoring in sociology and is set to graduate next semester. Recently Ben failed his midterm exam, and he shared with his professor how he had been extremely stressed out balancing school and his extracurricular activities. He is currently the president of his Filipino American student organization, he works 20 hours a week for a nonprofit organization, and he is taking a full course load for the semester. His professor recommends that he speak with someone

(Continued)

131

at the university counseling center to help him deal with his stress. Although initially Ben was hesitant to talk to a stranger about his problems, he reluctantly agrees because he feels overwhelmed and stressed with his life.

Upon meeting with a counselor for the first time, Ben explained his situation and talked about how he averages about 5 hours of sleep each night. He works every weekday morning and takes his classes in the early afternoon. His duties as president of his student group require that he attend meetings and events every night. Some evenings he also attends practice for the Pilipino Cultural Night that his organization is coordinating. When Ben gets home at around 11 p.m., he is exhausted, but he still tries to study for about 2 to 3 hours before going to bed. He wakes up the next morning at 7 and starts his routine all over again. When Ben's counselor asked if he would be willing to give up some of his activities, Ben said he "absolutely could not" give up his job or presidency, and he did not want to drop any of his classes. He stated that he needed his job to help pay for school, and he needed to fulfill his duties for the organization. He shared that he did not want to appear to be a failure, and he did not want to let anyone down. At the end of their first session, Ben agreed to go back to counseling on a weekly basis, especially since it was free and fit in his schedule.

During weekly counseling sessions, Ben reveals that he is under a lot of pressure to succeed as president of his organization. First, his three older siblings were all presidents of their organizations, and they each continued to become successful in their career fields. In fact, his parents are also leaders in their hometown Filipino association, and he knows his parents like to brag how all four of their children have been "presidents." Ben also discloses that none of his friends know he is struggling with school and how he pretends that he is a straight-A student who can balance all of his responsibilities. Finally, Ben admits he worries a great deal about what others think about him, particularly since two other candidates ran against him for president last year. Ben continues to attend counseling and said the sessions have been helpful; he said he liked being able to talk to someone about his problems, yet because of his busy schedule, nothing seems to improve. Ben refuses to give up any of his activities and hopes going to counseling will make his anxiety and stressors decrease.

Case 2: The Filipino American Community Center

Maritess is a 50-year-old first-generation Filipina American woman who has served as the executive director of the Filipino American Community Center (FACC) for the past 10 years. FACC is a nonprofit organization that services one Filipino American community in a major metropolitan area by offering youth empowerment programs, promoting community service projects, and hosting many social events in the neighborhood. Over the past five years, Maritess noticed there has been a decline in support for the organization. Donations have been decreasing, and there has been less participation in and attendance at all of the programs. She hires an organizational psychologist to conduct a program evaluation of the community center. The psychologist leads focus groups and individual interviews with members who are currently participating in FACC programs and those who have participated in FACC over the past five years.

The psychologist analyzes the data with a team of research assistants and presents the findings to Maritess and the FACC staff. First, it is revealed that there is tension among several groups: immigrants versus American-born Filipinos, youth versus adults, and Ilocanos versus Tagalogs (two Filipino regional/ethnic subgroups). American-born young professionals and youth claim that they do not want to participate anymore because they feel minimized and dismissed by older immigrant generations. Meanwhile, the Ilocano participants feel they are invisible in comparison to the Tagalogs (e.g., the FACC offers a Tagalog language class but not an Ilocano language class). Several group members have decided to drop out of FACC because they want to avoid tension and running into these people in the future. Additionally, many participants reported how *tsismis* (gossip) is very prevalent within the community and has led to several individuals distancing themselves from the FACC.

When Maritess is presented with this information, she does not know how to react. She asks her staff members for their input. and no one knows how to approach the situation. Maritess then presents the findings to the board of directors. Several members (who are first-generation, immigrant Filipino Americans) reply: "There's nothing you can do about this. This is just how Filipinos are!" Maritess decides to host a town

(Continued)

hall discussion where community members can share their views. At the meeting, several community members speak up about the various tensions at FACC, leading to some heated arguments among a few individuals. Throughout the meeting, Maritess tries to mediate and help everyone understand that they need to unite for the greater good of the community. And although she calmly reports that she will do everything she can to remedy the situation, community members leave the meeting angry, bitter, and upset. The next day, Maritess decides to contact the organizational psychologist to ask for additional help.

Case Study Discussion

In reviewing these two cases, one can notice the various ways that culture and community involvement has an impact on mental health on both individual and organizational levels. In the case of Ben, it is clear how it is very important for him to remain as president of his Filipino American student organization as a way of saving face and avoiding bringing *hiya* (shame) to himself and his family. He does not want to look like a failure, and he wants to avoid embarrassment or perceptions of failure at all costs. Additionally, Ben wants to uphold *pakikasama* (social acceptance) and hides his difficulties with school because he wants everyone to view him in a positive light. He likes his role as president and has difficulty setting better boundaries and balancing his time. Perhaps he wants to please everyone and wants to be involved in every aspect of the Filipino organization so that he feels acceptance and a sense of belonging. Given these factors, it is clear that these core Filipino values are so engrained in Ben that he does not consider that quitting his position as president is an option, even though he is not doing as well in school.

Issues of power also are manifest in Ben's situation, in that he feels the pressure to keep his position in order to uphold the power and pride it brings to his family. The fact that all of his older siblings were presidents of their Filipino American student organizations and that his parents are active in their own associations pressure Ben to continue with the position, even though it might not be the best idea for his mental health. Adding to this pressure is the knowledge that being president is bringing respect and satisfaction to his parents, who like to brag to their friends about their children's accomplishments. Even if quitting might be a healthier option for Ben's psychological well-being, the indirect pressure from his parents might prevent him from viewing quitting as an option.

In the case of the Filipino American Community Center, one may recognize how culture may influence community members in a variety of ways. First, it is clear that culture impacts coping mechanisms and how individuals deal with their problems. Before the organizational psychologist came on board to analyze the dynamic of the center, none of the community members shared their feelings about FACC with Maritess; instead, they just chose to avoid the situation altogether and stop coming to events. This situation exemplifies how Filipinos and Filipino Americans may choose to avoid situations instead of being confrontational or direct. Additionally, it appears that the American values of competition and individualism may be preventing members of the community from uniting together and looking past their differences. Instead of being able to discuss issues in a nondefensive way, the members present at the town hall meeting explode in anger and arguments.

Power manifests in the FACC in a few ways. It appears there are certain groups with privileges that may allow others to feel marginalized or afflicted. For example, the immigrant elders seem to maintain indirect power over the second-generation young professionals and youth, in that the younger individuals may feel silenced in their opinions. Concurrently, the Tagalog members may possess subtle power over the Ilocano persons, in that they have greater representation in the center's programming. Power conflicts between groups is often inevitable; however, the major problem here is that the group with power does not want to acknowledge that the other group may feel marginalized while the group with limited power does not want to work together with the other group. Instead, both groups avoid or deny the situation without attempting to resolve the situation in direct ways. Because this situation apparently has lasted for several years, tensions arise, emotions build, and individuals begin to drop out of the organization.

Finally, crab mentality takes overt and covert forms in both of these situations. In the case of Ben, it appears that he has a fear of crab mentality; he worries that quitting his position will result in others thinking or speaking negatively about him. As mentioned, Ben does not want to fail because he wants to bring pride to his family and to be viewed

(Continued)

positively by his peers. Perhaps he feels this way because he knows that *tsismis* (gossip) is prevalent in the community and he believes that those who ran against him for president may be vindictive or spiteful toward him. With the case of FACC, it appears that crab mentality is widespread across the community. Instead of trying to work together, group members are directly trying to fight with each other. When Maritess attempts to be a mediator among the groups, they still have difficulty seeing the greater picture and recognizing that working as a community would be in their best interests. Given the manifestation of crab mentality in other contexts, it would not be surprising if there were discussions or threats to "start a separate" Filipino American center in order to avoid the conflict at hand. However, in doing so, a new conflict would be formed, and history could likely repeat itself.

Case Study Discussion Questions

For undergraduate students and general readers, please consider these questions:

1. What are your reactions to Ben's situation? What are your reactions to the situation at the Filipino American Community Center?
2. How do you feel Ben is handling his situation? How do you feel Maritess is handling the situation with FACC? Explain your answers.
3. In what ways are Ben's situation and the situation at FACC similar to your own life?
4. Which social and organizational psychology concepts do you notice occurring in Ben's situation? In the FACC situation?

For helping professionals and graduate students of psychology, please consider these questions:

1. How would you approach Ben's situation if you were his counselor or clinician? How would you approach Maritess and the FACC if you were their organizational psychologist?
2. What countertransference issues would you (or might you) have in working with Ben? What countertransference issues would you (or might you) have in working with Maritess and the FACC?
3. Which theoretical orientation(s) would you use to work with Ben?
4. Which organizational psychology theories would be most helpful in working with the FACC?

CHAPTER SIX

Filipino Americans and the Model Minority Myth

Contemporary Experiences in Education, Health, and Society

Figure 6.1 Two Filipina American women hosting a community event
Photo courtesy of Ken Paprocki

CASE SYNOPSES

Beverly is a 17-year-old Filipina American high school senior who grew up in a traditional, upper-middle-class, Catholic Filipino American family. When she was 14 years old, she met Anthony, a Filipino American boy who was her age, and they began dating. Although Anthony came from a respectable Filipino American family, Beverly knew her parents would not approve of her having a boyfriend at such a young age, so she hid her relationship as best as she could. Beverly said she believed Anthony was "the one" and wanted to marry him when she was older. Consequently, when they were both 16 years old, she decided to have sex with him for the first time. Because they loved each other very much and because they were virgins, they did not wear condoms or use birth control on a regular basis. Last month, Beverly started to feel nauseous and learned she was pregnant.

Ryan is a 14-year-old second-generation Filipino American who was raised in a middle-class Filipino American family in a predominantly Filipino American community. When Ryan was in elementary school and junior high, he received very good grades and was always compliant and respectful toward his parents. However, when Ryan entered high school this past year, his parents noticed that his grades began to slip and he was spending a lot of time with his friends. Ryan and his friends were consistently getting into trouble in and outside of school. They were arrested by the police for painting graffiti on walls in a local park. A few months later, a teacher caught them drinking alcohol at school. Ryan's parents are fed up with him and do not understand why he is always getting into trouble. They have threatened to send him back to the Philippines to live with his extended family if he does not "shape up."

INTRODUCTION

The model minority myth defines all Asian Americans as being well-educated, successful, career-driven, and law-abiding citizens in the United States as compared to other racial/ethnic minority groups, such as African Americans and Latinos (Nadal & Sue, 2009). The notion of "model minority" is based on census data and other demographic statistics which indicate that Asian Americans achieve higher levels of education and household incomes than Whites and than other groups of color. Although these data may appear accurate (e.g., Asian Americans have higher family/household incomes than African Americans and Latinos), several factors are not taken into account when understanding this group's experience (e.g., Asian Americans may have higher household incomes because they have more contributors of the household income than Whites; Reeves & Bennett, 2004). Due to the model minority myth, society may be blind to or unaware of the experiences of many Asian Americans who do not fit this model. For example, Asian Americans are stereotyped as having fewer mental health problems than other people of color (Uba, 1994) and are presumed to have less significant experiences with racial discrimination (Delucchi & Do, 1996; Goto, Gee, & Takeuchi, 2002). Accordingly, Asian Americans may be neglected by educators, government officials, and clinicians despite the fact several Asian American groups are suffering in terms of their education, physical health, and mental health.

There are many ways in which the model minority myth allows society to ignore bleak educational and sociocultural experiences of many subgroups in the Asian American diaspora, including Southeast Asians (e.g., Vietnamese, Cambodian, Hmong Americans), Pacific Islanders (e.g., native Hawaiians, Samoans, Chamorros), and Filipino Americans. For example, previous data reported that about half of Southeast Asians do not have a high school diploma and an overwhelming amount of Hmong and Cambodian Americans live below the poverty level (Reeves & Bennett, 2004). For Filipino Americans specifically, statistics have shown that second-generation students experience higher rates of high school dropout and lower rates of college admission and retention than East Asian Americans (Okamura, 1998). It also has been shown that Filipino Americans have higher rates of HIV/AIDS (San Francisco Department of Public Health, 2008) and out-of-wedlock and teen pregnancy than other Asian American groups (National Center for Health Statistics, 2000; Tiongson, 1997). Previous research has shown that Filipino Americans may have a higher prevalence of substance abuse than East Asian Americans (see Nadal, 2000, for a review). Finally, several studies have noted that many Filipino American youth have participated in gangs or gang culture (Alsaybar, 1999; Sanders, 1994) and have been incarcerated at higher rates than East Asian Americans (Rumbaut & Ewing, 2007).

This chapter discusses how these statistics in education, health, and crime have a spectrum of influences on Filipino American mental health. First, due to the model minority myth, there are many expectations for all Asian Americans to do well; this chapter examines how Filipino Americans (and other Asian American subgroups) have encountered a number of experiences that are in direct contradiction to the myth. Second, the chapter discusses how these experiences may lead to a marginalized status within the Asian American community and may negatively impact Filipino Americans' self-esteem, self-efficacy, and worldviews. As a result of these experiences of marginalization from both the Asian American community and general American society, Filipino Americans face a different set of obstacles in psychotherapy than do members of other Asian American groups.

MODEL MINORITY MYTH

As mentioned, the model minority myth is a misleading stereotype that views all Asian Americans as well-educated, successful, career-driven, and law-abiding citizens. Some might argue that there is some truth to this stereotype. For example, Asian Americans as a whole tend to be admitted to college and attain bachelor's degrees at higher rates than African Americans and Latinos (Nadal & Sue, 2009). However, several points regarding the myth should be considered. First, by stereotyping the entire Asian American population to fit this label, individuals who are not educated, who are unsuccessful in their careers, or who are prone to criminal activities may be overlooked or underserved. Second, this generalization may create tension between Asian Americans and other racial/ethnic minority groups. Groups like African Americans and Latinos may feel resentment or anger toward Asian Americans because they are often compared to "the Model Minority" and asked "Why can't you be like the Asians?" As a result, a division between different racial/ethnic groups may occur, and a perceived hierarchy may lead to racial tension. This racial tension keeps various communities of color "fighting" against each other while lifting Whites up as the superior and dominant group (Nadal & Sue, 2009).

With these ideas in mind, it is important to examine the ways in which Filipino Americans exemplify some of the characteristics of the model minority category and identify the many ways in which they clearly do not. Chapter 1 covered some of the major statistics about socioeconomic status (SES) and income within the Filipino American community:

- Filipino American (and most other Asian American) families are likely to have two parents as the heads of households.
- Filipino Americans have a divorce rate that is less than that of the general American population but slightly greater than that of the general Asian American population.
- Filipino Americans are more likely than other Asian Americans to speak English very well.
- Filipina American women are more likely to enter the labor force than Asian American women and American women in general.
- Filipino Americans have the lowest poverty rate out of all Asian American groups and a rate significantly lower than that of the general American population.
- Filipino Americans have a higher median family income than other Asian American families and than the general American public.

At first glance, these statistics point to positive attributes in the Filipino American community. However, one must recognize how some of these statistics are misleading and have cultural explanations.

Chapter 1 examined the cultural implications of some of these positive qualities. For example, while Filipino American families may consist of two-parent households and Filipino American couples may divorce less than the general population, it is important to recognize how the influence of Catholicism may prevent married couples from divorcing. Although it appears that many Filipino American couples remain married, there is no way to know if these couples are happy or psychologically sound. Second, Filipino Americans speak English at higher rates than do other Asian Americans, which is likely due to U.S. colonization and the prevalence of English in the Philippines. Although English proficiency may be a positive quality, the influences of American colonialism may lead to other stressors resulting from colonial mentality. Moreover, it is imperative to acknowledge how matriarchal gender roles and cultural values like *kapwa* (fellow being) and *utang ng loob* (debt of reciprocity) may influence demographic trends, including a higher number of Filipina American women in the workplace or lower rates of poverty in Filipino American families.

141

Chapter 1 also explained how many of these statistics are misleading and need to be inspected further in order to fully understand the entire experience of Filipino Americans. First, although Filipino Americans may appear to have a higher median family income than other Asian American families and than the general American public, it is necessary to recognize that the average household size of individuals contributing to the family income for Filipino Americans is much higher than that for both the Asian American population and the general U.S. population. For Filipino Americans, there are 3.41 family members contributing to the household income, as opposed to 2.59 family members in general American households and 3.08 members in Asian American families. So, in reality, Filipino Americans average about $19,117 per person contributing to the family income, while the general American individual contributes $19,322 per person and Asian Americans as a whole contribute $19,266 per person. Thus, Filipino American families are making less money per person than others.

Second, it is also necessary to recognize that full-time Filipino American male workers make significantly less money than Asian American male and general American male populations. Filipino American men who work full-time earn an average of $35,560; Asian American men make an average of $40,650, and the average American man earns $37,057. One must wonder why Filipino American men are making less money than other Asians and the general population, despite the fact that a high percentage of Filipino Americans are college educated and speak English well. Although the model minority myth may work in favor of other Asian Americans, racism and discrimination may influence experiences of Filipino American men in different ways. The next section examines the experiences of Filipino Americans in education, which might shed light on why this discrepancy exists.

EXPERIENCES IN EDUCATION

As a consequence of the model minority myth, it is expected that Asian Americans will have higher levels of education than other racial and ethnic minority groups and the general U.S. population (Nadal & Sue, 2009). The most recent census has shown that 43.8% of Filipino Americans in the United States possess a bachelor's degree or higher, significantly above the 24.4% of the general American population and comparable to the 44.1% of the Asian American population (Reeves & Bennett, 2004). It was also revealed that only 27.6% of Filipino Americans have a high school diploma or less, a rate that is much lower than the average of 48.2% of Americans and 35.4% of Asian Americans who have a high school diploma or less (Reeves & Bennett, 2004).

It is important to analyze this data further to understand how it does not accurately reflect the true educational experiences of Filipino Americans. First, it does not indicate differences between generations. According to the 1990 U.S. Census, only 22% of second-generation Filipino Americans (those born and raised in the United States) achieved a bachelor's degree, which was significantly lower than the 43.8% of the general Filipino American population (U.S. Census Bureau, 1994). Bankston (2006) reports a higher percentage of educational attainment based on the 2000 U.S. Census, in which 30.7% of second-generation Filipino American men and 32.3% Filipina American women received college degrees, in comparison to the 41.1% of foreign-born Filipino American men and 46.9% of foreign-born Filipina American women. This educational trend is unique to Filipino Americans; no other major Asian American immigrant group shows such a discrepancy between their American-born and foreign-born groups.

The high college attainment of foreign-born Filipino Americans is likely due to the fact that Filipinos who immigrated to the United States after 1965 are predominantly professionals (e.g., doctors, nurses, engineers) who received their degrees in the Philippines. So while the population may be educated, the majority of Filipino Americans did not attend college in the United States. This is important to understand, because Filipino American parents may expect their children to attain the same educational levels as they earned in the Philippines, without recognizing the different academic obstacles and sociocultural experiences that their children face in the United States (Okamura & Agbayani, 1997). As a result, second-generation Filipino Americans may feel spoken and unspoken pressures to succeed, particularly given the sacrifices their parents made to immigrate to the United States.

Moreover, in comparison to other Asian American groups, while 22% of second-generation Filipino Americans achieved a bachelor's degree, a significantly higher number of East Asian Americans born and raised in the United States achieved a bachelor's degree (51% of native-born Chinese

Americans, 34% of native-born Japanese Americans, and 36.5% of native-born Korean Americans). Furthermore, despite the fact that many Filipino Americans are well educated, they do not reach the same levels of income and often have a lower occupational status compared to other Asian American groups with similar educational qualifications (Okamura & Agbayani, 1997). Although there are no clear explanations for these discrepancies, previous research has tried to identify some potential reasons.

Some authors argue that different experiences with racism in educational settings and in general society may influence distinct academic outcomes for Filipino Americans in comparison to Chinese Americans (Nadal, 2008c; Nadal, Pituc, et al., 2010; Teranishi, 2002). One study found that Filipino Americans were likely to experience similar types of racial discrimination as Black Americans and Latinos, in that Filipino Americans were more likely than Chinese Americans to encounter discrimination concerning being treated like a criminal or an intellectual inferior (Nadal, 2008c). Another study reported that Filipino American high school students were more likely than their Chinese American counterparts to be stereotyped by their teachers and school counselors as being "gang members" and "delinquent." These Filipino American students felt that teachers and school counselors were more likely to encourage their Chinese American counterparts to attend college (Teranishi, 2002). Perhaps as a result of these experiences, Filipino Americans are not applying to college or doing well in school because they have unconsciously internalized messages that they are intellectually inferior or incapable.

Other authors argue that a dearth of Filipino Americans in higher education may be due to a lack of community resources, support, and understanding (Nadal et al., 2009). In a study of Filipino American graduate students, some participants shared that they learned to "become [their] own mentor" and "develop a thick skin" (Nadal, Pituc, et al., 2010). Perhaps Filipino American parents and families may not be able to prepare their children for college because they are not familiar with American institutions of higher education. Another reason for these experiences in education may result from Filipino Americans' unique racial and ethnic identity (Nadal, 2004). Feeling different from other Asian Americans and feeling marginalized within the larger Asian American community may lead to lower self-esteem and self-efficacy, which may directly or indirectly impact educational performance and attainment.

Finally, SES may influence the lack of educational attainment for Filipino Americans. First, as mentioned, Filipino Americans may make less money than the average American families, and Filipino American individuals often get paid less for jobs in which they have the same education. Accordingly, Filipino Americans may not believe they can achieve a higher SES and therefore will not attain a college education. Second, because Filipino Americans are categorized with other marginalized groups, such as Black or African Americans and Hispanics or Latinos (Nadal, 2004), they may come to believe that they cannot achieve academically. They may internalize inferiority and may not expect to succeed because of the lack of resources or support from educational institutions. Also, the presence of teacher or counselor bias (e.g., Filipino Americans being stereotyped as being delinquents or gang members) also may lead to academic disparities. However, because Filipino Americans may also have similar sociocultural outcomes as Black or African Americans and Hispanics or Latinos (e.g., lower SES, experiences with racism, teen pregnancy, gang involvement, and juvenile delinquency), they may believe they are not meant to achieve higher levels of education and instead are meant to remain in the working or lower social classes.

Figure 6.2 A mother teaching her child how to use the computer
Photo courtesy of Kevin Nadal

HIV/AIDS AND TEEN AND OUT-OF-WEDLOCK PREGNANCY

Previous literature has discussed how Filipino Americans have higher incidences of HIV/AIDS and teen or out-of-wedlock pregnancy than other East Asian Americans (Nadal, 2004). In fact, since the disease first became prevalent in the 1980s, Filipino Americans have had the highest contraction rates of HIV/AIDS out of all Asian American and Pacific Islander groups, accounting for approximately 34% of AIDS cases among the Asian American community in California (Darbes, Kennedy, Peersman, Zohrabyan, & Rutherford, 2002; San Francisco Department of Public Health, 2008). Moreover, the Filipino Task Force on AIDS reported that the disease was the leading cause of death for Filipino American males ages 25 to 34 in the state of California in 2000 (Nadal, 2004).

Additionally, second-generation Filipina Americans have the highest rates of teen pregnancy and out-of-wedlock pregnancy of Asian American groups (National Center for Health Statistics, 2000; Tiongson, 1997; Weitz, Harper, & Mohllajee, 2001). Specifically, one study revealed that 6% of the total number of Filipina American birth mothers were teenagers, a rate higher than Chinese, Japanese, Vietnamese, Korean, and Indian Americans (Weitz et al., 2001). However, when looking at generational differences in teenage pregnancy, there are some discrepancies. Eleven percent of the total number of Filipina women who gave birth in the United States are second-generation Filipina American teenagers, or those who were born and raised in the United States. This contrasts with 2.7% of Filipina American teen mothers who were foreign-born (Martin, Hamilton, Sutton, Ventura, Menacker, & Munson, 2003). Given this statistic, one may deduce that teenage Filipina Americans who are born and raised in the United States are almost four times more likely to get pregnant and give birth than their immigrant-born counterparts.

One must wonder why Filipino Americans are contracting HIV/AIDS and becoming pregnant at rates higher than those of other Asian American groups. It is important to recognize that 88% of Filipino Americans who contract HIV/AIDS are gay and bisexual men (San Francisco Department of Public Health, 2008). This phenomenon is similar to other communities of color (e.g., Black Americans and Latinos), where men who have sex with men may be more likely to be closeted about their sexual identities (Nadal & Corpus, in press) and therefore may not practice safe sex (Choi, Han, Hudes, & Kegeles, 2002). For Asian Americans specifically, some literature has discussed how the lack of culturally appropriate HIV/AIDS prevention resources; racism in the mainstream lesbian, gay, bisexual, and transgender (LGBT) community; and internalized homophobia may lead to a decrease in safe sex practices (Han, 2008). Chapter 7 discusses various issues affecting lesbian, gay, and bisexual Filipino Americans and how the influence of Catholicism, gender role norms, and Filipino cultural values may negatively impact the mental health of such Filipino Americans.

In terms of teenage pregnancy, it can be hypothesized that a higher level of sexual activity during adolescence is one reason why Filipina American adolescents are becoming pregnant. In fact, one study found that for high school students, there was a significant difference between the number of Filipino American students who were sexually active (32%) versus Chinese Americans (13%). Rates of sexual activity among Filipino American teens was comparable to rates for White Americans (Horan & DiClemente, 1993). Other studies have found that up to 49% of Filipino American males engaged in sexual activity during their adolescent years (Grunbaum, Lowry, Kann, & Pateman, 2000). However, despite the fact that Filipino American teenagers are engaging in higher levels of sexual activity, they have little knowledge about safe sex (Weitz et al., 2001) and they are less likely to talk about safe sex practices with their parents (Chung et al., 2007). In fact, one study found that less than one-quarter of Filipino American adolescents regularly discuss sex with their parents and that varying acculturation levels of Filipino American parents influence their ability to discuss sex with their children (Chung et al., 2007). Filipino American parents may not talk to their children about sex because of cultural and religious stigmas; however, by not talking with their children (who may be exposed to sex and sex education in American media and educational systems), they may be doing a disservice to their children. Additionally, if their children (particularly their daughters) do become pregnant, Filipino American parents often wonder how this was possible. They may blame American society, and sometimes they even send their daughters back to the Philippines in order to avoid shame in their Filipino American communities in the United States.

ALCOHOL, DRUG, AND TOBACCO ABUSE

Numerous studies have examined how Filipino Americans may have higher rates of alcohol, drug, and tobacco use than other East Asian American groups (e.g., Berganio, Tacata, & Jamero, 1997; Nadal, 2000; Wong, Klingle, & Price, 2004). One study reported that Filipino Americans were the largest "abstainers" from alcohol in comparison to other Asian American groups, but at the same time Filipino Americans drank for pathological reasons significantly more than any other group (Johnson, Schwitters, Wilson, Nagoshi, & McClearn, 1985). While many Filipino Americans may not drink at all, the ones who do drink may be attempting to avoid psychological and emotional stressors. Gender also may play an influence in abstaining from alcohol; for example, one study found that 80% of the Filipino American men sampled were drinkers, while 50% of Filipina American women abstained from alcohol altogether (Lubben, Chi, & Kitano, 1988). This finding may be influenced by the gender role norms in which men are allowed to be macho and drink alcohol, while women are expected to be "pure and proper" and not drink alcohol. Another study revealed that alcohol use was lower among Filipinos born abroad (41.1%) than among those born in the United States; 64.8% of Filipinos born in Hawaii and 50% of Filipinos born in the mainland were alcohol users (Johnson, Nagoshi, Ahern, Wilson, & Yuen, 1987). Perhaps Filipinos in the Philippines abstain from alcohol for cultural reasons (e.g., they may not drink heavily as a way to avoid bringing shame to the family). It is also conceivable that Filipino Americans in the United States may use alcohol more as a way of coping with psychological stressors they would not encounter in the Philippines (e.g., acculturation or experiences with racism).

Many other studies examine different types of illicit drug use among the Filipino American community. One study reported that recent Filipino American immigrants admitted taking drugs when feeling isolated and depressed (Nemoto, Aoki, Huang, Morris, Nguyen, & Wong, 1999). This finding demonstrates how immigrants may turn to drugs as a way of dealing with acculturation and adjustment issues. Another study reported that Filipino American methamphetamine users in the San Francisco Bay Area often engaged in behavioral risk factors for HIV/AIDS infection, ranging from infrequent condom use, commercial sex activity, and low rates of HIV/AIDS testing (Nemoto et al., 2000). This finding is supported by another study of young Asian and Pacific Islander gay or bisexual men; more than half of the Filipino American males sampled had used ecstasy, hallucinogens, crack, amphetamines, and other types of drugs and had engaged in unprotected sex (Choi et al., 2002). These two studies show how drug use and risky sexual behaviors are highly related and how gay and bisexual men may turn to drugs as a way of dealing with their psychological stressors, emotional problems, and internalized homophobia.

In terms of smoking tobacco, one study found that Filipino American men smoke tobacco more than the general population (CAPIJLC, 2009). Data from the National Health Survey of 1992 to 1994 reported that 26.5% of Filipino American males were smokers and that an additional 23.2% were former smokers (Nadal, 2000). Another study revealed two important findings regarding Filipino Americans and smoking tobacco: Filipino Americans had the highest risks of smoking initiation in comparison to other Asian American groups and the highest prevalence of smoking among Asian Americans, while Filipina American women had the second lowest prevalence of smoking among Asian American groups (Klatzy & Armstrong, 1991). The same study revealed that Filipino Americans had higher levels of hypertension than any other Asian American group, supporting the potential correlation between stress and tobacco use (Klatzy & Armstrong, 1991). Smoking also may be viewed as a concern for younger generations of Filipino Americans; one study revealed that smoking cigarettes was more prevalent among Filipino Americans ages 18 to 29 than for those over age 45 (Romero, Messer, West, White, & Trinidad, 2008). Finally, a study involving Filipina American adolescents concluded that cigarette smoking is associated with depression and low self-esteem (Chen, Unger, Cruz, & Johnson, 1999). One can see several psychological and emotional reasons that may lead Filipino Americans to use alcohol, drugs, and tobacco.

GANGS AND JUVENILE CRIME

Gang membership and juvenile crime have been concerns in Filipino American communities (particularly for young men) in California and Hawaii since the 1980s (Alsaybar, 1999; Chesney-Lind, Pasko, Marker,

Freeman, & Nakano, 2004; De Leon, 2004; Mayeda, Hishinuma, Nishimura, Garcia-Santiago, & Mark, 2006; Sanders, 1994). Filipino gangs are unique because they may not fit societal stereotypical views of gangs. Urban gangs, for example, have formed in metropolitan cities in California, such as like Los Angeles or San Diego (Alsaybar, 1999; Sanders, 1994). These gangs tend to come from families of a lower SES and develop out of lower-SES neighborhoods, particularly those with a high population of Filipino immigrants. Many of these urban gangs consist of predominantly Philippine-born Filipino Americans who immigrated to the United States with their parents and speak primarily Tagalog with one another (Alsaybar, 1999). These gangs have been known to form out of a sense of survival and protection in tough urban neighborhoods that were predominantly Black or Latino. The gangs have been known to engage in a great deal of violence with other rival gangs (who tend to be of other racial or ethnic groups), and there has been an increase of arrests and complaints involving Filipino American gangs to local police departments (Alsaybar, 1999; Sanders, 1994). To demonstrate the amount of violence in Filipino American gangs, one author interviewed a gang member in Los Angeles who said:

When you gangbang, or if you were in danger of being attacked by enemies, everybody was down for you. Everything was suicidal, you know . . . we didn't care . . . all we do is like . . . whatever happens, happens. (Alsaybar, 1999, p. 125)

These Filipino Americans have learned many ways of surviving in their neighborhoods. Participating in gang violence seems to be a way for them to protect themselves and fit in. Moreover, it appears that the more acculturated these Filipino American immigrants are into American society, the more involved they became in gang life and violence. This trend is similar to other immigrant groups too. According to research on culture and youth violence, higher levels of acculturation into American life often is associated with higher levels of violence, gang membership, and substance abuse (Soriano, Rivera, Williams, Daley, & Reznik, 2004). Thus, it may be important for gang prevention programs for Filipino Americans to be created, as well as other services that address violence and substance abuse.

Besides urban Filipino American gangs, suburban gangs have formed outside of major metropolitan areas (e.g., Daly City, CA; Cerritos, CA), with members predominantly from middle-class Filipino American families whose family members are very well educated and have higher SES (Alsaybar, 1999; De Leon, 2004). Several reasons have been offered regarding why these gangs have formed, including a need for social support and identity development with other Filipino Americans (Pulido, 1991). These types of gangs are unique to Filipino Americans, in that other racial/ethnic groups form gangs in lower socioeconomic neighborhoods. And although the number of suburban gangs may have decreased over the past two decades, some might argue that these gangs merely have transformed or reconceptualized themselves as DJ crews (groups that are created around disc jockeys and follow hip-hop culture; De Leon, 2004). The formation of these crews is also indicative of the need these Filipino American youth feel for social support and identity development, as evidenced by one DJ who explains:

They knew they didn't fit into the white culture, so they rejected it and embraced hip-hop because hip-hop was already embraced by gang culture. . . . Filipino youth, not knowing anything about their own history or themselves, took to something they could identify with more. (De Leon, 2004, p. 196)

Although violence among these DJ crews has decreased since the late 1990s and early 2000s, there still may be heavy tensions between rival DJ groups, resulting in potential, rebellious criminal activities.

Even if Filipino American youth do not join organized gangs, they are involved in delinquent activity more than other Asian American groups. For example, one study in Hawaii found Filipino American youth, particularly boys, were more likely than any other Asian American group to engage in acts of property damage (Mayeda et al., 2006). Filipino American youth in Hawaii also were more likely than all other groups to be arrested for curfew violation, accounting for 33% of all juvenile arrests (Office of Youth Services, 2002). Another study in Hawaii found that Filipino Americans were more likely to engage in truancy (or "cutting school") than East Asian American groups (Chesney-Lind et al., 2004). Truancy often takes place in groups, and most truant youth are either at a friend's home or "cruising" (i.e., driving around local hot spots to try to meet other youth). There are many reasons why Filipino Americans may be truant, but the "fear of gangs" was stated as a reason more often for Filipino Americans than for other East Asian American groups (Chesney-Lind et al, 2004).

Although these studies concentrated on gang involvement in California and Hawaii, there is evidence that Filipino Americans nationwide may be involved in activities that are opposite of the "Model Minority." Researchers in a longitudinal study of Filipino American youth across the United States found that they reported more problem behaviors than Chinese, Korean, and Vietnamese American youth (Choi, 2008). These problem behaviors included a significantly lower grade point average in school, the likelihood of being expelled from school, experimentation with or abuse of alcohol and smoking, more aggressive and nonaggressive delinquent offenses, and more sexual experiences. Again, it is important to note that while the parents of these Filipino American youth are likely well educated and of a higher SES, their children are having such negative outcomes at school. Because Choi (2008) was a national study, perhaps the research on California and Hawaii represents the hardships Filipino American youth experience across the United States. However, very few studies are conducted on Filipino Americans outside of the West Coast and Hawaii, so little is known about the experiences of Filipino American youth in the Northeast, Midwest, Southeast, and Southwest (Nadal, 2008c).

As a final point, some authors have found Filipino American males to have higher rates of incarceration than members of other East Asian American groups (Rumbaut & Ewing, 2007). A little over 1.2% of Filipino American males are incarcerated, while less than 1% of other Asian American (Chinese, Korean, Japanese, and Indian American) males are incarcerated. Although this incarceration rate is significantly lower than that of Southeast Asian men (Laotians/Cambodians: over 7%; Vietnamese: over 5%) and men of other racial minority groups (African Americans: over 11%; Latinos: over 6%), it is important to notice and question why Filipino American incarceration rates are a bit higher than those of other East American groups.

One must wonder why incarceration, teen pregnancy, HIV/AIDS, substance use, and delinquency are almost always higher for Filipino

Americans than for East Asian Americans, despite their similar SES backgrounds and parents' higher levels of education. It is possible racism and discrimination may influence the ways Filipino Americans are perceived and treated by others (see Chapter 1). If others discriminate against Filipino Americans and if Filipino Americans internalize those messages of intellectual inferiority or criminality, perhaps they may unconsciously manifest these behaviors. Acculturation may influence one's ability to succeed (see Chapter 2). If Filipino Americans have difficulty adjusting to life in the United States (either when they immigrate or when they enter the real world outside of their families), there is a chance that they will have challenging experiences as a result of not being able to cope with their problems. Racial and ethnic identity development may influence these experiences (see Chapter 3). It is conceivable that Filipino Americans feel disconnected from Asian Americans and the model minority myth while feeling affinities or closeness to Black or African Americans and Latinos, which may lead to these experiences. Finally, colonial mentality may be a factor to consider when understanding these statistics (see Chapter 4). Concentrating too hard on materialistic things, such as beauty and social status (as a result of colonial mentality), may deter Filipino Americans from paying attention to other aspects that might be more important (e.g., understanding American educational systems or having open communication with children about their romantic relationships and friendships). A combination of all these factors might account for why Filipino Americans are suffering from such negative mental health outcomes. Therefore, counselors and clinicians must make efforts to understand the unique experiences of all Filipino Americans and examine how all of these cultural variables may impact each Filipino American in various ways.

ADDITIONAL SOCIOCULTURAL FACTORS

Many other sociocultural factors contradictory to the model minority myth may plague the Filipino American community. For example, gambling and body image issues are often viewed as "American" or "Western" problems that do not affect Asian American communities. However, because Filipino Americans tend to be lumped into the Asian American category, there are very few empirical articles to support that gambling or body image issues exist across the Filipino American community. For example, previous studies on gambling have found a higher prevalence of rates of pathological gambling among Filipino Americans when compared to the general population, and Filipino Americans were at risk for suffering maladaptive life consequences due to gambling behavior (Quiton, 2006). Again, further research is necessary to understand why Filipino Americans may be gambling at higher rates than other groups and how cultural values, colonial mentality, and other factors might influence this behavior.

Body image issues (and subsequent eating disorders) may be concerns for Filipino Americans, specifically because of colonial mentality and the need to be like the colonizer (see Chapter 4 for a review). One study reported Filipino American male college students to have the most body or self-dissatisfaction out of all other male groups (Yates, Edman, & Aruguete, 2004). This finding is important because eating disorders and body dissatisfaction usually are considered female disorders; however, such disorders also afflict Filipino American males. Another study found that Filipino American third-grade girls were likely to believe they were overweight and have body dissatisfaction that was similar to that of White American girls (Robinson, Chang, Haydel, & Killen, 2001). This finding may be of importance because eating disorders (anorexia and bulimia) are viewed as White adolescent female disorders and are not thought to be important among other racial/ethnic communities. Since Filipino Americans have similar statistics to White Americans in these studies, counselors and clinicians may want to consider how eating disorders specifically affect the Filipino American community. Nonetheless, further research on this subject (as well as other psychological disorders) is required to fully understand the complete experiences of Filipino Americans.

DISCUSSION QUESTIONS

1. How do you feel about the model minority myth? Are there positive or negative aspects to the model minority myth? Explain your answer.
2. What do you think are reasons why Filipino Americans experience shortcomings in education (e.g., higher rates of high school dropouts and lower rates of college admission and retention)?

3. What do you think are reasons why Filipino Americans experience higher incidences of HIV/AIDS, teen pregnancy, and drug use?

4. What do you think are reasons why Filipino Americans join gangs or engage in criminal activity?

5. How do you think these unique experiences influence how Filipino Americans are perceived and treated by others? By Whites? By other Asian Americans? By Black Americans and Latinos? By Filipinos in the Philippines?

SUMMARY

This chapter discussed the model minority myth, which describes all Asian Americans as being law-abiding citizens who are successful in educational systems and in their careers. However, the chapter highlighted some of the negative aspects of the myth, particularly when certain Asian American groups are not succeeding in stereotypical ways. Previous literature has asserted Filipino Americans have disparate experiences in higher education, have a higher prevalence of HIV/AIDS and out-of-wedlock pregnancy, suffer substance abuse issues, and often get involved in gang culture and crime. In discussing these issues, the chapter highlighted how the sociocultural experiences of Filipino Americans are distinctive from other Asian American groups, which may lead to differential mental health experiences. This next section presents two case studies that may not be typical of what is assumed of the model minority. It may be useful to brainstorm other factors discussed in previous chapters (e.g., racial/ethnic identity development, colonial mentality) and explore how these variables may influence the scenarios directly and indirectly.

Case Studies

Case 1: Beverly and Her Teenage Pregnancy

Beverly is a 17-year-old Filipina American high school student who grew up in a traditional, upper-middle-class, Catholic Filipino American family in New Jersey. When she was 14 years old, she met Anthony, a Filipino American boy (who was her age), at a neighboring high school, and they

(Continued)

began dating. Anthony came from a respectable Filipino American family. However, Beverly knew her parents would not approve of her having a boyfriend at such a young age, so she hid her relationship as best as she could and avoided talking to her parents about anything. Beverly's parents suspected she had a boyfriend because she was very private and spent a lot of time on the phone in her bedroom. In fact, they asked her younger siblings about Beverly, and they confirmed that Anthony was her boyfriend. Even though her parents learned that Beverly was dating, they chose not to ask her about the relationship because they "trusted her" to be a "good Catholic girl." However, the main reason they did not bring it up was because they were embarrassed to talk about dating, relationships, and sex, as this was a topic parents never discussed with their children in the Philippines.

Beverly and Anthony's relationship became very serious. In fact, Beverly said she believed Anthony was "the one" and wanted to marry him when she was older. So after two years of dating, Beverly and Anthony decided to have sex with each other for the first time. Because they loved each other so much and because they were virgins (and therefore had not been exposed to any sexually transmitted diseases), they chose not to use condoms or other birth control. A month later, Beverly starts to feel nauseous and learns she is pregnant. She is conflicted about keeping the baby because she does not want to be a teen mom and sees her whole life ahead of her. However, because of her Catholic upbringing, she believes abortion is a mortal sin. After a week of talking about the situation with Anthony, she decides to keep the baby.

Beverly knows she should probably tell her parents about her pregnancy, but she is worried they will judge and punish her. She is afraid of bringing shame to the family for having premarital sex, for being a teen mother, and for potentially not going to college. Three months pass, and Beverly still does not tell her parents. Because of her small frame (and because she wears very baggy clothing), they do not seem to notice. Additionally, Beverly spends most of her time in her room and refuses to eat dinner with her family. In the morning, she rushes out of the house as quickly as she can so she does not have to see her parents. After her fifth month of pregnancy, Beverly's mother finally confronts her in the morning, while Beverly is on her way to the shower. She asks Beverly why she is so distant from the rest of the family. The two begin to argue before Beverly eventually blurts out "Because I'm pregnant!" She runs out of the house crying and goes to school. When she shows up in her first class in tears, her teacher instructs her to go to the school counselor.

Case 2: Ryan: The Teenager who Always Gets into Trouble

Ryan is a 14-year-old second-generation Filipino American teenager who was raised in a typical middle-class Filipino American family in a predominantly Filipino American community in Daly City, California. When Ryan was in elementary school and junior high, he performed very well and was always compliant and respectful toward his parents. This had been especially helpful because his parents were both working full-time and expected him to be independent with his homework and obedient toward his *lola* (grandmother) when she baby-sat him after school. When Ryan was in middle school, he began to be more rebellious, wanting to spend more time with his friends and not with his *lola*. He started to hang out with his friends after school for hours at a time but managed to return home before his parents came back from work. However, because he was still getting good grades with school, his *lola* did not tell his parents, and his parents never knew of this behavior.

When Ryan entered high school this past year, his parents noticed his grades began to slip significantly. While he used to earn mostly As and Bs in his classes, he was now receiving Cs and Ds. They recognized he was spending a lot more time with his friends on the weekends and discovered from his *lola* that he was with his friends most of the time after school on the weekdays too. They also learned that Ryan was consistently getting into trouble with his friends at school and with law enforcement officers. First, his parents got a phone call from a teacher who caught Ryan cheating on an exam with one of his friends. Then Ryan and his friends were arrested by the police for painting graffiti on walls in a park. After both of these incidents, his parents would yell at Ryan; he would just roll his eyes, laugh, and eventually leave the room. Finally, Ryan and his friends were caught cutting class and drinking alcohol at school. When his parents confronted him, Ryan yelled back at his dad: "You're the one who gets drunk with the uncles all the time!"

Ryan's parents are fed up with him and do not understand why he is always getting into trouble. They threaten to send him back to the

(Continued)

Philippines to live with his extended family if he does not "shape up." However, Ryan does not take their threats seriously and ignores them as much as he can. Ryan's parents do not know what to do. They do not want to talk to their relatives or friends about the situation because they do not want to bring hiya (shame) to the family. They believe they are bad parents and that this would not have happened if they did not have to work all the time. They decide to pray to God, in hopes that prayer will solve the situation, and to ask forgiveness for being "bad parents."

Case Study Discussion

In understanding these two cases, it is important to acknowledge that they definitely do not fit the stereotypes of the model minority. Both cases consider adolescents who engage in behaviors that may not be expected of Asian Americans. Beverly is a Filipina American who became sexually active and pregnant during adolescence, while Ryan is a young Filipino American who is not performing well in school and is getting into trouble with his teachers and police officers. Although these situations may not be perceived as typical for Asian Americans because of the model minority myth, they may be viewed as fairly standard situations for Filipino Americans, particularly those on the West Coast and Hawaii.

One can notice how the lack of parental involvement might be a reason for these incidents to occur. For Beverly, it appears that both parents (particularly her mother) have difficulty talking to her about her relationship and about sex. This is likely due to their upbringing in the Philippines, where sex was a taboo subject and their own parents likely never had such talks with them when they were adolescents. The taboo or embarrassment of talking about sex is multiplied due to Catholicism; because the Catholic church forbids premarital sex, many parents will not discuss the issue with their children, even if it may help them be prepared in making good decisions. As a result, Beverly does not learn about proper birth control, contraception, or safe sex, which may have led to her pregnancy.

For Ryan, it appears that both parents might be uninvolved in his life and may not recognize some warning signs that he is getting into trouble with his friends. As a result, when Ryan starts to engage in criminal behaviors, it appears as if the situation may have gotten out of control.

Perhaps if his parents had been more knowledgeable of their son's whereabouts from a younger age, Ryan may have learned more about boundaries, and his parents may have gained more control over his life. Perhaps Ryan's parents were not as involved in his life because he is a boy, and adolescent boys are expected to have more freedom and independence than adolescent girls. Ryan may have learned to take advantage of the fact that his parents were always at work, which eventually led to his excessive amounts of freedom and lack of consequences.

Because both sets of parents are uninvolved in different ways, they may rely on indirect communication as ways of gathering information about their children and conveying messages to them. For example, Filipinos and Filipino Americans often discover information by "asking around." This includes talking to family members when they are too embarrassed or hesitant about asking someone directly. In the case of Beverly, it appears her parents question Beverly's younger siblings instead of talking to her straightforwardly. Ryan's parents rely on his grandmother to find out about his behaviors, instead of maintaining a closer relationship where they would directly be aware of what he was doing.

In both cases, it is important to acknowledge that there are various ways Filipino Americans cope with unanticipated problems. First, in the case of Ryan, it appears that turning to religion is a main way that his parents deal with stress. Filipino Americans often turn to prayer and God as a way to cope with problems. Their reasons are usually twofold: (1) to seek answers and solutions and (2) to repent for their sins, ask forgiveness, or both, because the situation is somehow their "fault." Second, it is apparent in both scenarios that all of these characters may use avoidance as a primary defense mechanism. Beverly and her parents seem reluctant to cause tension or interpersonal conflict; they choose to avoid the problem by not talking and evading each other physically. In Ryan's case, he and his parents avoid confrontations, conflicts, and interactions with each other altogether. Perhaps Ryan's parents want to be oblivious to his actions, so they do not have to deal with the guilt they experience for working hard and not developing a close relationship with him.

Although all parties seem to use avoidant coping styles, there are various ways that the avoidance in both situations is culture based

(Continued)

and generation specific. For Beverly and Ryan, who are both second-generation Filipino Americans, it may be desirable to shun their parents because they believe their parents "do not understand" and come from a different generation born in the Philippines. At the same time, both sets of parents may want to avoid their children because they do not know how to deal with issues facing youth in America. As a result, both sides do not know how to communicate with each other and may not learn proactive ways of dealing with their current situations.

Case Study Discussion Questions

For undergraduate students and general readers, please consider these questions:

1. What are your initial reactions to these two case examples? To Beverly? To Ryan? To Beverly's parents? To Ryan's parents?
2. What do you believe were the major factors that led Beverly to her current situation?
3. What do you believe were the major factors that led Ryan to his current situation?
4. How might the experiences of Beverly or Ryan relate to your own experiences or to those of someone in your family or life?

For helping professionals and graduate students of psychology, please consider these questions:

1. What would be the most difficult part of working with Beverly? What would be the most difficult part of working with Ryan?
2. How might different cultural identities (e.g., race, ethnicity, gender, social class, or religion) influence Beverly? How would these influence Ryan?
3. How would your cultural identities (e.g., race, ethnicity, gender, social class, or religion) impact your work with Beverly and with Ryan? How do you think they would react to you based on your cultural identities?
4. What would be helpful to create a therapeutic alliance with Beverly? What would be helpful to create a therapeutic alliance with Ryan?

CHAPTER SEVEN

Filipino American Experiences With Gender and Sexual Orientation

Figure 7.1 A spoken word artist who discusses what it is like to be an LGBTQ Filipino/a American
Photo courtesy of Kevin Nadal

CASE SYNOPSES

Melissa is a 41-year-old second-generation Filipina American woman who works as a successful attorney for a major law firm. She is single, has never been married, and does not intend on having any children. She constantly gets into arguments with her 62-year-old mother, Teresa, who says that Melissa needs to get married in order to be happy. Teresa believes that Melissa is too Americanized and too focused on her career, and that she needs to be more "proper" and "ladylike." Melissa thinks her mother is too traditional and needs to accept her daughter's life. Melissa begins to withdraw from her family, especially her mother, and begins to feel depressed.

Valentino is a 30-year-old Filipino American man who immigrated to the United States over 15 years ago. His parents live in the Philippines, and he sends them money every month, so they can live a comfortable life. Valentino realized when he was younger that he was probably *bakla* (gay) but vowed never to come out to his family, because he knew his parents were conservative Catholics and it would bring shame to them. A few years ago, Valentino met Jason, and they have been in a serious relationship since. However, Valentino refuses to tell his parents about Jason, which leads to much tension in their romantic relationship. Lately, Valentino has been experiencing physical symptoms, such as chest pains, heart palpitations, and muscle tension. When he goes to the doctor, he is told that the symptoms are likely psychosomatic and due to anxiety.

INTRODUCTION

This chapter focuses specifically on issues of gender and sexual orientation within the Filipino American community. Through exploring the history of gender and sexuality in the Philippines, one can learn how the Filipino culture was a matriarchal society prior to colonial rule. By describing various gender roles in the Filipino American community, the chapter highlights specific experiences with Filipina American women, particularly with incidents of sexism, misogyny, and gender role expectations. Previous literature has supported the fact that Filipina American women often experience family obligations differently from their male counterparts (Heras, 2007; Maramba, 2008). Additionally, the impact of gender roles on men is be considered, citing various psychological issues that may occur, including gender role conflict, which manifests through restrictive emotionality, restrictive affectionate behavior with other men, health care problems, obsession with achievement and success, restricted sexual and affectionate behavior, socialized control, power, competition issues, and homophobia (O'Neil, 2008). Finally, this chapter describes the experiences of lesbian, gay, bisexual, and transgender Filipino Americans, citing previous research which states that the intersections of identities may lead to various mental health problems, including depression, anxiety, and lower self-esteem (Nadal & Corpus, in press). Two identity development models are presented: a model of intersecting identities for Filipina American feminists and one for lesbian and gay Filipino Americans.

INFLUENCES OF GENDER AND GENDER ROLES

Chapter 2 analyzed how gender roles may have shifted in the Philippines as a result of Spanish and American colonialism. The indigenous Philippines often is described as a gender-neutral country, in that men and women were treated equally (Mananzan, 2003). In family systems, men and women had equal power; they shared household and parenting duties and had equal voice in decision-making processes. In mainstream Philippine society, women had equal opportunities in leadership and were encouraged in educational pursuits. However, when the Spanish arrived in the Philippines in 1521, they brutally forced the Filipino people to adapt to Spanish cultural values and religion. In doing so, gender roles began to shift from a gender-neutral society to that of a patriarchy. Women were objectified and mistreated by Spanish friars and colonizers; some were raped and physically abused. The Filipino people were taught directly and indirectly about Spanish gender role values such as *machismo* (male dominance) and *marianismo* (female submissiveness). As a result of colonial mentality, both Filipino men and women adapted these Spanish gender roles as their own.

When the Americans colonized the Philippines in 1899, gender roles began to shift further. The Philippines were taught American values, such as individualism and competition, which were in direct opposition

to the Filipino values of *kapwa* (fellow being), *utang ng loob* (debt of reciprocity), and *pakikasama* (social acceptance). As a result, Filipinos may
have learned to become more independent and goal-oriented in their
educational and career pursuits. Concurrently, Filipinos learned of different events in the United States and idealized various events they read
about in American newspapers. When the women's suffrage movement
formed and American women were granted the right to vote in 1920,
Filipina women also organized their own suffrage movement and were
granted the right to vote in 1937 (Santos, 1984). As a result, Filipina
women became more independent and began to endorse the gender-
neutral roles that existed prior to Spanish rule.

Current Filipino and Filipino American gender roles may reflect a
combination of indigenous, Spanish, and American values. Previous literature has argued that the present-day Philippines has reverted back to
the gender-neutral or egalitarian society in which Filipinos give recognition, deference, and opportunities to any family member (regardless
of sex) who shows potential to increase the family's status and position (Pido, 1986). Some authors argue that the Philippines may be a
matriarchal society, as evidenced by the notion that Filipina women are
encouraged to be community leaders and hold the "purse strings" in the
family (Nadal, 2004). However, regardless of whether the Philippines is
viewed as gender neutral, egalitarian, or matriarchal, one must consider
how Spanish values of male dominance and female submissiveness still
seep into interpersonal dynamics between men and women. For example, while Filipina women may no longer be expected to be submissive
to men, Filipino men still may insist on being hyper-masculine, emotionally controlling, and prideful when it comes to asking for help or
assistance. At the same time, although Filipina women are encouraged
to be successful in their educations and careers, some women may insist
on maintaining *marianismo* roles, by viewing getting married and having
children as a primary life goal.

Gender roles can be determined through a number of factors, including traditional stereotypes, career choices, dress/clothing, and personality/
behaviors (Nadal, 2010b). There are many ways in which Filipinos and
Filipino Americans may or may not subscribe to these various forms of
gender roles while other Asian Americans and other racial/ethnic groups
might. First, some gender roles are based on traditional stereotypes for

women and men and transcend culture. For example, in many cultures (including Filipino culture), women are expected to engage in indoor household chores (e.g., cooking, cleaning, doing laundry) while men are expected to be involved in outdoor household chores (e.g., fixing the car, taking out the garbage, raking leaves). Second, gender roles may be based on one's career choices, in which men are expected or encouraged to enter certain careers (e.g., medicine, law, or sports) while women are expected or encouraged to enter other fields (e.g., nursing, teaching, or social work). It is important to note that Filipino Americans do not tend to choose careers based on gender roles. In fact, there are an equal number of female medical doctors as there are male medical doctors in the Philippines, and there has been an increase in Filipino male nurses. Additionally, two of the last four presidents of the Philippines have been women, signifying the value and respect for female leadership on the national level, which may not be a value in most other Asian countries or even in the United States.

Gender roles may be expressed through clothing or styles of dress, which appears to be salient in the Philippines, particularly for women. For example, one study reported that Filipina American women were often discouraged from or punished for cutting their hair short and were pushed directly by their parents to wear skirts, even as adults (Nadal & Corpus, in press). Finally, gender roles may take form in personality traits and behaviors that may be more desirable for men and women. For example, in American society, men are encouraged to act as leaders or be aggressive while women are encouraged to be affectionate or cheerful (Bem, 1981). Although Filipino gender roles do not fit these exact characteristics (e.g., men and women are both encouraged to be leaders), there are definite ways men and women are "supposed" to act based on gender role norms. For example, one study reported that Filipino American men are encouraged by their families to maintain masculine mannerisms while being emotionally strong, whereas Filipina American women are encouraged to be proper, pure, and pretty (Nadal & Corpus, in press).

In general American society, gender role socialization also may influence how individuals cope with stress and how men and women may develop mental health problems (Nadal, 2010b). For example, previous literature has indicated that in the general population, there is a higher prevalence of depression in adolescent girls while there is a higher prevalence of substance use and antisocial behavior in adolescent boys

(Lengua, 2000). Perhaps depression manifests more in girls because they are taught to be emotionally expressive, which allows them to connect to feelings of sadness, hopelessness, or worthlessness. Perhaps substance abuse and antisocial behavior manifests in boys because they do not know how to cope with their emotions and turn to drugs, alcohol, or risky behaviors as defense mechanisms. To further support this notion of gender role influencing coping skills, several studies have found that men are likely to be more aggressive, engage in violent behaviors, and have more conduct problems than women (Cohn & Zeichner, 2006). Although these studies appear to describe the impacts of gender roles well, further research needs to be conducted on the influences of gender roles on Filipino American men and women.

Gender Role Expectations and Gender Role Conflict

Failing to conform to these gender roles may lead to much conflict for Filipino Americans. For both men and women, there are many contradictory messages about gender roles, likely due to the conflicting indigenous Filipino, Spanish, and American values. As a result, many Filipino American men and women may experience varying levels of psychological distress and acculturative stress. For example, it is common for Filipina Americans to have difficulties negotiating their individualistic needs and family needs (Heras, 2007). One qualitative study revealed that Filipina American college students feel a great deal of pressure to do well in school while simultaneously expected to maintain their duties at home (Maramba, 2008). Although they are encouraged to pursue their education and careers, Filipina Americans are expected to fulfill their family roles as obedient daughters, sisters, nieces, and granddaughters (Galapon, 1997). Negotiating between two sets of pressures may lead to psychological distress and even physical exhaustion. Moreover, many authors report that Filipina Americans experience gender role expectations that are greater than or different from those of their male counterparts (e.g., brothers or male cousins), representing the "gender double standards" that exist within Filipino American families (Maramba, 2008; Wolf, 1997). For example, women are expected to: care for their parents as elders; help their parents with household chores (even when they are adults who no longer live in the home); and take leadership roles in the family, such as organizing family parties, coordinating weddings and funerals, and maintaining communication within the family during times of illness or death.

Men may have different gender expectations in Filipino American families, but they may experience a gender role conflict that women do not. Gender role conflict refers to the experience of psychological distress for men and manifests itself in four areas:

1. Success, power, and competition
2. Restrictive emotionality
3. Restrictive affectionate behavior between men
4. Conflict between work and family (Iwamoto & Liu, 2008; O'Neil, 2008)

Success, power, and competition involve a man's focus on wealth and accomplishments as a means of self-worth; the need to have authority over another person; and the need to triumph, or "win," over another. Restrictive emotionality is defined as a man's inability to express emotions while also hindering others from expressing their emotions. Restrictive affectionate behavior between men concerns a man's inability to or difficulty in expressing intimacy and affection toward men and women. Conflict between work and family concerns a man's difficulty in balancing problems at home and at work (Iwamoto & Liu, 2008; O'Neil, 2008).

All of these factors may be specific to Filipino American men in many ways. For example, success, power, and competition may be heavily influenced by the Spanish value of *machismo* (male dominance), as well as American values of competition and individualism. Because men have internalized the need to be masculine and dominant, they may feel a desire to compete with others to assert their manhood and power. Moreover, because Americans introduced competition and individualism to the Philippines (which is indigenously a collectivist nation), Filipino American men may feel compelled to imitate the American colonizer by being successful, powerful, or competitive. Restrictive emotionality and restrictive affectionate behavior between men also may be influenced by the Spanish value of *machismo*. Since men may feel the need to be masculine, they have internalized the view that expressing one's emotions is a feminine quality and a sign of weakness. Because of *machismo*, they may feel a need to limit their intimate expressions with other men in order to not feel effeminate or appear homosexual. Finally, conflict between work and family may be applicable to Filipino American men, in that they have internalized through Spanish *machismo* and American individualism and competition the belief that they need to be providers for their families and cannot show signs of weakness to their family or peers.

Experiences With Sexism

Many authors recognize that women will face various forms of discrimination based on their gender (Nadal, 2010a; Sue & Capodilupo, 2008). However, because the United States has become increasingly more "politically correct," women are likely to experience subtle and covert forms of discrimination, otherwise known as gender microaggressions, rather than overt discrimination. Women might encounter several types of gender microaggressions on a daily basis:

- *Sexual objectification.* This occurs when a woman is treated as a sexual object.
- *Invisibility.* This occurs when a woman is overlooked and/or when men are given preferential treatment.
- *Assumptions of inferiority.* Such assumptions are seen when a woman is assumed to be less competent than men (e.g., physically or intellectually).
- *Denial of reality of sexism.* This denial occurs when a woman is told that sexism does not exist.
- *Assumptions of traditional gender roles.* Such assumptions occur when an individual assumes that a woman should maintain traditional gender roles.
- *Denial of individual sexism.* This denial occurs when a man denies his gender biases or prejudice.
- *Use of sexist language.* This occurs when language is used to degrade a woman.
- *Environmental invalidations.* These occur when institutions and systems convey sexist messages toward women (Nadal, 2010a).

Examples of sexual objectification include women being sexually harassed at work or men calling out to women on the street. Illustrations of invisibility include a woman being passed up for a job promotion in place of a less qualified man or being ignored for service by a bartender, computer salesperson, or mechanic. Examples of assumptions of inferiority include times when men assume a woman would not be able to carry a heavy box or make an effective leader. Denial of the reality of sexism may occur when a man tells a woman she is being paranoid when she believes that something sexist happened. Assumptions of traditional gender roles are demonstrated when men expect women to perform traditional gender roles, such as cooking and cleaning. An example of denial of individual sexism may include when a man tells a woman: "I can't be sexist. I have a wife and daughters." Use of sexist language comprises of instances when a woman is referred to as "bitch," "whore," or "slut." Finally, environmental invalidations occur on systemic and environmental levels, including the fact that a woman has never been president of the United States or that women make up only a small percentage of leaders of Fortune 500 companies.

Experiences with gender microaggressions may have several implications for the mental health of Filipina Americans. Although these discriminatory experiences may appear subtle or insignificant, their cumulative nature may impact a woman's self-esteem, leading to depression, anxiety, and an array of other emotions, including anger, sadness, frustration, fear, and resentment (Nadal, 2010a). Moreover, for Filipina Americans who are also women of color, the stressors of racial microaggressions and gender microaggressions may have a double impact, in that they experience racism, sexism, or the combination of both (Galapon, 1997). For example, a Filipina American might be exoticized when a man says "Filipina women are so beautiful and obedient." Although the man who makes this statement might be attempting a compliment, a Filipina American who hears this statement is objectified as a woman and as a person of color. The subtle messages being conveyed are that Filipina Americans are inferior to men and Filipina Americans are abnormal or bizarre compared to White women. When Filipina American and other Asian American women are exoticized, they may feel invalidated by the men who enact the microaggression and antagonistic toward White women who do not have to experience such discrimination (Sue, Bucceri, Lin, Nadal, & Torino, 2007).

Experiences of Sexual Orientation

This section shifts to examining experiences of sexual orientation for Filipino Americans. Gender roles influence one's perceptions of sexual orientation in a myriad of ways, particularly in shaping one's view of how individuals are supposed to act, whom they are supposed to be attracted to, and what life path they are supposed to take. This section focuses primarily on one subgroup of Filipino Americans who often are invisible in the literature: lesbian, gay, bisexual, and transgender (LGBT) Filipino Americans.

First it is important to understand what is meant by the term "sexual orientation" and how it differs from "sexual identity" and "gender identity." "Sexual orientation" can be defined as an individual's sense of personal and social identity based on sexual attractions, behaviors expressing those sexual attractions, and membership in a community of others who share them (Nadal, 2010c). Examples of sexual orientations may include gay, lesbian, bisexual, or heterosexual. Gender identity reflects an individual's personal sense of identification as male or female. Most individuals will identify their gender as their biological sex (i.e., if they were born with male genitals, they will identify as a male). Individuals who do not identify their gender with their birth sex are considered transgender. Finally, the term "sexual identity" can be defined as the understanding of one's values, beliefs, and roles as a sexual being, through the comprehensive process of exploring, assessing, and committing to one's sexual orientation and gender identity (Nadal, 2010a). All individuals develop a sexual identity, regardless of whether it is a salient part of their lives. For example, heterosexual individuals may not be aware of their sexual identity due to the privilege of belonging to the dominant sexual orientation and gender identity. However, their values, beliefs, and roles may be heavily influenced by these two parts of their sexual identity.

Various terms are used to identify sexual orientation for Filipino Americans. In the United States, the major terms used to describe sexual orientation include "gay," "lesbian," and "bisexual;" the term "transgender" is used for individuals with a nonconforming gender identity. In the Philippines (and in the Filipino American community), the term used to describe gay men is *bakla,* which literally translates to "effeminate or flamboyant gay man." *Baklas* take on traditional female roles, such as hairstylists and domestic workers, and are stereotyped as being drag queens or cross-dressers. The term used to describe lesbian women in the Philippines and in the Filipino American community is "tomboy," which has a similar definition in Philippine culture as it does in American culture: a girl who takes on male gender roles (e.g., through mannerisms, behaviors, and interests). In examining these two terms, it is vital to identify two issues for Filipino Americans: (1) "Gender roles" and "sexual orientation" are synonymous, in that a man who is gay is assumed to be feminine and a woman who is a lesbian is assumed to be masculine; and (2) "sexual orientation" and "gender identity" are synonymous, in that lesbian and gay individuals are assumed to be transgender or have a desire to live as a member of the opposite gender. It is important to understand these two concepts as they may offer some insight into how sexual orientation is perceived in Filipino and Filipino American communities.

It is important for counselors and clinicians to understand the experiences of LGBT Filipino Americans. Most of the psychology research that focuses on LGBT individuals assumes that there is a "universal" experience for lesbian and gay individuals (Nadal & Corpus, in press; Nadal, Rivera, & Corpus, 2010). Accordingly, it may be assumed that all lesbian and gay persons will have similar identity development processes and experiences, regardless of race, ethnicity, gender, sexual orientation, religion, and social class. Moreover, this assumed universal experience is usually based on gay White men and women and tends to view experiences of lesbian and gay people of color as abnormal or deviant. This is problematic for individuals of racial/ethnic minority groups because they often are expected by the LGBT community to conform to the norms of White lesbian and gay culture. For example, many psychologists view "coming out of the closet" as an imperative and necessary process for optimal psychological health (Brady & Busse, 1994). However, cultural obstacles may prevent many individuals from various racial and ethnic groups (including Filipino Americans) from fully coming out to their families or communities (Nadal & Corpus, in press; Nadal, Rivera, & Corpus, 2010). It also is important to understand that research on LGBT populations tends to focus primarily on lesbians and gays and does not examine experiences of bisexuals or transgender persons. Although lesbians and gays are marginalized in society, bisexuals and transgender persons are even more invisible.

Some research has focused on the experiences of lesbian and gay Filipino Americans. The few articles on the subject concentrate primarily on gay Filipino men in the Philippines and may not be necessarily applicable to lesbian and gay Filipino Americans in the United States. However, some concepts in these Philippine-based studies can help to underscore experiences of Filipino Americans. For example, similar to Latino culture and contrary to Western culture, the Filipino culture does not stringently associate sexual behavior with sexual orientation or sexual identity (Manalansan, 2003). This finding is demonstrated particularly with men who have sex with men (or men on the "downlow") who may not identify as gay because they participate in the dominant role during anal sex (Nadal & Corpus, in press; Tan, 1995). In fact, many call boys, or male sex workers, in the Philippines engage in same-sex sexual activities as a way of surviving poverty and may not consider themselves to be gay. This process of behavior not equating identity may be similar for Filipina and Filipina Americans who may be considered to be "tomboys" for behaving or dressing in masculine ways yet who may not identify as lesbians.

Given the complexities of identifying as lesbian or gay, it is important to understand the processes of "coming out of the closet" for Filipinos and Filipino Americans. As mentioned, some psychologists view coming out as a necessary stage of accepting one's identity (Brady & Busse, 1994). However, Filipino culture may view coming out as an unnecessary American trait that is excessive and gratuitous (Manalansan, 2003). In fact, for lesbian and gay Filipinos and Filipino Americans, sexual orientation is often understood, intuited, and not necessary to be talked about by one's friends or family (Manalansan, 2003; Nadal & Corpus, in press). Perhaps lesbian and gay Filipino Americans have difficulty coming out of the closet due to the influence of religion (Nadal & Corpus, in press). Because of Catholicism, many report having conflictual relationships with religious family members (who sometimes will even initiate religious interventions toward them). Additionally, many lesbian and gay Filipino Americans report feeling excessive amounts of guilt and shame, which may prevent them from accepting their sexual identities (Nadal & Corpus, in press).

172

If Filipino Americans decide to come out, they often might have to tell their parents more than once because their parents are not accepting. In one qualitative study, a Filipina American lesbian says:

When I was in my 20s, I felt like I had to come out to my mother like several times before she realized I was gay. . . . And I would just be like "I really have something to tell you" in college and I'd tell her and she'd cry . . . and then after four or five years, I'm still coming out to my parents. (Nadal & Corpus, in press)

Filipino American parents and families may have difficulty in accepting the lesbian or gay identity of their children or family members because of the influence of Catholicism and because of the stigma and fear of lesbian and gay individuals.

Finally, lesbian and gay Filipino Americans report unique experiences with the intersections of race, ethnicity, and sexual orientation. Many say that they have difficulty navigating through their distinctive communities; they may not feel fully accepted by Filipino Americans because of their sexual orientation while they may not feel fully accepted by LGBT persons because of their race and ethnicity (Nadal & Corpus, in press). Other gay and lesbian persons of color who would like to identify with both their racial/ethnic and sexual identities but struggle as they feel negative repercussions from both groups describe a similar process (Espin, 1987). An additional struggle may occur in members of multiple oppressed identities, who often are questioned whether they identify as lesbian or gay first or as a person of color first (Conerly, 1996).

Lesbian and gay Filipino Americans also report unique experiences with race that may not be experienced by other ethnic groups, including other Asian American ethnic groups. First, as with the general Filipino American community, some lesbian and gay Filipino Americans report the struggles in identifying as "Asian" or "Filipino." This struggle with racial and ethnic identity development is described in detail in Chapter 3. Lesbian and gay Filipinos may experience racism within the LGBT community when they recognize they may be treated, stereotyped, or exoticized differently from East Asian Americans. Second, gay Filipino American men report that race influences perceptions of gender roles. For example, many gay Filipino American males (and other gay Asian

American men) are stereotyped as subordinate, passive, and sexually submissive as well as the recipients of anal sex (Nadal & Corpus, in press). This leads to a racialized experience for Filipino Americans within the LGBT community that may negatively impact their sense of connection or kinship.

It is important to note that all of these studies focus primarily on lesbian and gay Filipino Americans and do not highlight the experiences of bisexual or transgender Filipino Americans. This omission is not due to a lack of interest in the topic but rather because little has been written about these two populations. There are no known studies that focus on bisexual Filipino Americans. The few psychology studies that focus on bisexual Asian Americans tend to lump them with lesbians and gays, without discussing unique experiences or processes that may occur for them as a subgroup. For example, some authors state that bisexual individuals often feel discriminated against within the LGBT community because gays or lesbians often suggest that they need to "choose" to be either lesbian/gay or heterosexual (Nadal, Rivera, et al., 2010). Moreover, studies on bisexual individuals of color tend to focus primarily on men and their sexual behaviors (Siegel, Schrimshaw, Lekas, & Parsons, 2008). In fact, many of these studies use the terms "bisexual" and "men who have sex with men" interchangeably, failing to consider the distinctive identity development that occurs for bisexuals.

Although there is some work on Filipino American gay men who cross-dress (Manalansan, 2003), no known studies focus specifically on the experiences of Filipino American transgender persons. Some studies that center on Asian American transgender persons include Filipino American transgender participants yet concentrate primarily on behaviors, not on identity development or psychological processes. For example, in one study involving Asian American transgender females (those born with a male sex but who now live as females), the majority of the sample consisted of Filipina American transgender females (Operario & Nemoto, 2005). The study concentrated on how Asian American transgender women are likely to engage in risky sexual behaviors and substance abuse but did not discuss other issues relating to their experiences with race, ethnicity, sexuality, or gender. Because of this lack of information, psychologists and other practitioners may not fully understand the experiences of transgender Filipino Americans.

The few studies on bisexual and transgender individuals that exist are exclusive and limited, primarily underscoring the experiences of bisexual men and transgender male-to-female individuals. As a result, bisexual women and transgender female-to-male individuals may be completely invisible or nonexistent in the literature. Because of this, it is essential for practitioners to be aware of the marginalization of bisexuals and transgender persons in general society as well as in the LGBT community. This omission in the literature may speak to the assumed universality of the LGBT experience, in which society tends to assume all bisexuals and transgender persons are the same, regardless of gender identity, sexual orientation, or experiences. Additionally, it is imperative to note that bisexual and transgender persons of color, particularly those of an underrepresented ethnic group, such as Filipino Americans, become even more invisible and oppressed.

Figure 7.2 A young Filipino American man marching in the Lesbian, Gay, Bisexual, and Transgender Pride parade
Photo courtesy of Kevin Nadal

Experiences With LGBT Discrimination

Like women and other minority groups, LGBT individuals are the recipients of "sexual orientation" and "transgender microaggressions," which are defined as subtle forms of discrimination based on sexual orientation and gender identity (Nadal, Rivera, et al., 2010). For LGBT individuals, likely these forms of discrimination take the form of micro-assaults, microinsults, and microinvalidations. A sexual minority micro-assault may include a heterosexual person calling a gay man a "faggot" or calling a lesbian a "dyke." A sexual minority microinsult might include an individual staring at same-sex couples or transgender persons in disgust. Examples of sexual minority microinvalidations might include a heterosexual telling a lesbian, gay, or bisexual person, "You think about your sexual orientation too much" or telling a transgender person "You're paranoid for thinking you were discriminated against." These types of statements or behaviors convey a negative and derogatory message toward sexual minorities. The cumulative nature of these experiences may impact an individual's mental health and self-esteem (Nadal, Rivera, et al., 2010).

LGBT individuals may face several categories of sexual minority microaggressions on a regular basis. These include:

- *Use of heterosexist terminology.* In this situation. heterosexist language is used to degrade LGBT persons.
- *Endorsement of heteronormative culture/behaviors.* This occurs when LGBT persons are expected to be or act like heterosexuals.
- *Assumption of universal LGBT experience.* In this case, individuals assume that all LGBT persons are the same.
- *Exoticization.* This occurs when LGBT persons are dehumanized or treated like objects.
- *Discomfort with/disapproval of LGBT experience.* This situation occurs when LGBT individuals are treated with disrespect or condemnation.
- *Denial of reality of heterosexism.* Here individuals deny to LGBT persons that heterosexist/homophobic experiences exist.
- *Assumption of sexual pathology/abnormality.* Here LGBT persons are presumed to be oversexualized and/or sexual deviants.

- *Denial of individual heterosexism.* This occurs when a heterosexual denies her or his heterosexist biases or prejudice.
- *Environmental microaggressions.* These occur when institutions and systems convey heterosexist messages toward LGBT persons (Nadal, Rivera, et al., 2010).

An example of a heterosexist terminology may include someone saying "That's so gay" (in reference to something negative) in front of an LGBT person. Endorsement of heteronormative culture may be exemplified by persons who tell LGBT individuals they need to "act straight" or "stop acting gay." An example of assumption of the universal LGBT experience occurs when someone passes judgment if an LGBT person has not come out of the closet. Examples of exoticization include instances when a heterosexual man asks a lesbian couple to engage in sexual activities or someone refers to an individual as their "gay friend." Denial of reality of heterosexism is demonstrated by an individual telling an LGBT person "You're being hypersensitive. That wasn't homophobic." An example of assumption of sexual pathology/abnormality includes an individual believing that all LGBT people have HIV/AIDS. Denial of individual heterosexism may be expressed by a person saying "I'm not homophobic. I have a gay friend." Finally, environmental microaggressions include societal and institutional messages conveyed through the media or other systems. For example, this can occur when an LGBT person notices that there are no LGBT individuals or couples on television, when legislation or proposition passes that bans same-sex marriage or gay adoption, or when a person observes that the leaders in the U.S. government are not LGBT or out of the closet.

Experiences with sexual minority microaggressions may have several implications for the mental health processes of LGBT individuals. As with gender microaggressions discussed earlier, although these sexual minority microaggressions may appear to be minor or meaningless, their cumulative nature may impact a LGBT individual's self-esteem, increase her or his likelihood of developing a psychological disorder, such as depression or anxiety, and may lead to a spectrum of emotions, including fear, anger, grief, disappointment, and disparagement (Nadal, Rivera, et al., 2010). Additionally, LGBT Filipino Americans may experience the double impact of racial microaggressions and sexual minority microaggressions, and Filipina American lesbians also experience gender microaggressions. For example, when a same-sex Filipino couple is refused service or stared at in disgust, one might wonder if they are experiencing a racial microaggression, a sexual minority microaggression, or both. Such experiences may lead for LGBT Filipino Americans to feel like "double minorities" (Conerly, 1996), which may result in psychological distress and other mental health problems.

FILIPINA FEMINIST IDENTITY DEVELOPMENT MODEL

After recognizing the different ways in which gender and gender roles influence Filipino American experiences, it is necessary to examine the various ways by which women might learn to identify as women and as Filipina Americans. It is important to recognize that both of these identities may influence each other in a variety of ways (e.g., race/ethnicity influences experiences of gender, while gender influences experiences of race/ethnicity) while also leading to a unique identity as a result of the two. In order to understand these intersections of identity, it is useful to review the identity models presented in Chapter 3, bearing in mind the gender identity development models that are present for women.

One model of feminist identity development (Downing & Roush, 1985) was proposed to demonstrate how women learn to achieve a positive feminist identity. Through the processes of accepting, grappling, and dealing with their feelings about sexism and gender discrimination, individuals potentially can navigate through five unique stages.

> *Stage 1: Passive acceptance.* A woman is unaware of sexism and may even deny that individual or institutional sexism exists. This may be demonstrated by a woman who believes men are superior intellectually or physically or a woman who allows men to objectify her.
>
> *Stage 2: Revelation.* A woman initially becomes conscious of individual or institutional sexism, either through personal experience or by being educated on women's issues. This stage may involve conflicting feelings of anger and guilt, in which the woman wonders how she was ever oblivious to sexism.
>
> *Stage 3: Embeddedness-emanation.* Here women may develop deep, intimate connections with other women as a way of feeling affirmed

and validated in their new identities. They may recognize these relationships as a "sisterhood" where others understand them and their worldviews, communicating validation and positive regard to other women

Stage 4: Synthesis. Here a woman learns to value herself and her gender by surpassing traditional sex roles and valuing men individually instead of stereotypically.

Stage 5: Active commitment. A woman learns to be fully accepting of herself as a woman and makes a lifetime vow to combat sexism in practical and peaceful ways.

Since racial and ethnic experiences influence one's gender and feminist development and vice versa, a new model (Nadal, 2008d) was created to demonstrate how this feminist identity may be influenced by one's Filipino American identity and experiences. Utilizing the Filipino American Identity Development Model described in Chapter 3, Table 7.1 outlines the various statuses in which racial/ethnic and gender identities may intersect and result in a unique identity for Filipina American women. In this model, stages 4 and 5 in the Feminist Identity Development Model are combined because of similarities in processes that occur in each. Stage 1 of the Filipino American Identity Development Model is dropped as it occurs during childhood.

In this model (Nadal, in press), 20 unique identity statuses represent the spectrum of experiences for Filipina Americans. *Status 1 (Passive-Acceptance/Assimilation)* occurs when a woman may have both internalized racism and sexism, where she does not like being Asian, Filipina, or a woman. A woman with this status may allow men to make sexist or racist jokes regarding her and may even allow White men to exoticize her. *Status 4 (Passive-Acceptance/Ethnocentric Consciousness)* might occur when a woman interacts only with other Filipino Americans yet might allow Filipino American men to take advantage of her and treat her as an inferior. *Status 7 (Revelation/Sociopolitical Awakening)* takes place when a woman feels conflicted as she learns about the sexism she experiences as a woman while also realizing the racism she experiences as a person of color. Statuses 13 and 14 represent instances where a Filipina American may identity primarily with her Asian American identity or her Filipina American identity. For example, a woman in *Status 13*

Table 7.1 Filipina American Feminist Identity Development Model

	Assimilation	Sociopolitical Awakening	Panethnic Consciousness	Ethnocentric Consciousness	Integration
Passive Acceptance	Status 1: Low Feminist ID, Low RI, Low EI	Status 2: Low Feminist ID, Conflicted RI, Conflicted EI	Status 3: Low Feminist ID, Hi RI, Neutral EI	Status 4: Low Feminist ID, Low RI, High EI	Status 5: Low Feminist ID, Integrated RI, Integrated EI
Revelation	Status 6: Conflicted Feminist ID, Low RI, Low EI	Status 7: Conflicted Feminist ID, Conflicted RI, Conflicted EI	Status 8: Conflicted Feminist ID, Hi RI, Neutral EI	Status 9: Conflicted Feminist ID, Low RI, High EI	Status 10: Conflicted Feminist ID, Integrated RI, Integrated EI
Embeddedness/ Emanation	Status 11: High Feminist ID, Low RI, Low EI	Status 12: High Feminist ID, Conflicted RI, Conflicted EI	Status 13: High Feminist ID, Hi RI, Neutral EI	Status 14: High Feminist ID, Low RI, High EI	Status 15: High Feminist ID, Integrated RI, Integrated EI
Synthesis/Active Commitment	Status 16: Integrated Feminist ID, Low RI, Low EI	Status 17: Integrated Feminist ID, Conflicted RI, Conflicted EI	Status 18: Integrated Feminist ID, Neutral EI	Status 19: Integrated Feminist ID, Low RI, High EI	Status 20: Integrated Feminist ID, Integrated RI, Integrated EI

*RI = Racial Identity

*EI = Ethnic Identity

(Embeddedness-Emanation/Panethnic Consciousness) may seek a general community of Asian American women while a woman in *Status 14 (Embeddedness-Emanation/Ethnocentric Consciousness)* may need to find a community of only other Filipina American women for support and solidarity. *Status 16 (Synthesis-Assimilation)* might represent a woman who is comfortable with her identity as a woman yet may possess internalized racism and may reject her identity as a person of color. For example, this woman may have White, feminist friends yet may not be concerned about issues impacting people of color. *Status 20 (Synthesis-Active Commitment/ Integration)* represents an individual who has completely accepted herself as a Filipina, Asian, person of color, and woman.

SEXUAL IDENTITY DEVELOPMENT MODEL FOR LESBIAN AND GAY FILIPINO AMERICANS

Several models describe the identity development of lesbian and gay individuals, citing that they will advance through a series of stages or phases, ranging from questioning one's heterosexuality to fully accepting one's gay identity. Cass (1979) and Troiden (1989) are two of the most widely cited of these stage models and are similar in many ways; however, Troiden's model captures an individual's identity development into four succinct stages.

Stage 1: Sensitization. An individual begins to feel same-sex attraction during childhood or adolescence, leading her or him to feel marginalized and different from peers.

Stage 2: Identity confusion. An individual begins to recognize feelings and behaviors that can be labeled as homosexual. People in this stage may cope with their confusion by denying feelings and impulses, by avoiding situations that may force them to confront their sexual impulses, by compensating for their internalized hatred by behaving heterosexual, or by accepting their impulses as a part of their identity.

Stage 3: Identity assumption. Here the individual may still feel the stigma from society, but they may begin with an increase in contact with other lesbians and gays. In this stage, individuals may begin to

disclose their sexuality to others on a limited basis, eventually leading to telling more people about their "true selves."

Stage 4: Commitment. This stage involves the integration of homosexuality into one's personality and way of being; a person is
comfortable with her or his sexuality and is able to achieve self-
actualization as a lesbian or gay person.

Similar in the Filipina Feminist Identity Model, racial and ethnic
experiences influence one's sexual identity development. In turn, sexual
orientation experiences influence one's racial and ethnic identity development. Accordingly, Troiden's (1989) model of sexual identity development
cannot be applied to lesbian and bisexual Filipino Americans alone but
should be used in conjunction with racial and ethnic identity development models. Therefore, this chapter presents a model for lesbian and
gay Filipino Americans that combines Troiden's (1989) lesbian and gay
identity development with the Filipino American Identity Development
Model outlined in Chapter 3 (see Table 3.1). Identity development of
transgender persons is not included in the model, as transgender persons
may undergo different processes because of gender identity. Identity
development of bisexual persons is not included in the model either,
because of the unique experiences that may occur as a result of being
attracted to both men and women. Future research should examine the
distinctive identity development of bisexual and transgender Filipino
Americans.

In examining this model, one can identify several ways in which
race, ethnicity, and sexual identity intersect. As a result, any lesbian or
gay Filipino American may maintain 20 different identity statuses (see
Table 7.2). *Status 1 (Sensitization Assimilation)* occurs when an individual has internalized *homophobia* and internalized racism and is unaware
of her or his status as a lesbian or gay person and as a racial or ethnic
minority. This individual might be unhappy about being a person of
color while also denying some of the sexual feelings for members of the
same sex. *Status 4 (Sensitization/Ethnocentric Consciousness)* may include a
lesbian or gay Filipino American who is still completely in the closet and
is heavily involved in the Filipino American community. This person
might be compelled to stay closeted because she or he is afraid of stigma
or rejection from other Filipino Americans. *Status 7 (Identity Confusion/*

Table 7.2 Identity Development for Lesbian and Gay Filipino Americans

	Assimilation	Sociopolitical Awakening	Panethnic Consciousness	Ethnocentric Consciousness	Integration
Sensitization	Status 1: Low Sexual ID, Low RI, Low EI	Status 2: Low Sexual ID, Conflicted RI, Conflicted EI	Status 3: Low Sexual ID, Hi RI, Neutral EI	Status 4: Low Sexual ID, Low RI, High EI	Status 5: Low Sexual ID, Integrated RI, Integrated EI
Identity Confusion	Status 6: Conflicted Sexual ID, Low RI, Low EI	Status 7: Conflicted Sexual ID, Conflicted RI, Conflicted EI	Status 8: Conflicted Sexual ID, Hi RI, Neutral EI	Status 9: Conflicted Sexual ID, Low RI, High EI	Status 10: Conflicted Sexual ID, Integrated RI, Integrated EI
Identity Assumption	Status 11: High Sexual ID, Low RI, Low EI	Status 12: High Sexual ID, Conflicted RI, Conflicted EI	Status 13: High Sexual ID, Hi RI, Neutral EI	Status 14: High Sexual ID, Low RI, High EI	Status 15: High Sexual ID, Integrated RI, Integrated EI
Commitment	Status 16: Integrated Sexual ID, Low RI, Low EI	Status 17: Integrated Sexual ID, Conflicted RI, Conflicted EI	Status 18: Integrated Sexual ID, Hi RI, Neutral EI	Status 19: Integrated Sexual ID, Low RI, High EI	Status 20: Integrated Sexual ID, Integrated RI, Integrated EI

*RI = Racial Identity
*EI = Ethnic Identity

Sociopolitical Awakening) may occur when an individual is confused about her or his racial and sexual identities. This person may recognize for the first time that racism exists while also recognizing she or he may be lesbian or gay. *Status 13 (Identity Assumption/Panethnic Consciousness)* may include an individual who is active in the general Asian American community and is starting to feel comfortable with coming out to some lesbian or gay individuals. *Status 14 (Identity Assumption/Ethnocentric Consciousness)* is when an individual may start to identify her- or himself as a lesbian or gay person while being involved in the Filipino American community. *Status 16 (Commitment/Assimilation)* is demonstrated by a lesbian or gay person who is fully comfortable with her or himself as a lesbian or gay person but who may be unhappy with being a person of color. Finally, *Status 20 (Commitment/Integration)* represents an individual implementing a level of accepting her- or himself as a lesbian or gay person, Filipino American, and person of color.

DISCUSSION QUESTIONS

1. What messages about gender did you receive from your family, school systems, religion, or the media? What messages about sexual orientation did you receive from your family, school systems, religion, or the media?
2. In what ways has gender affected you personally and your everyday life (e.g., how do people treat you based on gender, how do family members treat each other based on gender?)
3. In what ways has sexual orientation affected you personally in your everyday life (e.g., how do people treat you based on sexual orientation, how do family members treat each other based on sexual orientation?)
4. How do you consciously or subconsciously abide by gender roles?
5. Do you believe that gender roles are necessary in society? Why or why not?

SUMMARY

This chapter highlighted numerous issues of gender and sexual orientation within the Filipino American community. As mentioned, previous authors have stated that indigenous Filipino culture was a matriarchal or gender-neutral society prior to colonization. Gender roles within the Filipino American community were explored, and how gender role expectations and gender role conflict may lead to psychological distress for both men and women was discussed. The chapter emphasized the experiences of lesbian, gay, bisexual, and transgender Filipino Americans, underscoring their struggles with multiple identities and oppressions. Finally, two identity development models were presented: one for Filipina American women and one for lesbian and gay Filipino Americans. These models aim to educate readers about the various ways Filipina American women and LGBT Filipino Americans may view the world and interact with others. Two case studies display how gender, gender roles, and sexual orientation may influence the mental health of a Filipino American. In reading these cases, it may be beneficial to consider how gender and sexual orientation may influence people's abilities to relate with others, cope with problems, and develop multifaceted identities.

Figure 7.3 Three Filipina American cousins who grew up together in the United States
Photo courtesy of Ken Paprocki

Case Studies

Case 1: Melissa and Her Opposition to Gender Roles

Melissa is a 41-year-old second-generation heterosexual Filipina American woman who works as a successful attorney for a major law firm in Florida. She is single, has never been married, and thoroughly enjoys her career. She would be interested in entering a romantic relationship, but she does not view it as a necessity in her life; she also has no intention of having or desire to have children. Because of this, Melissa constantly gets into arguments with her mother, Teresa, 62, who says that Melissa needs to get married and have children in order to be happy. Teresa believes that Melissa is too Americanized, focuses too much on her career, and needs to be more "proper" and "ladylike."

In fact, when Melissa was a teenager, her mother was very strict with her. Her brothers had more freedom to leave the house on nights and weekends, but Melissa was not allowed to spend time with her friends, especially with boys, even though she had good grades and did not get into trouble at school. When Melissa graduated from high school, she purposefully wanted to attend college far away from home. After graduating from college, she chose to live 500 miles away from her parents' home, where she worked as a paralegal and eventually entered law school. She graduated from law school when she was 29 and had no intention of moving back to her hometown. She did promise that she would visit her parents and family members at least once every other month, and she kept her word.

Melissa enjoys her work as an attorney and has been trying to make partner at her law firm for the past several years. In doing so, she has little time for dating and has not been able to sustain a successful romantic relationship since she was in college. In fact, every time she goes home to visit her parents, she is consistently asked, "Why aren't you married?" or "Do you have a boyfriend?" by her mother and aunts. This aggravates Melissa each time because she recognizes that they do not bother her brothers or male cousins about getting married as much as they nag her and her female cousins. Melissa believes that her mother and aunts are too traditional and that they (especially her mother) need to accept her life. This leads to many arguments between Melissa and Teresa, which causes significant tension for them both. After a huge blowout argument over the holidays, Melissa decides to withdraw from her family, especially from her mother. She no longer visits her parents and begins to feel isolated and depressed. Although she has a strong support network of friends, she is very sad that there is a strain in her relationship with her mother. Her depression begins to affect her work, particularly in decreasing her motivation, concentration, and ability to sleep.

Case 2: Valentino and His Refusal to Come Out to His Parents

Valentino is a 40-year-old Filipino American man who immigrated to the United States over 15 years ago. He moved to Chicago, Illinois, where he currently works as a computer engineer. When he graduated from college in the Philippines, he told his family he wanted to move to the United States to pursue career opportunities; however, one of the major reasons was that he knew he was gay and wanted to be able to feel "free" in the United States. Valentino realized when he was younger that he was probably *bakla* (gay) but vowed never to come out to his family, because he knew his parents were conservative Catholics and because he felt it would bring shame to the family. When he finally settled in the United States, he began sending money to his parents every month, so they can live a comfortable life in the Philippines. Valentino speaks with his parents on the phone at least once a month, and each time, they ask him whether he had a girlfriend or if he was getting married soon. Valentino usually laughed or brushed off the subject, without ever hinting he was gay. Meanwhile, Valentino has been living in the United States as a gay man: He casually dated several men over the past 10 years; he developed many gay friendships; and he has even become comfortable in telling many of his heterosexual friends and coworkers about his sexual orientation.

A few years ago, Valentino met Jason, a 38-year-old Mexican American man, and the two fell in love. They developed a serious, monogamous relationship and moved in together after dating for 1 1/2 years. While Valentino has met and is accepted by Jason's family, Valentino refuses to tell his parents about Jason. This leads to much tension in their relationship because Jason feels as if Valentino is ashamed of him. Jason, who is the child of two immigrant parents, believes Valentino needs to come out of the closet to his parents in order to fully accept himself as a gay man. However, Valentino refuses to do so and continues

(Continued)

his facade with his parents. Additionally, Jason has become increasingly frustrated with Valentino because he feels Valentino does not know how to communicate his feelings. Jason believes that Valentino represses his emotions, runs away from his problems, and hides his true feelings toward him. This causes significant distress for both men yet is a topic Valentino does not want to discuss.

Lately, Valentino has been experiencing physical symptoms, such as chest pains, heart palpitations, and muscle tension. He goes to see his doctor, and he is told the symptoms are likely psychosomatic and due to anxiety. The doctor asks Valentino if he is stressed or anxious about anything, and Valentino denies he is feeling anxious about anything. When the doctor refers him to a hospital psychologist, Valentino is compliant and attends his first appointment. He tells the psychologist about his situation but insists he cannot come out of the closet to his parents. He says he fears if his parents found out about his sexual orientation, they would disown him and if he ever went back to the Philippines, his father might become violent toward him.

Case Study Discussion

In reviewing these two cases, it is clear how gender and sexual orientation may have an impact on people's problems. Both cases involve gender roles that appear to cause tension with others (particularly family members) if the person does not conform to what is expected by family or society. In the case of Melissa, gender role expectations lead to conflict with her mother. Her mother appears to be a more traditional Filipina woman who maintains the rigid gender roles taught in the Philippines: Women are supposed to be submissive to men, and the primary role of women is to become mothers and wives. It would be unacceptable for a woman in the Philippines to concentrate solely on her career, not be interested in getting married and having a family, or both. In fact, if a woman does not get married or have children, she is either ostracized as being undesirable or an "old maid" or she is assumed to be a "tomboy," or lesbian.

Because Melissa was born and raised in the United States, she may have learned different gender roles from those of her mother. Gender roles in the United States are more flexible. Women are allowed to be independent and career-driven, and a woman's happiness or success may not necessarily involve getting married and/or having children. Due to the difference in worldviews and gender role expectations, Melissa argues consistently with her mother, which leads to significant distress for both. Moreover, Melissa appears to be experiencing acculturative stress, which is the process of negotiating between acculturation and assimilation. She may not agree with what Filipino culture defines as gender role norms, and instead may want to be more career-driven, which would be more acceptable in the United States. Nonetheless, the fact that she may not want to dismiss her Filipino American family or identity leads to internal conflict and depression.

With Valentino, one can see how gender role expectations may influence his inability to come out of the closet to his parents. Because he has learned that men are supposed to be masculine and macho (and therefore heterosexual), he chooses to escape his family and move to the United States, where he can feel free. Men in the Philippines are expected to be heads of households and providers, so his parents constantly ask him if he has a girlfriend or if he is planning to get married. Valentino may have internalized these gender role expectations and messages of homophobia and heterosexism, which may impact his inability to feel fully comfortable with himself as a gay man. It also appears that Valentino believes it would be impossible for him to come out of the closet to his parents. This may be a common situation for Filipinos and Filipino Americans who do not come out to their parents or family because of shame, stigma, or because hiding their sexuality is viewed as necessary. However, keeping this secret from his parents appears to be a source of anxiety for Valentino and leads to physical (and potentially psychosomatic) health problems.

Furthermore, Valentino may be expressing gender role conflict, in which he may not have learned appropriate ways of communicating his feelings. Most Filipino men have been given messages at an early age that it is unacceptable for men to cry or express negative emotions. This trend for Filipinos and Filipino Americans is in line with factors described in gender role conflict: restrictive emotionality (inability to express emotions toward anyone) or restrictive sexual and affectionate behavior (inability to express intimate emotions toward one's partner or loved ones). Perhaps Valentino views his emotions as a sign of weakness and therefore chooses to ignore and repress them. However, not

(Continued)

189

addressing his emotions causes significant distress for him, which leads to physical and psychosomatic symptoms as well as conflict in his relationship with his partner, Jason.

There are many reasons why Valentino might not come out of the closet to his parents. For example, he fears that coming out would bring shame to the family and result in his parents disowning him. This may not be paranoid thinking; it actually may be the case if his parents are conservative Catholics, since many Catholic Filipinos have negative and fearful views of LGBT people. Valentino also fears that his father may become violent, which also may be a real concern, especially if his father has a history of violence or maintains a *machismo* attitude. It is important for psychologists to recognize how Filipino Americans and other racial/ethnic minorities might have difficulty coming out of the closet. In fact, forcing or encouraging clients to come out actually may be two forms of microaggression.

1. It may be considered an assumption-of-universal-experience microaggression in presuming that all LGBT persons need to come out of the closet as an optimal stage of acceptance.
2. It may be considered a cultural invalidation, if the psychologist encourages Valentino to endorse American values (e.g., coming out of the closet as optimal) and not such Filipino values as collectivism, putting one's family and community before the self, *hiya* (shame), *utang ng loob* (debt of reciprocity), *kapwa* (fellow being), and *pakikasama* (social acceptance). Even though the psychologist may feel she or he is working in Valentino's best interests, the psychologist must be aware of how personal biases have an impact on her or his perceptions of Valentino. The psychologist must also be aware of how failing to understand the cultural influences in Valentino's life may result in cultural mistrust or tension in the counseling and psychotherapy relationship.

Case Study Discussion Questions

For undergraduate students and general readers, please consider these questions:

1. What are your initial reactions to these two case examples? Do you agree with the choices that Melissa has made? Do you agree with the choices Valentino has made? Why or why not?

2. How do you feel about the ways gender roles or sexual orientation impact Melissa's mental health? Valentino's mental health?
3. How might the experiences of Melissa or Valentino relate to your own experiences or those of someone in your family or life?
4. What status of Filipina feminist identity development do you believe Melissa may be in?
5. What status of Filipina feminist identity development do you believe Melissa's mother may be in?
6. What status of lesbian or gay Filipino American identity development do you believe Valentino may be in?

For helping professionals and graduate students of psychology, please consider these questions:

1. What would be the most difficult part in working with Melissa? What would be the most difficult part in working with Valentino?
2. What might be some of your transference or countertransference issues with Melissa? With Valentino? With Melissa's mother? With Jason (Valentino's partner)?
3. What is your theoretical orientation? Which theoretical orientation do you think would be most effective in working with Melissa? With Valentino?
4. What therapeutic techniques or interventions do you think would be most helpful in working with Melissa? With Valentino?

ACTIVITY 4: SELF-REFLECTION

The purpose of this activity is to examine how the intersections of racial, ethnic, gender, and sexual orientation identities may manifest in popular media forms. Many Filipino American comedians, hip-hop artists, performance artists, poets, and spoken word artists address Filipino American issues. A select few address gender and sexual orientation. (See Appendix B for a list of Filipino American artists.)

1. Review the work of Filipino American artists on www.youtube .com, particularly searching for the work of Kay Barrett, Regie Cabico, Alison dela Cruz, Rich Kiamco, and Emily Lawsin.

2. Reflect on your cognitive and emotional reactions to the artists' works.

3. How do you believe the presence of Filipino American artists in the media impacts the views of gender and sexual orientation in the Filipino American community?

Multiracial, Multiethnic, and Adopted Filipino Americans

Figure 8.1   A Filipina American adoptee and her biracial son
Photo courtesy of JoAnn Garcia

CASE SYNOPSES

Wesley is a 12-year-old biracial boy who lives with his mixed race family in a predominantly White, middle-class, suburban town. His father is a White American of Irish Italian descent, while his mother is a Filipina

American who immigrated to the United States when she was 22 years old. Wesley's parents met in the United States about 20 years ago and were married after dating for 4 years. Although it is obvious that his mother has an accent and looks different from all of his friends' mothers, Wesley assumes he is "just like the other kids." He plays soccer, is in the choir at his school, and recently joined an after-school swimming team. One day he is sitting with his new swimming teammates waiting to be picked up when his mother pulls up in her car. One of the other boys asks, "Your parents send your maid to pick you up?" Wesley is distressed by this comment but hides his feelings in front of his new friends. When he enters the car, his mother asks him if something is wrong; Wesley says everything is fine and is quiet for the remainder of the car ride.

Karen is a 20-year-old biracial woman of Filipino and Mexican heritage; her father is a second-generation Filipino American and her mother is a third-generation Mexican American. Her parents were high school sweethearts who had an 8-year relationship before they were married. Karen has one older sister, and the family grew up in a mixed Filipino and Mexican American neighborhood in Southern California. When Karen attended a multicultural college in another part of the state, she decided she wanted to meet other Filipino and Mexican Americans. So, she went to two campus organization meetings: Kaibigan, which is the Filipino and Tagalog word for "friend" as well as the Filipino American social and political organization on campus, and MEChA, which stands for Movimiento Estudiantil Chicano de Aztlán, and is the Chicano and Mexican American political student organization on campus. When she attended the Filipino club meeting, one club member said, "That's so great that you would join our group even though you're not Filipino." When she attended the MEChA meeting, one member started talking with her in Spanish; when she told them she did not understand because her parents spoke English at home, the member said, "That's a shame."

Noah is a 16-year-old teenager who was adopted as a little boy by an upper-middle-class Jewish, White American family in Connecticut. He was born in the Philippines, and his mother gave him up when he was born. He spent his early years in an orphanage until his adoptive parents were able to adopt him when he was five years old; he has not had any contact with his birth parents since he was born. Despite his Filipino appearance, Noah lived his life as any Jewish boy would; he attended synagogue with his family on a regular basis, celebrated Jewish holidays, and even had his Bar Mitzvah a few years ago. Several weeks after Noah got his driver's license, he was pulled over by a police officer while driving in his neighborhood. The police officer was condescending toward Noah, with accusations that he had a fake driver's license and that his luxury car was stolen. Noah went home feeling confused, angry, and frustrated.

INTRODUCTION

This chapter firsts spotlights the experiences of biracial, multiracial, biethnic, and multiethnic Filipino Americans, subgroups often overlooked when discussing Filipino American issues. The term "multiracial" will be used as an umbrella term for this group, but "biracial" will be used when specifically discussing individuals who belong to two distinct racial groups. According to the U.S. Census, about 22% of the entire Filipino American population is multiracial, multiethnic, or both (Barnes & Bennett, 2002). Previous research has found that multiracial and multiethnic individuals often are forced to "choose" one identity over the other, leading to potential psychological distress (Root, 1990, 1995). Additionally, because of phenotype, multiracial and multiethnic individuals will experience various levels of racial discrimination due to how they are perceived. Four major subgroups of multiracial Filipino Americans are examined: (1) Filipino/White, (2) Filipino/Black, (3) Filipino/Latino, and (4) Filipino/Other Asian. The chapter cites specific experiences and identity processes that may occur with each of these subgroups. In addition, the chapter reviews various mental health experiences of this population, including how one develops a multiracial or multiethnic identity, how one deals with cultural value conflicts, and how one overcomes racial discrimination and stereotypes.

This chapter also examines the experiences of Filipino American adoptees, a group that has been growing in the United States over the past 20 years. Although most of the literature on Asian adoptees focuses on those from Korea, China, and Vietnam, the number of adoptees from the Philippines has grown exponentially in the past 10 years (Lee & Miller, 2008). In fact, the U.S. Census reports that about 4,000 Filipino Americans were adopted between 1989 and 2004, and there have been

195

an average of 252 adoptions from the Philippines every year since that time (Le, 2008a). Despite this relatively small number, it is likely that the number of Filipino adoptees will increase in the future, given the rise in adoptions from other Asian countries. Yet little has been written on this population, leaving adoptive parents (who are primarily White American) and Filipino adopted children without any resources to assist them in their child rearing or identity development. Given this dearth of literature, this chapter examines the mental health experiences of this hidden population and provides recommendations for working with it.

FILIPINO AMERICANS OF INTERRACIAL RELATIONSHIPS

History of Interracial Relationships With Filipino Americans

In order to understand multiracial Filipino Americans, it is important to be familiar with the context of interracial relationships in Filipino and Filipino American history. Interracial relationships involving Filipinos and Filipino Americans dates back to precolonial and colonial Philippines, when Filipinos married outside of their race, namely to: individuals of Chinese, Indian, and Muslim descent; Spanish colonizers; and missionaries from other countries (Root, 1997b). Filipinos who immigrated to the United States in large numbers in the early 1900s were mainly male and settled mostly on the West Coast (Cordova, 1983; Posadas, 1999). In fact, for every 10 to 15 Filipino American men, there was only 1 Filipina American woman (Cordova, 1983; Posadas, 1999). As a result, many Filipino American men had to search outside their race for romantic relationships and companionship, and many courted and dated White and Mexican women.

However, because of antimiscegenation laws in California (which were enacted as early as the state's admission to the Union in 1850), White people were not allowed to marry outside of their race. In 1880, the California government passed specific laws that prohibited "Mongolians" (a term used broadly to describe people of Asian descent) from marrying "White persons" (a term that included people of European descent and also Mexicans; Posadas, 1999; Takaki, 1998). From the 1900s to early 1930s, many Filipino men wanted to marry White women and were not allowed to do so because of these laws. Technically they were not permitted to marry Mexican women either because the U.S. Census at the time considered Mexican women as "White." However, because of the lack of concern about non-European groups marrying each other, the government put up few roadblocks to Filipinos and Mexicans from marrying each other (Guevarra, 2008).

During the 1920s and 1930s, there was also an anti-Filipino sentiment in California, in which Filipino men were viewed as sexual competition for Whites (Guevarra, 2008). There were three main reasons for this stereotyping and prejudice.

1. Many White women expressed interest in Filipino men, because Filipino men were respectful, romantic, and were not as sexist as White men.
2. Many Filipino men courted White women because there were no Filipina women around.
3. During the Great Depression, when many Whites lost their jobs, Filipino men were still working in various menial positions; Whites viewed this as Filipinos "stealing jobs" away from Whites, when in fact they had held these positions when they first started to arrive in the early 1900s (Guevarra, 2008; Posadas, 1999).

This anti-Filipino sentiment also stereotyped Filipino American men as hypersexual or sexual deviants, similar to how Black or African American men have been portrayed in the past. This can be demonstrated in some published quotes from newspapers in the 1920s:

"The love-making of the Filipino is primitive, even heathenish . . . more elaborate."

"The Filipinos are hot little rabbits, and many of these white women like them for this reason." (Takaki, 1998, pp. 328–329)

While laws were in place preventing interracial marriage, there were also many attempts to keep Filipino men at a distance from White women altogether. Filipino men became the targets of discrimination, with many acts of anti-Filipino interpersonal violence and anti-Filipino riots (Guevarra, 2008; Posadas, 1999). For example, the infamous anti-Filipino riots in Watsonville, California, in 1930 led to the murder of Fermin Tobera, a Filipino migrant worker (Jamero, 2006), making Tobera the first documented Filipino American victim of a hate crime in the United States. Thus, anti-Filipino sentiment grew above and beyond the stereotypes of Filipino men being sexual predators; discrimination and hate crimes occurred as a way of Whites exerting power over the Filipinos.

Eventually, interracial marriage for Filipino Americans and all other groups was debated in the court systems. In 1933, the California Supreme Court ruled Filipino Americans to be of the "Malay" race (and not the "Mongolian" race), which then allowed them to marry Whites and Mexicans (Posadas, 1999; Takaki, 1998). This decision allowed Filipinos to marry outside of their race; other Asians (who were considered Mongolian) still were not allowed to marry Whites at this time. It was not until 1948 that the extensive repeal of antimiscegenation laws occurred in California, allowing all people to marry interracially. Nationally, antimiscegenation laws were repealed in 1967 by the U.S. Supreme Court in the *Loving v. Virginia* case, which stated that such laws were a violation of the Fourteenth Amendment of the U.S. Constitution (Suyemoto & Tawa, 2008).

Contemporary Interracial Relationships With Filipino Americans

In present times, Filipino and Filipino Americans are different from many Asian and Asian American groups in that they may not adhere to a "pure race" mentality (Spickard, 1997). In fact, according to the U.S. Census, 21.8% of Filipino Americans are of mixed heritage, a rate that is significantly higher than Asian Indian, Chinese, Korean, and Vietnamese American populations and lower only than Japanese Americans (Barnes & Bennett, 2002). The number of multiracial Japanese Americans is also high likely because of their duration of stay in the United States, the smaller number of immigrants, and because many Japanese Americans are second, third, and fourth generation. If Filipino Americans continue their rates of interracial marriage and follow a path similar to that of Japanese Americans, the number of multiracial Filipino Americans can be expected to continue to grow in the near future.

Additionally, many specific trends in interracial and interethnic marriage are noticeably different for Filipino Americans than for other Asian American groups. Three points are notable.

1. The Census revealed that Filipino Americans were the least endogamous Asian American group, which means they are least likely to marry within their ethnic group (Le, 2008b).

2. Although both Filipino American men and Filipina American women have higher rates of interracial marriages than other Asian American groups, the number for Filipina Americans is much higher. While 82.4% of Filipino American men marry Filipina Americans, only 61.1% of Filipina Americans are likely to marry Filipino Americans. As a result, the next generation of Filipino Americans will likely include a higher percentage of multiracial Filipino Americans (Le, 2008b).

3. There are differences between the various racial and ethnic groups that Filipino American men and women marry. Filipino American men are the most likely of all Asian American men to marry White, Hispanic or Latina, and multiracial women; Filipina Americans are the most likely of all Asian American women to marry Black, Hispanic, or Latino men (Le, 2008b).

In examining this data, there are several points to notice. First, these statistics support the concept that Filipino Americans may not endorse a "pure race" mentality other Asian American groups might. For example, while 82.4% of Filipino American men and 61.1% of Filipina American women marry within their ethnicity, the percentages of other groups marrying within their race include: 89.5% of Chinese American men, 81.5% of Chinese American women, 91.9% of Asian Indian men, and 93.6% of Asian Indian women. Second, while other Asian American interracial marriages consist mainly of marriages to Whites, Filipino Americans may enter interracial marriages of all combinations, particularly with Latinos and Black or African Americans. For example, while marriages involving Filipina American women with White American men was 27.2% of all Filipina American marriages, the percentages of Filipina Americans who married Hispanic or Latino men (3.6%), Black or African American men (2.8%), other Asian men (2.8%) and multiracial men (2.5%) are fairly similar (Le, 2008b). Similarly, although marriages with White American women consisted of 9.2% of all marriages for Filipino American men, the percentages of Filipino American men who married Hispanic or Latina women (2.9%), other Asian women (2.8%), and multiracial women (2.3%) are also similar. The only percentage significantly lower involved Filipino American men marrying Black or African American women (0.3%); however, this statistic aligned with those from other Asian American male groups, in which only 0.1% to 0.5% of the male population married Black or African American women.

There are many reasons why Filipino Americans may enter interracial relationships and why they tend not to adhere to a "pure race" mentality. Previous literature suggests this may be due to the Spanish and American colonialism in the Philippines in which marrying a White individual or person of Spanish descent would give a Filipino or Filipino American a higher social status, envy, or respect (Nadal, 2008a). This would be an example of colonial mentality, in which individuals internalize the standards of beauty of the colonizers as the norm while viewing the physical appearance of their own group as inferior. In addition, openness to interracial marriage may be due to the strong American presence in the Philippines, which has led to Filipinos being exposed to other racial and ethnic groups and subsequently may have led to openness in interracial romantic relationships (Root, 1997a). The fact that Filipino Americans have higher English-speaking proficiencies (Reeves & Bennett, 2004) may allow them to communicate more easily with White or Black Americans when they first arrive in the United States. The similarities in cultural values due to Spanish colonization (Guevarra, 2004; Nadal, 2004) possibly may encourage Filipino Americans to marry Hispanic or Latinos more than other Asian groups do. Filipino Americans may be more open to interracial romantic relationships and marriages with African Americans or Latinos because of similarities in family values, experiences with racism, and sociocultural issues (see Chapter 6 for a review) or due to historical allegiances and similar interests in hip-hop, art, and activism, (Nadal, 2004). Additionally, since a majority of Filipinos and Filipino Americans are Catholic or Christian, they may be encouraged to "love everyone" and not be restricted by racial barriers when choosing romantic partners. Finally, it can be argued that Filipinos and Filipino Americans may not deem it important to marry other Filipinos because the Philippines itself may already be considered a mixed or multiracial country, due to the history of Spanish colonialism and trade from China, the Pacific Islands, Australia, and Portugal.

MULTIRACIAL AND MULTIETHNIC IDENTITY DEVELOPMENT

Chapter 4 examined the racial and ethnic identity development Filipino Americans may undergo in their lifetimes. Using the Filipino American Identity Development Model (Nadal, 2004), one can understand how individuals navigate through various statuses of identity, in which their feelings about themselves, about their racial group, and about other racial groups have an impact on their self-esteem, their interpersonal relationships, and their worldviews. However, a major limitation to racial and ethnic models of identity development is that they assume that individuals are monoracial or monoethnic while failing to examine the experiences of persons who are biracial, biethnic, multiracial, or multiethnic (Renn, 2008). It is important to be aware of the unique experiences of people who are multiracial as well as specific implications of being multiracial within the Filipino American community.

A common experience for multiracial persons is that they often are forced to "choose" an identity (Suyemoto & Tawa, 2008). This can occur in official forms (e.g., census forms or demographic sheets) or in social settings (e.g., in interpersonal interactions with questions like "What are you?"). When multiracial and multiethnic persons are asked to choose, they may experience psychological distress that monoracial persons may not encounter (Hall, 1992). It is important to give multiracial persons the ability to identify however they please, using terminology that is salient for them (Root, 1990). Some of the ways multiracial individuals may identify include: *hapa*, biracial, multiracial, mixed, Amerasian, or Eurasian (Suyemoto & Tawa, 2008). *Hapa* is a Hawaiian word that literally translates to "half" and has been used to describe multiracial persons in Hawaii (by self and others). Originally derived from the Hawaiian term *hapa haole* (which translates to half White or half mainlander), the label currently is used even on the mainland as a term of identity and empowerment (Fulbeck, Lennon, & Spickard, 2006). Some individuals may choose to identify with one race or ethnicity over the other, sometimes even denying their other race and ethnicity altogether. Some biracial or multiracial Filipinos and Filipino Americans may identify (or are identified by others) with the term *mestizo*, which originally was defined as someone who is part Spanish but also refers to fair-skinned persons (Nadal, 2008a).

Many studies examine how multiracial and multiethnic individuals distinguish themselves and experience the world, recognizing that persons can have positive, negative, and neutral experiences as a result of their multiracial and multiethnic identity. Although few bodies of work focus on experiences of multiracial persons of Filipino American heritage, some applications of the general literature may be salient to the multiracial and multiethnic Filipino American population. For example, some studies suggest that being multiracial and multiethnic is positive, in that individuals can have the "best of both worlds," navigating both groups encouragingly and learning positive aspects of both identities (Guevarra, 2004; Root, 1995). Studies also have found biracial and multiracial persons to be less susceptible to racial stereotypes than monoracial individuals (Shih, Bonam, Sanchez, & Peck, 2007). Moreover, multiracial and multiethnic persons can claim an "ambiguous identity" in that they may navigate the world without others knowing what their racial and ethnic backgrounds might be (Guevarra, 2004; Root, 1995). Finally, some multiracial and multiethnic persons may identify with "multiple passing" in that they may determine their racial and ethnic identity by certain situations, places, or geographic locations (Guevarra, 2004; Root, 1995). For example, when multiracial Filipino/White people live in predominantly Latino areas, they might be treated like Latinos. When multiracial Filipino/Black individuals move into a predominantly Black community, they might attempt to "blend in" with their neighbors, without publicly announcing or denying their Filipino American identity.

A few studies focus specifically on multiracial and multiethnic identity within the Filipino American community. One author describes the experiences of multiracial and multiethnic Filipino Americans in Hawaii (Nayani, 2010), citing five major themes of experiences:

1. Ethnic identity switching
2. Environment
3. In group versus out group

4. Competing social rewards
5. Local and *hapa* identity

Ethnic identity switching is similar to the "ambiguous identity" mentioned earlier, where multiracial persons have the ability to alternate identities depending on certain situations. *Environment* discusses the influence of the outside surroundings on one's ethnic identity. This is similar to the "multiple passing" mentioned earlier, in which environment has an influence on how one is perceived. The *in group versus out group* concept discusses the various ways in which individuals may feel like insiders and outsiders based on various identities, including generation, ethnicity, or social class. *Competing social rewards* involves the processes by which multiracial and multiethnic individuals decide whether it is acceptable or desirable to "out" themselves as multiracial or multiethnic. Finally, *local and* hapa *identity* discusses the ways in which multiracial and multiethnic people in Hawaii have learned to identify as a unique multiracial group.

Nayani's (2010) study of multiracial and multiethnic Filipino Americans in Hawaii also established that individuals might have some "ease" in navigating through their conflicting cultures. Individuals report being able to honor both sides of their identities and can highlight different parts of their selves when they are among various groups and in diverse situations. However, one conflict that did exist with participants in this study was the difficulty in "fitting in" with new Filipino immigrants who spoke native Filipino languages. Regardless, the overall experiences of this population seemed to be generally positive, which contradicts findings of previous works that state that multiracial and multiethnic persons tend to experience an identity conflict and psychological distress (e.g., Root, 1990, 1995). However, there is one major difference with this study compared with others: geographic location. In Hawaii, the presence of multiracial and multiethnic persons is considered more common and therefore more normalized than it would be in the mainland United States. Given this fact, it is possible that as the U.S. population becomes more multicultural (with an increase of multiracial persons), the ethnic makeup of a certain region may play an influential role in the acceptance of multiracial persons.

Multiracial Identity Development Model

One identity development model for multiracial persons examines the ways individuals may identify with their racial groups, impacts of societal racism, and influences of internalized oppression (Root, 1990). This model focuses specifically on biracial individuals of White and racial minority heritage (e.g., Asian, Black, or Latino). Biracial individuals can identify with five statuses:

1. Acceptance of the identity society assigns (e.g., the person's phenotype appears White, so the individual accepts a White identity).
2. Identification with both racial groups (e.g., the person identifies with both Asian or Filipino and White).
3. Identification with a single racial group (e.g., the person was raised in a Filipino community so only identifies as Asian or Filipino).
4. Identification with a new racial group (e.g., the person identifies most with others who are Asian or Filipino and White).
5. The individual may move fluidly among racial groups but identifies most strongly with other biracial people, regardless of specific heritage backgrounds (e.g., the individual identifies most with other biracial or multiracial persons including those who are Black and White, Asian and Latino, Black and Asian, etc.).

This identity development model sheds light on the experience of having two racial and cultural identities. Racial heritage, phenotype, and experiences with racism will influence multiracial and multiethnic identity for various combinations of multiracial and multiethnic heritage. For example, if someone is perceived as being "ambiguous" or "mixed," she or he is likely to be treated or discriminated against in a variety of ways. However, an individual who is perceived primarily as a member of a monoracial group (e.g., an individual who is always perceived as White or Black) will have a different experience with racism than the individual who can "pass" in multiple ways. Moreover, the combination of being Filipino American with another racial and ethnic background may have specific implications for cultural conflicts, identity confusion, community acceptance, racial and family tensions, and attitudes and beliefs toward the dominant, White group.

Figure 8.2 A biracial Filipina American woman with her multiracial newborn son
Photo courtesy of Lorial Crowder

The next section examines experiences of various multiracial or multiethnic Filipino American groups: multiracial Filipino/White, multiracial Filipino/Black, multiracial Filipino/Latino, and multiethnic Filipino/Other Asian. In reading about these various subgroups, recall the case synopses presented at the beginning of the chapter. Brainstorm ways in which being multiracial may impact these persons' identities and how being a member of these specific racial groups may lead to unique experiences within the Filipino American community.

SUBGROUPS OF MULTIRACIAL AND MULTIETHNIC FILIPINO AMERICANS

Multiracial Filipino/White Individuals

Most of the studies that focus on multiracial Asian Americans tend to discuss those who are mixed with Asian and White backgrounds. This is likely because most multiracial Asian Americans have parents who

205

are White. For multiracial Filipino Americans specifically, individuals may have White and Filipino parents of both genders, which may be in contrast for multiracial persons of different Asian ethnicities, who may be more likely to have a White mother than a White father (Le, 2008b). Some biracial and multiracial individuals with Asian and White parents have found that individuals experience a "dual existence" in which they may appear to be confident and popular but instead feel some inner turmoil and conflict about not fitting into any one social group (Root, 1990). This dual identity of being a part of the majority (White) group but also being a part of the minority (Filipino/Asian) group may lead to identity clashes for the individual. The person may receive messages that she or he is a member of the privileged group, because Whites are the cultural norm and the group to compare standards of beauty. However, the person may internalize messages that she or he is a member of the oppressed group, because Filipinos (or other minorities) are culturally different or physically inferior.

For biracial and multiracial persons of Filipino and White descent, there are specific implications of belonging to both groups. Because of colonial mentality, Filipinos and Filipino Americans may highly value individuals who are more like the colonizer (e.g., those who have Spanish or American ethnicity, who have fair or light skin, or who have a Spanish surname; Nadal, 2008c). As a result, many Filipino and Filipino American parents encourage their children to marry someone who is White, so their children and grandchildren can be *mestizo*, or light-skinned. In fact, most celebrities in the Philippines are biracial Filipino/White and set the standards of beauty there, even though most Filipinos in the Philippines are more likely to have darker skin (Nadal, 2008a). Accordingly, multiracial persons who are Filipino and White are more likely to be accepted within the Filipino American community than multiracial persons of other backgrounds. However, biracial and multiracial Filipino/White individuals are also likely to be exoticized within the Filipino American community (and general White society), in that they may be objectified or viewed as exotic because of their appearances. Nonetheless, despite this perceived acceptance in the Filipino American community, biracial and multiracial Filipino/White individuals still may feel psychological stressors of not fitting in completely with other Filipino Americans. Additionally, members of the Filipino American community may value the colonial or physical appearance of biracial and multiracial Filipino/White individuals but still may force them to choose to identify culturally as Filipinos.

Depending on a person's phenotype, she or he may face a spectrum of experiences. Some biracial and multiracial Filipino/White individuals may appear to be monoracial White (particularly when they have European surnames), which may result in these individuals experiencing similar privileges as monoracial Whites. This can be problematic if these individuals find themselves in situations where Whites make racial remarks about minority groups (or even their own Filipino group). While this person may be "passing" as White, she or he may experience an array of internalized psychological stressors. Some biracial and multiracial Filipino/White individuals may be perceived as racially ambiguous, which may result in the consistent questioning of their racial identities. This can lead to the constant stress of having to announce, or "out," one's racial background, which is something that monoracial individuals do not face. Some biracial and multiracial Filipino/White individuals are perceived as Hispanic or Latino, which may lead the individual to receive discrimination common for Hispanic or Latinos. Finally, some biracial and multiracial Filipino/White persons may appear to be completely Filipino. In this case, the individuals may be fully accepted in the Filipino American community but may feel cultural conflict for balancing the two cultures of their parents.

Multiracial Filipino/Black Individuals

The experience of being multiracial with Asian/Black backgrounds is unique and has several racial implications. First, because of racial hierarchies, Black or African Americans often are discriminated against by Asian Americans (Suyemoto & Tawa, 2008); this may be reflected in the significantly smaller number of Asian/Black interracial relationships (Le, 2008b). As a result of this discrimination, biracial and multiracial persons who are Asian/Black are discriminated against more within the Asian American community than biracial and multiracial persons who are Asian/White (Valverde, 1992). Second, when they are asked to choose a single racial identity, multiracial persons who are Asian/Black often tend to choose their Black identity over their Asian identity (Hall,

1992; Herman, 2004). This may be due to the greater acceptance of biracial and multiracial Asian/Blacks in the Black community or the greater exclusion or discrimination of biracial/multiracial Asian/Blacks within the Asian community (Suyemoto & Tawa, 2008).

Phenotype also may play a role in the acceptance of a Black identity over a biracial and multiracial identity. Because of dominant genes, multiracial Asian/Blacks might often be perceived as Black" and not as biracial/multiracial. For example, several biracial and multiracial persons in the entertainment industry are viewed as Black only; the general populace may not realize they are also of Filipino descent. Some of these entertainers include Apl de Ap (Black Eyed Peas), Cassie (R&B singer), Melissa Howard (*MTV Real World*), and Sharon Leal (*Dreamgirls*). Similarly, because these biracial and multiracial Asian/Black persons are perceived as Black, they may experience racism and racial discrimination that other Asian Americans may not face. As a result, they may feel more allegiance toward monoracial Black and African Americans who can fully empathize with their struggles accompanied with prejudice and discrimination.

For biracial and multiracial persons who are Black and Filipino, there are experiences that may be different for both monoracial Filipino Americans and multiracial Filipino Americans of different racial/ethnic combinations. First, it is essential to note that Filipina Americans may marry Black or African American men at higher rates than other Asian American female subgroups. Accordingly, it is becoming more accepted for Filipino/Black interracial relationships to exist than it may be in other Asian ethnic communities. Perhaps the increase in these relationships may be due to the fact that second-generation Filipino Americans may feel strong alliances with Black or African Americans due to similar sociocultural experiences and interests (e.g., experiences with racism or interests in hip-hop culture).

In fact, many second-generation Filipino Americans have been referred to as the "Black Asians" a term that has both positive and negative implications. When the term is used by Black or African Americans, it can convey a sense of solidarity and unity, in that Black or African Americans recognize cultural similarities with the Filipino American community that they may not share with other Asian American groups. This label is especially attributed to Filipino Americans in hip-hop culture, particularly those who succeed as break dancers, disc jockeys, spoken word artists, and graffiti artists. When Filipino Americans are referred to as Black Asians by other Asian groups or by Whites, the term can have negative insinuations, in that the speakers may be attributing to Filipino Americans negative stereotypes often given to Black or African Americans (e.g., Filipinos and African Americans are stereotyped to be unintelligent, criminals or gangsters, "ghetto," or lazy). When Filipino Americans refer to themselves as the Black Asians, the term can be viewed as either positive or negative. If the individual is recognizing the history of Filipino people and how aboriginal Filipino ancestors were considered *Negritos* (or of the Black race), aligning themselves with this term may be positive, as the person has pride in her or his Filipino identity. However, if the individual is denying that Filipino American identity and instead wishes to be Black or African American, it may be considered a negative trait.

Finally, it is essential to acknowledge generational differences in the acceptance of Filipino/Black interracial relationships. Although there may be strong allegiances between second-generation Filipino Americans and the Black or African American community, racist views may still thrive among older Filipino American (especially older Filipino immigrant) populations. Racism toward Black or African Americans can be viewed as a direct result of colonial mentality, in which Filipinos and Filipino Americans may have learned to adopt the stereotypes and prejudices of the colonizer (e.g., Spanish and Americans). However, Filipino Americans who were born and raised in the United States may recognize the benefits of allying with other people of color and having support systems with other Black or African Americans. Because of these generational differences, the biracial and multiracial Filipino/Black population is likely to increase as a result of interracial relationships with second-generation Filipino Americans but may not increase as a result of interracial relationships with Filipino immigrants.

Multiracial Filipino/Latino Individuals

Some research has highlighted the experiences of *Mexipinos*, or biracial and multiracial individuals of Mexican and Filipino descent (Guevarra, 2004, 2008). Mexipino persons are prevalent mainly in California, where there have been an increasing number of Filipino and Mexican immigrant populations for the past century, with both groups residing in the same geographic areas and where both groups have had a similar history with racism and civil rights. For example, during the United Farm Workers (UFW) movements in California in the 1960s, Filipino American farmworkers organized alongside Chicano (the political term for Mexican American) farmworkers to fight for employment rights and equal treatment (Posadas, 1999). While César Chávez (a Mexican American) is often credited with organizing the boycott of table grapes, Filipino Americans such as Philip Vera Cruz and Larry Itliong were cofounders and organizers in the UFW. Because of close allegiances during this movement and for 30 years prior, many Filipino men and Mexican women lived in close proximity to one another, leading to courtship, marriage, and the birth of Mexipino children. Antimiscegenation laws prohibiting Filipinos from marrying Whites may have pushed them to marry Mexicans, but it is more likely that the convergences of these two groups can be attributed to a similarity in cultural values, family structures, religion, and language (Guevarra, 2004, 2008).

Although other studies on multiracial persons of Asian/White backgrounds state that the two cultures often may be at odds with each other, leading to cultural clashes (e.g., Root, 1990), studies recognize that Mexipino individuals may navigate both of their identities with greater ease. Due to numerous similarities between Filipino and Mexican Americans (e.g., colonial history, language, Catholic religion, socioeconomic status, phenotype, and experiences with racism), Mexipino children may not even recognize the differences in their two cultures until they become adults (Guevarra, 2008). Since both their cultural groups may be accepting of each other, there may be less conflict between groups, leading to a celebration of being multiracial instead of dissent or tension. Moreover, many Mexipinos who grow up in Mexipino communities state that they prefer to be mixed with both Filipino and Mexican heritage, and they value both groups equally (Guevarra, 2008). Although the research focuses primarily on Mexipinos' experiences, these findings can be very similar and applicable to biracial individuals who are Filipino and another Latino ethnicity. Indeed, other Filipino/Latino identities exist, including Filirican (Filipino and Puerto Rican) (Guevarra, 2008).

Phenotype also may play a factor in the identity development of Mexipinos, Filiricans, and other biracial persons of Filipino/Latino heritage. It appears more likely for biracial Filipino/Latino individuals to present with a more Latino phenotype, although some biracial and multiracial individuals may appear to be more Filipino (Guevarra, 2008). What appears to be unique with this group is when a monoracial Filipino or Latino person "discovers" the person is biracial, they are welcomed with statements like "Oh, that explains your eyes" or "You look like you're Filipino but you have [insert physical feature]" (Guevarra, 2008, p. 386). Unlike experiences of biracial Filipino/White individuals, where there may be a discomfort upon discovery of the Filipino status, or biracial Filipino/Black individuals, where they might still be forced to "choose" a Black racial identity, biracial Filipino/Latino individuals may experience acceptance by monoracial individuals with greater ease.

Multiethnic Filipino/Other Asian Individuals

No known research articles have examined the experience of multiethnic Asian Americans. Perhaps multiethnic persons are assumed to be of the same racial group and are assumed to experience limited psychological distress or cultural clashes despite having parents of different ethnic heritages. However, as with multiracial individuals, multiethnic Asian Americans still may be pressured to choosing one identity over the other or feel cultural clashes between their ethnic groups. For example, an individual of Filipino and Chinese descent may be pressured to "act more Filipino" or "act more Chinese." There may be a conflict in religion, in that the Filipino parent or extended family may prefer the child be raised Catholic, while the Chinese parents or extended family may prefer the child be raised Buddhist, Confucian, or Christian. There may even be intraracial tension between the two groups, where the Chinese extended family may stereotype the person's Filipino family as criminal, lazy, or "too dark," while the Filipino extended family may stereotype the individual's Chinese family as stingy, nerdy, or uncivilized.

Individuals who identify as multiethnic, with Filipino and another Asian heritage, may feel at ease in identifying with an Asian racial group instead of focusing on ethnicity. In fact, utilizing the Pilipino American Identity Development Model (Nadal, 2004) presented in Chapter 3, the individual may be completely comfortable with a panethnic Asian American identity (or identify fully with other Asian Americans, regardless of specific heritage or ethnic groups), because it is a way to unite one's two ethnic identities. Moreover, this individual may not fully comprehend or want to accept the marginalized experiences of Filipino Americans within the Asian American community because it forces her or him to recognize status differences in the Asian American hierarchy. This may be a similar conflict experienced by biracial persons who are of White and non-White backgrounds, who may recognize privileges from one part of their identity while recognizing the oppression received from the other part of their identity.

Phenotype may influence how a biethnic or multiethnic individual of Filipino and another Asian descent identifies and experiences the world. Depending on genetic makeup and parents' phenotype, individuals can look a variety of ways. For example, if a Filipino individual has darker skin and conceives a child with an East Asian with light skin, it is probable that the biethnic child will appear to be more Filipino, as darker skin is typically a dominant gene, while lighter skin is typically a recessive gene. However, if the Filipino individual has lighter skin and conceives a child with an East Asian with light skin, it is likely that the child's skin color will be light, but her or his facial features, eye shape, and hair texture may determine whether she or he is viewed as Filipino or East Asian. Similarly, if a Filipino individual conceives a child with a South Asian with darker skin (e.g., Indian, Pakistani), the biethnic child likely will appear more South Asian, because darker skin is a dominant gene. Finally, if a Filipino individual marries or conceives a child with a Thai, Vietnamese, or Cambodian individual (who have a very similar phenotype as Filipinos), it is likely that the biethnic individual will appear to be Filipino within Filipino American communities, Thai within Thai American communities, Vietnamese within Vietnamese American communities, and Cambodian within Cambodian American communities.

FILIPINO ADOPTEES

There has been an increase in research focusing on the experiences of Asian adoptees. However, most of the research has concentrated on adoptees from Korea, China, and Vietnam without examining outcomes

of adoptions from the Philippines or other Asian countries. It is estimated that there are about 252 U.S. adoptions from the Philippines per
year. Between the years 1989 and 2004, there were about 4,034 U.S.
adoptions from the Philippines (Le, 2008a). International adoptions
from any country have multiplied by 300% in the United States between
1990 and 2005, Two Asian countries (Korea and China) have been
among the top sending countries (Lee & Miller, 2008). As a result, it is
likely that this number will increase significantly for all Asian countries,
including the Philippines. It is imperative to recognize the experiences of
this subpopulation in order to provide culturally competent and appropriate resources for them. The next section examines various aspects of
Filipino adoptee experiences, including mental health, encounters with
racism, and identity development.

Mental Health Experiences

The issue of transracially adopted children, or *transracial adoptees*, has
been a source of controversy since the 1970s (Lee, 2003; Lee & Miller,
2008). Some believed having a child of a racial minority background
adopted into a White American family would lead to mental health
stressors, unprotected and vulnerable racial and ethnic identity development, and potential psychological problems. However, most of the
research on transracial adoptions has found that adoptees adjust well
into their environments and experience similar mental health issues as
nonadoptees; in fact, most studies support that 80% to 90% of adoptees
have few serious behavioral or emotional problems (Lee, 2003; Lee &
Miller, 2008). When transracial adoptees do exhibit psychological problems, research has concluded that other factors are involved, including age at adoption, length of institutional care, and birth country of
origin (Lee, 2003). However, when examining the research on transracial adoptions, one must recognize that these studies are based on the
countries with the largest adoption numbers, including China, Korea,
Russia, and Romania, and fail to account for countries with smaller
adoption numbers, such as the Philippines.

Because of this fact, it is important to acknowledge that these studies *may* be applicable to the experiences of Filipino adoptees while also
being conscious of the limitations of studies that do not refer explicitly

to adoptees from the Philippines. First, because the Philippines is a poverty-stricken country in which 90% of the population lives below the poverty line, it is important to investigate the impacts on adoptees who live in orphanages before moving to the United States. While poverty is prevalent in many of these countries, it is possible that the extreme conditions of the Philippines may influence the early childhoods of these adoptees, which may then affect their mental health experiences as adults. Second, because Filipino Americans have encounters with racism and identity development different from those of other East Asian American groups, it is unclear how the experiences of Filipino adoptees may differ from those of Korean or Chinese adoptees. As a result, the mental health outcomes of Filipino adoptees is unclear, and further research is necessary to understand if results of studies on Korean and Chinese adoptees apply to Filipinos as well.

Ethnic Identity and Adoptive Identity Development

Although previous research finds that Asian adoptees may adjust well into their adoptive families, many studies examine the spectrum of ethnic identity experiences adoptees may face (see Lee & Miller, 2008, for a review). Some adoptees may identify primarily with their ethnic identity (i.e., identity of their country of origin) while others may identify as "American" or try to assimilate into the dominant culture as best as they can. Similarly, some adoptees may identify primarily with their adoptive identity (i.e., accept and celebrate their identity as adopted) while others may deny that they are adopted and hide this from others altogether. One author suggests that Asian adoptees have developed a hybrid identity, inclusive of both their ethnic identity and adoptive identity (Hübinette, 2004). Table 8.1 reveals the various levels of ethnic and adoptive identity development that Filipino adoptees may experience.

In examining the table, one can notice the different statuses of identity that individuals may experience. In these nine different identity combinations, there are ways individuals can identify positively with both groups, feel conflict about both groups, or feel negatively about both groups. Concurrently, there are ways individuals may feel positively about one group but feel conflict or negatively about other groups. Understanding the various statuses of ethnic and adoptive

214

Table 8.1 Ethnic and Adoptive Identity Development for Filipino American Adoptees

	Ethnic Identity Rejection/ Assimilation	Ethnic Identity Conflict/ Dissonance	Ethnic Identity Acceptance/ Integration
Adoptive Identity Rejection/ Assimilation	Negative EI, Negative AI	Negative EI, Conflicting AI	Negative EI, Positive AI
Adoptive Identity Conflict/ Dissonance	Conflicting EI, Negative AI	Conflicting EI, Conflicting AI	Conflicting EI, Positive AI
Adoptive Identity Acceptance/ Integration	Positive EI, Negative AI	Positive EI, Conflicting AI	Positive EI, Positive AI

EI= Ethnic Identity
AI= Adoptive Identity

identity development is essential so that one can gain an understanding of others' worldviews and learn how they interact with people of different racial and ethnic groups, as well as differing adoption statuses. Also, one can develop greater empathy for Filipino adoptees and appreciate the spectrum of ways their experiences are unique from those of Filipino Americans who were raised with their birth families as well as from adoptees who were raised with families of their own racial group.

It is also important to identify how experiences with racism may influence one's ethnic and adoptive identity development. Many published works have described the experiences of being a transracial adoptee, citing various encounters with racism that range from being teased to being assaulted (e.g., Trenka, Oparah, & Shin, 2006). A problem with being a transracial adoptee and dealing with racism is that the adoptee may not know where to turn, how to handle such situations, or both. Whereas individuals who were born into their birth families can talk to parents or siblings of their same race about various discriminatory experiences, transracial adoptees may not feel comfortable discussing race issues with their adoptive family members (particularly if the adoptive family is White). Additionally, White adoptive families may not be prepared or comfortable in discussing issues of race with their transracially adopted child. Accordingly, it is important that the issues of race are brought up early in the child's life, in order to create a safe space for when the child actually encounters racism for the first time. Transracial adoptive parents must learn to become comfortable with race in order to be supportive of their children and prevent psychological distress that often occurs when people of color encounter racism, discrimination, and/or racial microaggressions.

DISCUSSION QUESTIONS

1. How do you feel about interracial relationships?
2. How do you feel about transracial adoption?
3. What are the similarities and differences between multiracial Filipino Americans and monoracial Filipino Americans?
4. What are the similarities and differences between Filipino adoptees and Filipino Americans raised by their birth families?
5. What do you believe are the major issues impacting biracial and multiracial individuals?
6. What do you believe are the major issues impacting Filipino adoptees?

SUMMARY

This chapter discussed the experiences of multiracial Filipino Americans and Filipino adoptees by sharing the history of interracial relationships and how the Filipino American population is increasingly becoming more multiracial and multiethnic. The chapter also examined how culture, colonial mentality, identity development, and phenotype may influence the lives of various multiracial Filipino Americans, particularly those of various racial combinations (e.g., Filipino/White, Filipino/Black, Filipino/Latino, and Filipino/Other Asian). Finally, the chapter introduced the experiences of Filipino adoptees, citing various mental health experiences and one's intersectional development of ethnicity and adoptive identities. Now this chapter presents three case studies, two which concentrate on multiracial identity and one that concentrates on identity development of a Filipino adoptee. Two cases are provided for multiracial individuals, but it is essential to note that several factors would differ based on other racial and cultural combinations. For example, these cases here involve a multiracial Filipino/White individual and a multiracial Filipino/Latino person. Their experiences may be completely different from those of a multiracial Filipino/Black or a Filipino/Other Asian individual. For all three cases, it would be useful to speculate how the individuals' multiracial or adoptive identities may influence their situations and how they cope with their problems.

Case Studies

Case 1: Wesley and His Hidden Biracial Identity

Wesley is a 12-year-old biracial boy who lives with his mixed race family in a predominantly White, middle-class, suburban town in upstate New York. His father is a White American of Irish Italian descent, while his mother is a Filipina American who immigrated to the United States when she was 22 years old. His parents met in the United States about 20 years ago and were married after dating for 4 years. Wesley has two younger siblings: Andrea, 11, and Jonathan, 8. Although it is obvious that his mother has an accent and looks different from all of his friends' mothers, he just assumes he is "just like the other kids." He plays soccer, is in the choir at his school, and recently joined an after-school swimming team. One day he is sitting with his new swimming teammates waiting to be picked up when his mother pulls up in her car. One of the other boys asks, "Your parents send your maid to pick you up?" Wesley is distressed by this comment but hides his feelings in front of his new friends. When he enters the car, his mother asks him if something is wrong; Wesley says everything is fine and is quiet for the remainder of the car ride.

When Wesley goes to school the next day, he starts to feel different from the other kids. In addition to the comment he heard from his friends from swimming, he reflects on the subtle ways his school friends may have teased him about his mother in the past (e.g., making fun

(Continued)

217

of her accent or the Filipino "duster" dresses she wears around the house). He feels sad about this realization but tries to ignore it and continues his life as he normally would. However, his friends notice that he has become distant and quiet during their extracurricular activities. His teacher, Ms. Green, notes that Wesley's behavior has changed significantly (in that he appears withdrawn and silent most of the time), and she informs his parents about this transformation. Ms. Green asks if everything is stable at home; Wesley's parents tell her everything is fine, and they do not know what is bothering their son. Ms. Green then suggests that Wesley see the school psychologist, and his parents reluctantly agree.

Case 2: Karen and Feeling Forced to "Choose" an Identity

Karen is a 20-year-old biracial woman of Filipino and Mexican heritage; her father is a second-generation Filipino American and her mother is a third-generation Mexican American. Her parents were high school sweethearts who had an 8-year relationship before they were married. She has one older sibling, Laura, 23, and the family grew up in a mixed Filipino and Mexican American neighborhood in Southern California. However, Karen chose to attend a college that was more multicultural; the population was about 50% White and with the remainder equally divided among Black, Latino, and Asian populations. Because she missed the friends she had back home, Karen decided she wanted to make more Filipino and Mexican friends at school.

She attended two campus organization meetings: Kaibigan, which is the Filipino and Tagalog word for "friend" as well as the Filipino American social and political organization on campus and MEChA, which stands for Movimiento Estudiantil Chicano de Aztlán, and is the Chicano or Mexican American student organization on campus. When she attended the Filipino club meeting, one of the club members said to her, "That's so great that you would join our group even though you're not Filipino." She felt invalidated and upset that someone would assume she was not Filipina and left the meeting immediately. When she attended the MEChA meeting, one member started talking with her in Spanish. When she told them she did not understand because her parents spoke in English at home, the member said, "That's a shame." Karen felt upset that someone would assume she could speak Spanish because she was Mexican, and she also felt hurt because someone did not recognize she was part Filipina. She left the meeting just as distressed as she did upon leaving the Filipino student group meeting.

Karen is distressed by this experience and calls her parents to tell them about it. Her parents are empathetic and encourage her to attend the meetings again. Karen tells them she would consider it but decides she really does not want to put herself in those situations again. Karen calls her sister, Laura, who tells her that she had similar experiences when she attended college. Laura encouraged Karen to find the college's multicultural center or office of multicultural affairs, to see if there were any other "mixed" people on campus. Karen discovers that there is a multicultural center and learns that there is an organization called Hapa that is a multiracial student group. She attends her first meeting and meets several multiracial students, including Mimi (a senior and a club officer for Hapa) who identifies as Mexipino. Karen tells Mimi she is excited about meeting other multiracial individuals but that she is still saddened by not feeling accepted by the Filipino and Mexican students on campus. Mimi offers to take Karen to both the Kaibigan and MEChA meetings and also suggests that Karen talk to a college counselor as another source of support.

Case 3: Noah and His Experience With Racism

Noah is a 16-year-old teenager who was adopted by an upper-middle-class, Jewish, White American family and grew up in a small town in Connecticut. He was born in the Philippines, and his mother gave him up when he was born. He spent his early years in an orphanage until his parents were able to adopt him when he was 5 years old; he has not had any contact with his birth parents since birth. Noah's adoptive family is of mixed European descent (his great-grandparents immigrated from Russia and Poland three and four generations ago). Despite his Filipino appearance, Noah lived his life as any Jewish boy would; he attended synagogue with his family on a regular basis, celebrated Jewish holidays, and even had his Bar Mitzvah a few years ago. Noah knows he is adopted and loves his adoptive family very much. He wants to fit in as

(Continued)

much as possible and does not have interest in searching for his birth parents in the Philippines.

A few weeks after Noah first got his driver's license, he was pulled over by a police officer while driving in his neighborhood. Noah did not think he was speeding or doing anything wrong, so he did not know why he was being stopped. When the police officer asked to see Noah's driver's license, the officer claimed the ID was fake because he could not believe that Noah's last name was Goldman. Noah told him that he was adopted, and the officer snickered. When Noah asked why he was being pulled over, the officer asked to see his proof of insurance and car registration; he also asked Noah if the luxury car he was driving was stolen. Noah assured him the car belonged to his parents and showed him that his license matched his car insurance. The police officer let Noah go without a citation, but Noah went home feeling confused, angry, and frustrated.

When Noah arrived home, he immediately told his parents, because he had a very close relationship with them. His father told him the police officer was a "jerk" and he should not let it bother him. Noah asked his father why this happened and Noah's father did not have an answer. He insisted that Noah "forget about the situation" and move on with his life. A few months later, Noah experienced a different form of racism. This time he was in a store, and he noticed the White store owner kept following him around as he shopped. Noah felt paranoid that he was being watched but also felt that he was being treated like a criminal. Noah again told his parents about the situation, and now both parents told him to "forget about it" and not let the situation bother him. Over the next few months, Noah starts to notice other forms of potential discrimination but decides not to tell his parents. He knows what they will tell him and how it makes them uncomfortable. He also feels isolated and alone because he starts to recognize how race has an impact on his life. However, because he does not have anyone in his life who would understand, he represses these emotions, which then makes him feel low self-esteem, frustration, and disconnected from his family.

Case Study Discussion

In reviewing these three cases, it is clear that the experiences of Wesley, Karen, and Noah may be similar to those of the other case studies involving Filipino Americans (e.g., experiences with racism, struggles in identity development) while also recognizing how these scenarios may be different because of their multiracial or adoptive identities. Wesley appears to be encountering what is similar to the social political awakening status of the Pilipino American Identity Development Model (PAIDM). For the first time, when his monoracial White friends make unintentional racist insults about his mother, Wesley realizes that he is different from them. While dissonance and confusion may reflect a typical occurrence of racial identity development, it is different because of Wesley's biracial identity. He may feel conflicted, angry, and hurt that his friends insulted his mother, but he also may have feelings of guilt, shame, or embarrassment for being biracial. In other words, although monoracial persons can feel anger toward the dominant group, biracial and multiracial persons (who are part White) may feel conflict for being a part of the dominant group and of the marginalized group. So while monoracial people may not intend to discriminate against multiracial people, the multiracial person may have a negative reaction to this unintentional discrimination. And when multiracial people continually experience these subtle forms of discrimination (also known as microaggressions), they may have difficulty feeling part of any of their racial or ethnic groups (Johnston & Nadal, 2010).

This struggle with identity is also present in the case of Karen. Although she may be experiencing conflict or feelings of rejection from both Mexicans and Filipinos, she may have difficulty expressing anger toward her Mexican or Filipino sides. In the PAIDM, monoracial Filipino Americans may experience feelings of anger or frustration toward the dominant, White group; Karen's current struggle with identity does not involve the dominant, White group at all, however. In fact, for multiracial or biracial persons of two or more minority groups, there may be two different processes of identity development: (1) the struggle of identifying with their two or more racial groups and (2) the struggle of recognizing oneself as a person of color in the United States. Perhaps at a later time Karen will be discriminated against by a member of the White racial group, which will drive her toward the second struggle with identity. However, in the present scenario, her biggest concern is her disconnect from both of her racial groups.

In the case of Noah, identity development may also appear very similar to the PAIDM. When he experiences racism for the first time, he feels

(Continued)

221

confused and conflicted about it, just as other persons of color would feel. This is a common experience for people of color who may initially believe the world is color-blind and attempt to assimilate and align themselves with the dominant, White group. However, this worldview may be shattered when people of color experience racism for the first time. Noah may especially be confused because he grew up in a White family and never knew that blatant racism still existed. Moreover, because his parents are White, they are not able to understand what it is like for him to be a person of color who has to deal with racism. Noah's experience demonstrates one of the difficulties of growing up as a transracial adoptee. Although he may have the love and support of his adoptive family, they may not completely understand his struggles with race, racism, and racial identity.

For each of these cases, phenotype may play a role in how others may perceive or treat the individuals. Noah, who may self-identify as a Jewish American teenager, is identified by the police officer (and others) to be a person of color. It is unclear whether the officer views him to as Filipino, Asian, Latino, or of another racial group, because Filipinos often are mistaken for various races. Wesley is multiracial of Filipino and White descent and "passes" in that he is perceived by his new acquaintances to be White. Therefore, they feel comfortable making a racist comment about his mother being a maid, because they had no idea he was part Asian or Filipino. Finally, Karen, who is Mexipino, is perceived by other Filipino Americans to be Mexican (or Latina) and is perceived by Mexican Americans to be full Mexican (or full Latina). As a result, the other Filipino Americans may view Karen as an outsider while the Mexican Americans may assume she is monoracial and therefore that her experience would be identical to theirs.

Finally, in exploring these three cases, counselors and clinicians can recognize the various ways multiracial individuals and adoptees cope with their problems. Wesley appears to repress his problems and does not disclose his feelings to anyone. Eventually, this leads him to feel withdrawn and perhaps even depressed, which eventually leads to difficulties in his academic and social functioning. His parents do not know what is wrong, and even when they ask, he does not feel comfortable in telling them how he is feeling. Since Wesley is the oldest child and does not have any biracial role models, he feels alone and isolated from everyone else. Karen seems to have a good support system, in that she is able to reveal her troubles to her parents and her sister. However, her parents, who are both monoracial ethnic minorities, may not know what it is like to be biracial. Accordingly, Karen seems to feel the greatest support from other biracial individuals, particularly other Mexipinos, like her sister Laura and her new friend Mimi. Sometimes monoracial persons may be well intentioned and empathetic but cannot provide the full support multiracial persons need when racial stressors occur. Finally, Noah may attempt to talk to his family about his hardships, but because they are not people of color, they may not be able to offer the support he needs. So while his coping mechanisms tend to include expressing his emotions to others, he may have learned to repress his feelings because he felt invalidated, misunderstood, or alone.

Case Study Discussion Questions

For undergraduate students and general readers, please consider these questions:

1. What are your initial reactions to these three cases?
2. What multiracial identity status do you believe Wesley is in? What multiracial identity status do you believe Karen is in?
3. What ethnic identity and adoptive identity statuses do you believe that Noah is in?
4. How might the experiences of Wesley, Karen, and Noah relate to your own experiences or experiences of people in your life?

For helping professionals and graduate students of psychology, please consider these questions:

1. Based on their various identity statuses, what would be the most important issues to discuss with Wesley? With Karen? With Noah?
2. What are your biases about biracial and multiracial individuals? What are your biases about transracial adoptees? How would these biases influence your work with Wesley? With Karen? With Noah?
3. What theoretical orientation or therapeutic approaches would you utilize with Wesley? With Karen? With Noah? Explain your answer.
4. Do you believe the counselor's or clinician's race, ethnicity, or gender would make a difference in working with Wesley, Karen, or Noah? Why or why not?

ACTIVITY 5: SUGGESTED READING AND SELF-REFLECTION

The purpose of this activity is to understand how multiracial Filipino Americans may have different experiences from monoracial Filipino Americans. For this activity, read the book *American Son: A Novel* (2001) by Brian Ascalon Roley (see Appendix B for full citation).

1. Reflect on your cognitive and emotional reactions throughout the novel.
2. How do you believe multiracial identities impact the multiracial Filipino American character(s) in the book?
3. What statuses of multiracial identity do you believe exemplify the character(s) best?

CHAPTER NINE

Mental Health Experiences and Psychotherapy With Filipino Americans

Figure 9.1 A Filipino American couple who both grew up in the United States
Photo courtesy of K. M. Escobar

CASE SYNOPSES

Maria is a 54-year-old Filipina American woman who immigrated to the United States over 25 years ago. She met her husband in the Philippines, and they raised three children in a multiracial neighborhood in an average U.S. suburb. All three of her children moved out of the house when they graduated from high school; two are currently college students, and the other pursued a career in fashion. Maria's husband, Emilio, has worked as a mechanic for several years but recently was laid off due to troubles in the economy. As a result, Maria is the sole source of income in the family with her job as a post office worker, where she worked for 20 years. Recently, Maria went to her primary care physician to complain of back and chest pains and difficulty breathing. She also stated that sometimes when she is stressed, she gets dizzy and faints. She admits this usually occurs after major arguments with her family members (in which she is involved or sometimes uninvolved). Her doctor runs medical tests and also refers her to a psychologist.

Arthur is a 22-year-old second-generation Filipino American who grew up in a predominantly working-class Filipino American neighborhood. He worked at a retail electronics store after high school for several years, where he felt like he was "wasting his life away." He became depressed, exhibiting such symptoms as difficulties in sleeping, loss of appetite, and feelings of hopelessness and worthlessness. For the past six months, Arthur has been hearing voices that tell him he is "no good." He also began to believe his boss was planting small video cameras to "catch him making mistakes." Arthur became increasingly tense at work, particularly during busy hours, and began "talking strangely" to customers. He quit his job, after yelling at his boss that he could not take the constant abuse of being videotaped all the time. His family noticed this behavior and checked Arthur into a hospital.

INTRODUCTION

Throughout this book, it has been emphasized that the mental health of Filipino Americans is often invisible for many reasons. One reason is that many studies concentrate on the mental health experiences of Filipino immigrants or Filipinos in the Philippines (Nadal, 2004); another is that studies in the United States tend to generalize the experience of Asian Americans to apply to Filipino Americans (Agbayani-Siewert, 2004; David & Okazaki, 2006a; Nadal, 2004, 2008c; Root, 1997a). As a result, information regarding mental health treatment of

Filipino Americans is limited. Therefore, group members may receive culturally incompetent mental health services, which may in turn result in the underutilization of services by and decrease in overall mental health in the Filipino American community.

This chapter discusses existing research on Filipino American mental health disorders and treatment. By focusing on help-seeking behaviors and cultural values of this population, one may learn how Filipino Americans perceive mental health treatment. The chapter also reviews the most common psychological disorders from the *Diagnostic and Statistical Manual of Mental Disorders, Fourth Edition, Text Revision (DSM-IV-TR)* (American Psychiatric Association [APA], 2000), highlighting symptoms of these disorders, their cultural manifestations, and culturally appropriate treatment for Filipino Americans who may be diagnosed with these disorders. Additionally, several psychological theoretical orientations are introduced, with culturally appropriate suggestions for each one.

Because of the dearth of literature concentrating on Filipino Americans, this chapter also highlights the mental health experiences and treatment of other cultural groups, which may be helpful in understanding Filipino Americans. These groups include Filipinos in the Philippines, first- and second-generation Asian Americans, and Latino Americans. Some may argue these groups have parallel experiences with Filipino Americans and therefore studies on these groups can be applicable to mental health treatment of Filipino Americans. For example, understanding Filipinos in the Philippines can be useful for considering the impacts of Filipino cultural values on coping skills, family dynamics, and perceptions of psychotherapy. Moreover, examining the experiences of other Asian Americans can reveal how biculturalism and balancing two cultural value sets can impact a person's mental health. Finally, exploring experiences of Latino Americans may be useful because of the cultural and religious values they may share with Filipino Americans.

FILIPINO AMERICANS' MENTAL HEALTH HELP-SEEKING BEHAVIORS

Previous literature has established that Asian Americans utilize mental health services less than any other racial/ethnic group, including Whites and other people of color (David, 2010; Uba, 1994). Moreover, when Asian Americans do attend mental health services, they prematurely terminate (Leong, 1985; Snowden & Cheung, 1990; S. Sue, 1977). For Filipino Americans specifically, there has been some research regarding mental health help-seeking behaviors. One study found that Filipino Americans in San Francisco had low utilization rates of health services, which was likely a result of limited health care access (Ziguras, Klimidis, Lewis, & Stuart, 2003). The same study discovered that a lack of Filipino American staff members or culturally and linguistically competent providers may have been a barrier to services for Filipino Americans (Ziguras et al., 2003). Although this study concerned general health help-seeking behaviors, it can be applied to mental health help-seeking behaviors as well. A lack of Filipino American counselors and clinicians or a lack of culturally and linguistically competent providers may be one reason why Filipino Americans do not seek mental health treatment.

Other authors have reported that Filipino Americans had lower rates of treatment of mental illness than the general population; however, those who did seek treatment had more severe or dysfunctional psychological disorders (Sanchez & Gaw, 2007). This notion falls in line with previous literature that reports that Asian Americans in general have lower utilization rates of mental health treatment and higher rates of pathologies when they do seek help (e.g., Leong, 1985; Snowden & Cheung, 1990; Sue, 1977). So although it may be thought that under-utilization of resources may be a sign that Filipino Americans have fewer mental health issues, it is more likely that they do not seek treatment until their problems have worsened or become unbearable.

When Asian Americans do seek mental health treatment, there may be ethnic differences with the types of issues discussed. According to one study, Filipino Americans and biracial Asian/White individuals were more likely to discuss personal and emotional problems in counseling than other Asian American groups, who were more likely to voice educational and vocational concerns (Tracey, Leong, & Glidden, 1986). This study suggests that Filipino Americans may have different worldviews and communication styles from other Asian Americans due to colonial mentality and other cultural values. It also implies that when Filipino Americans enter mental health treatment, it can prove to be a useful experience, because of their general tendency to be interpersonally warm and emotionally expressive. However, because Filipino Americans may not utilize mental health services, they may not have opportunities for these positive experiences with counselors or clinicians.

Cultural stigma is cited as a main reason why Filipino Americans underutilize mental health services (David, 2010; Sanchez & Gaw, 2007). As mentioned throughout this book, Filipinos and Filipino Americans may do everything possible to avoid bringing *hiya* (shame) to themselves and their families. Seeking mental health treatment might be seen as disgraceful to oneself and one's family and therefore may deter Filipino Americans from obtaining mental health treatment. Filipino Americans may feel embarrassed to talk to counselors and clinicians about their problems and admit that they are having difficulties handling life situations. Moreover, Filipino Americans may be afraid to seek help for their psychological problems out of fear that others in their community or extended family may discover this, leading to *tsismis* (gossip) and shame. Even though the counselor or clinician and other staff members would protect the client's privacy, there may be fear that a mental health practitioner may break confidentiality. There may also be a fear that other community members may see the client sitting in a waiting room of a mental health clinic or clinician's office.

As a result of this shame, Filipino Americans may not seek traditional mental health treatment but may find alternative resources. According to some authors, Filipino Americans may be more comfortable seeking help from laypersons instead of mental health counselors and clinicians; these individuals include specialists, general practitioners, religious leaders, or other folk systems (Gong, Gage, & Tacata, 2003). Similar to other Asian American and Latino groups, it is common for Filipino Americans to present their primary care physicians with physical complaints (e.g., headaches, backaches, muscle pain) instead of realizing that these may be psychosomatic symptoms and seeking mental health treatment. And if their physicians do tell patients that their problems are indeed psychologically based and not medically based, Filipino Americans are likely to remain in denial and seek a second opinion or alternative medicine.

Additionally, Filipino Americans who are more culturally "traditional" and conservative may turn to religious leaders or clergy for assistance

229

with their mental health problems (Abe-Kim, Gong, & Takeuchi, 2004). Due to the strong presence of Catholic and Christian values, they may feel that it would be less shameful to "turn to God" or religion for help with their mental health problems than it would be to seek help from psychotherapists (Nadal & Monzones, 2010). Finally, Filipino and Filipino Americans may seek help from folk leaders, faith healers, or shamans (Demetrio, 1991; Henry, 1986; Hwang, Miranda, & Chung, 2007). Although they may be Catholic or Christian, many Filipinos and Filipino Americans also seek alternative and indigenous healing methods to cope with mental health problems. For example, it is common for Filipinos in provincial areas of the Philippines to use *hilots* (or massage techniques) during childbirth and other medical ailments. In addition, Filipinos in the Philippines frequently use herbal remedies for symptomatic relief (e.g., ginger for nausea). So while Filipinos and Filipino Americans initially may turn to Catholic and Christian religious leaders, they also may rely on guidance and healing from folk healers. This may be viewed as a similar practice for Latino groups who may practice Catholicism and Santeria concurrently.

Gender roles also may contribute to cultural stigma regarding mental health treatment. As discussed in Chapter 7, Filipino American men are expected to obtain rigid gender roles, which may lead to restrictive emotionality and other psychological distress. Because of Spanish colonialism and the prevalence of *machismo* (male dominance) in the Filipino American community, men may be encouraged to repress their emotions and hide their mental health problems from their loved ones. Expressing emotions, asking for help, and not being able to handle one's own problems may be viewed as a sign of weakness for Filipino American men. As a result, they may have more difficulties in seeking counseling or psychotherapy than their female counterparts.

Finally, like other racial/ethnic minority groups, Filipino Americans may harbor "cultural mistrust" or patient suspiciousness against mental health services, which may impact their ability to seek mental health services (David, 2010). "Cultural mistrust" or "patient suspiciousness" refers to the inclination to mistrust Whites, particularly in education and training, business and work, interpersonal and social relations, and politics and law (Bell & Tracey, 2006; F. Terrell & Terrell, 1981). Although the term "cultural mistrust" is used more commonly regarding Black

Americans, Asian Americans may experience patient suspiciousness, in which they too may feel distrustful of mental health services, particularly from White American individuals (Uba, 1994). Individuals' levels of cultural mistrust would likely be contingent on their racial identity status and colonial mentality (see Chapters 4 and 5 for a review). For example, if an individual is highly assimilated, has higher levels of colonial mentality, or both, she or he may have lower levels of cultural mistrust than an individual who is ethnocentric, has lower levels of colonial mentality, or both.

FILIPINO AMERICAN PSYCHOPATHOLOGY

As mentioned in Chapter 1, there are very few studies that examine psychological disorders among Filipino Americans. While there may be some studies that focus on Filipinos in the Philippines and about the general Asian American population, there is a lack of literature that concentrates specifically on Filipino Americans. This next section will highlight some of the most prevalent psychological disorders in American society, including depression, bipolar disorder, anxiety disorders, schizophrenia, and personality disorders. By reviewing the symptoms of these disorders, as well as the ways culture may influence the development of these disorders, one can identify effective treatment plans for Filipino Americans.

Depression and Bipolar Disorder

Depression and bipolar disorder are two examples of mood disorders; in this *DSM-IV-TR* category of diagnoses, a disturbance in the person's emotional mood is hypothesized to be the main underlying feature (APA, 2000). Major depressive disorder is the clinical diagnosis for depression, and occurs when a person has two or more major depressive episodes. Symptoms of depression may include *anhedonia* (or loss of interest in normal daily activities); chronic feelings of sadness, hopelessness, and worthlessness; crying spells; difficulty in sleeping, eating, or concentration; irritability, and sometimes suicidal thoughts. Bipolar disorder is a mood disorder involving alternating periods of mania and depression. Mania usually occurs when individuals have an extremely elevated mood and energy, unusual thought patterns, impulsivity, and sometimes psychosis. Individuals with bipolar disorder may alternate between mania and depression for various periods of time. Often manic episodes last for days or weeks, while depression can last for months or years.

There are various reports of the prevalence of major depressive disorder and bipolar disorder in the Filipino American population. One study reported that 27% of a random Filipino American community sample had a major depressive episode or clinical depression of varying severity, which is significantly higher than that of the general U.S. population, which is typically reported at 10% to 20% (Tompar-Tiu & Sustento-Seneriches, 1995). According to another older study, the prevalence of depression for Asian American patients in primary care settings is estimated to be 14%, but Filipino Americans have higher rates compared to Chinese and Japanese American patients (Kuo, 1984).

These studies highlight important statistics about depression within the Filipino American community, but it is important to recognize that these numbers may be inaccurate because Filipino Americans tend to underutilize mental health services. Perhaps there are more Filipino Americans who are depressed but are not seeking treatment; therefore, the prevalence of mood disorders may be higher than what is reported. Additionally, many Filipino Americans may suffer from what is known as smiling depression, which occurs when people manage to conceal their emotions and maintain a happy demeanor externally (Sanchez & Gaw, 2007). Since depression may be viewed as a sign of weakness and because mental health issues may bring *hiya* (shame) to the family, individuals may cope with depression by smiling or pretending everything is fine while hurting and suffering internally.

Finally, the 2004 Surgeon General's report indicates that Filipino Americans have the lowest rates of suicide, in comparison to White Americans and other racial/ethnic minority groups (as cited in Sanchez & Gaw, 2007). There are two major implications for this statistic. First, while the rate of suicide completion is low, the prevalence of suicide ideation may be high. For example, one study estimates that 45% of Filipino American teenage girls have seriously contemplated suicide (Wolf, 1997), which is significantly higher than reports of suicidal ideation in the general adolescent population—24% of females and 14% of males (Grunbaum et al., 2002). It is likely that Filipinos and Filipino Americans are not completing suicidal acts due to the influences of Catholicism (Sanchez & Gaw, 2007). Because Catholics view suicide as a mortal sin, many Filipino Americans may not follow through on suicide because they believe they will be punished by God while bringing shame to their families.

Second, it is common for suicide to be underreported across all Asian countries due to the cultural shame and stigma it would bring to one's family (Vijayakumar, 2004). In fact, in the Philippines, suicide and sexual assault often are underreported due to cultural factors, including shame and embarrassment (Consunji & Hyder, 2004). Similarly, suicide may be more common causes of death for Filipino Americans but may not be reported officially as the cause of death. Finally, despite lower reported occurrences of suicide than the general population, Filipino Americans still may have a higher prevalence of depression that goes undetected or untreated, which may lead to alternative psychological disorders (e.g., substance abuse) or other forms of self-harm (e.g., cutting).

Anxiety Disorders

Anxiety is a normal reaction to stressors in life; however, when the anxiety becomes so pervasive that it impacts everyday functioning, it can be a problematic disorder. The *DSM-IV-TR* lists four major types of anxiety disorders: generalized anxiety disorder (GAD), panic disorder, obsessive-compulsive disorder (OCD), and posttraumatic stress disorder (PTSD). GAD is characterized by chronic anxiety, exaggerated worry, and tension even when there is little to provoke it (APA, 2000). Panic disorder typically consists of unexpected and repeated episodes of intense fear accompanied by physical symptoms, which may include chest pain, heart palpitations, shortness of breath, dizziness, or abdominal distress. OCD involves recurrent, unwanted thoughts (obsessions) and repetitive behaviors (compulsions). Repetitive behaviors (e.g., hand washing, counting, checking, or cleaning) often are performed with the purpose of preventing or eliminating obsessive thoughts. PTSD may develop after exposure to a terrorizing event or ordeal in which grave physical harm occurred or was threatened.

Traumatic events may include war, rape, or physical assault. For example, one study found 37% of Asian American Vietnam veterans (including Filipino Americans) suffered from PTSD upon returning from war (Loo et al., 2001).

Although anxiety disorders exist across all racial/ethnic groups, there are many cultural implications for anxiety disorders with Filipino Americans. As mentioned in Chapter 1, research has found that Filipino American men and women have a higher prevalence of hypertension in comparison to Whites and other Asian subgroups (Klatsky, Tekawa, & Armstrong, 1996; Ryan et al., 2000). Moreover, the overall prevalence of hypertension is second highest for Filipino Americans, next to African Americans (Stavig, Igra, & Leonard, 1998). Many physiological reasons may lead to these health disparities (e.g., bad diet, lack of exercise, or both), it is important to recognize that many older immigrant Filipino Americans often complain about having "high blood pressure" (whether this is medically diagnosed or not). In taxing or confrontational situations, sometimes these individuals may faint (actually or dramatically) or announce they have "high blood" as a way of distracting from the stressful encounter or of receiving attention from others.

Complaining about high blood pressure is similar to the phenomena in Latino culture known as *ataques de nervios*. Ataques are characterized by episodes of uncontrollable shouting and crying, trembling, palpitations, and aggressiveness, particularly during times of distress (Lewis-Fernández, Guarnaccia, Martínez, Salmán, Schmidt, & Liebowitz, 2002). Although ataques are most prevalent in the Latino and Caribbean communities, because Filipino Americans share similar cultural values and colonial mentalities from Spain, they also experience these attacks. Ataques de nervios sometimes are associated with panic disorders but often are viewed as hysterical reactions and attention-seeking behaviors. For example, it is quite common for Filipinos and Filipino Americans at funerals to experience ataques, as a way of substantiating their personal closeness to the deceased or of receiving sympathy or attention from others.

There may also be cultural implications for PTSD in the Filipino American community. Because Filipino Americans may have difficulty expressing their emotions and seeking help for their problems, they may use repression as a primary coping mechanism. In fact, it is difficult to measure mental health in the community because Filipino Americans tend to deny, somatize, and endure emotional problems instead of seeking help (Araneta, 1993). As a result, when Filipino Americans experience something traumatic or terrifying, they may repress their emotions and never fully cope with or heal from the experience. For example, it is common for Filipino American men to restrict their emotions, even with psychologically traumatic events. Because of this, they may repress feelings of fear, anger, or anxiety, which then manifest in their dreams and intrude on their thoughts and concentration when they are awake.

Schizophrenia

Schizophrenia is a chronic, severe, and disabling brain disorder that affects about 1% of the U.S. population. There are many symptoms of schizophrenia, including unusual thoughts or perceptions, hallucinations, delusions, disorganized speech, and an inability to find pleasure in everyday life (APA, 2000). Persons who are diagnosed with schizophrenia usually have difficulty with everyday functioning, including sustaining a job or career and maintaining social and familial relationships; as a result, they often suffer from social isolation and an inability to maintain basic human needs. There are several types of schizophrenia, including paranoid schizophrenia (which occurs when delusions and hallucinations are present but thought disorder, disorganized behavior, and affective flattening are absent), disorganized schizophrenia (which occurs when thought disorder and flat affect are present together), and catatonic schizophrenia (which occurs when an individual exhibits agitated, purposeless movement or is completely immobile).

There have been a few studies involving Filipino Americans and schizophrenia. Studies in the 1960s and 1970s reported that Filipino Americans in Hawaii tended to have a higher incidence of schizophrenia than other Asian ethnic groups (Sanchez & Gaw, 2007; Young & Kinzie, 1974). For example, one study discovered that Filipino Americans were diagnosed with schizophrenia at a somewhat later age than other groups (about 43 years for male patients and 36 years for female patients) while also finding there was an unusually high mortality ratio (2 out of 7) for Filipina Americans with schizophrenia (Weiner & Marvit, 1977). Another study revealed that Filipino American patients with schizophrenia were more likely to express feelings freely and directly and were characterized by greater violence, more bizarre behavior, and more dramatic delusions of persecution and of grandeur than similar Japanese American patients (Enright & Jaeckle, 1963).

A few cultural implications for schizophrenia exist in the Filipino American community. For one thing, it is important to understand that Filipinos and Filipino Americans may consider schizophrenia to have religious or spiritual manifestations. For example, a person who has hallucinations may believe him- or herself to be cursed by evil spirits or to be punished by God. Concurrently, some visual hallucinations may not be viewed as psychotic in the Filipino community at all but rather as spirits of deceased loved ones making appearances to the living. This finding aligns with previous researchers who have asserted that it is common (and accepted) for Filipino Americans to describe how deceased spirits make "visits" to family members after they die (Shimabukuro, Daniels, & D'Andrea, 1999). Although this phenomena may be culturally ordinary in Filipino American families, Western psychologists may view these individuals as having visual or auditory hallucinations or even schizophrenia. Yet many individuals who experience these "visits" may not seek help from mental professionals but rather may seek guidance from religious leaders and spiritual healers. In other cases, individuals might enjoy the "visits" and not view them as problematic or harmful.

If Filipino Americans truly do exhibit symptoms of schizophrenia, family members may ignore the problem, due to *hiya* (shame) and the cultural stigmas of receiving mental health treatment. It is common for persons with schizophrenia to be "hidden" within family homes or shipped to far away relatives. Moreover, in Filipino and Filipino American families, schizophrenia may be viewed as a punishment from God, which may dissuade families from seeking help or telling extended family or community members. Instead of addressing the disease with medication or psychological treatment, families may turn to religion and pray for these relatives to "heal." As a result, many Filipino and Filipino American individuals who exhibit schizophrenic symptoms remain undiagnosed and untreated.

It is vital to realize how racism may have an impact on individuals with schizophrenia. According to some reports, disproportionate numbers of African Americans are diagnosed with schizophrenia compared to Whites (Keith, Regier, & Rae, 1991), and some studies suggest that racism and race-related stress may be a psychological factor contributing to paranoia or schizophrenia (Boydell et al., 2001; Combs, Penn, & Fenigstein, 2002). For example, if an African American individual develops paranoid schizophrenia, perhaps experiences of racism have allowed the individual to develop auditory hallucinations or become paranoid about others. Although it is understood that Filipino Americans and African Americans are different in a number of ways, according to one study, Filipino Americans are more likely than Chinese Americans to experience similar forms of racism as African Americans (Nadal, 2008c). Because of this finding, there is a possibility that racism may impact Filipino Americans and lead to psychoses in the same ways as among African Americans. Further empirical studies are necessary to understand the impact of race and race-related stress on Filipino American patients diagnosed with schizophrenia.

Figure 9.2 Like many other young Filipino American couples, this couple met during their college years
Photo courtesy of Ken Paprocki

Personality Disorders

Personality disorders are a group of psychological disorders listed in the *DSM-IV-TR* that are characterized by rigid and enduring patterns of feeling, thinking, and behaving that deviates markedly from other members of a given culture or society (APA, 2000). These disorders may influence overall functioning, including ability to form and maintain relationships, be successful in one's career, or maintain healthy levels of self-esteem and self-worth. The *DSM-IV-TR* describes 10 distinct personality disorders that are categorized into 3 clusters: (1) odd or eccentric disorders; (2) dramatic, emotional, or erratic disorders; and (3) anxious or fearful disorders. An example of an odd or eccentric disorder is paranoid personality disorder, which is characterized by irrational suspicions and mistrust of others. An example of a dramatic, emotional, or erratic disorder is histrionic personality disorder, which is defined as consistent attention-seeking behavior, which often includes inappropriate exaggerated emotions or sexual seductiveness. Another common example of a dramatic, emotional, or erratic disorder is narcissistic personality disorder, which is characterized as a persistent pattern of grandiosity, need for admiration, and a lack of empathy. Finally, an example of an anxious or fearful disorder is dependent personality disorder, which is classified as a pervasive psychological dependence on other people.

No known studies examine these personality disorders in the Filipino American community. However, there are several cultural implications for all of these disorders, which demonstrate the need for empirical research on personality disorders with Filipino American populations. For example, one might wonder if a Filipino American who develops paranoid personality disorder has become suspicious of others due to the competition, colonial mentality, and "crab mentality" that occur in Filipino American groups and organizations (see Chapter 5 for a review). When examining histrionic personality disorder, one might explore how gender roles and the cultural expectation for Filipina Americans to be emotionally expressive may impact their need to gain attention from others (see Chapter 7 for a review). Filipino American individuals who are diagnosed with narcissistic personality disorder also may have higher levels of colonial mentality, in which they may feel a need to be grandiose and admired because they want to be viewed as superior to other Filipinos and Filipino Americans. Finally, perhaps Filipino Americans who develop dependent personality disorder may become reliant on others because of the cultural value of *kapwa* (fellow being) and *utang ng loob* (debt of reciprocity), in which family members depend on each other for help and support in all situations. For example, children or adolescents may not learn how to make decisions on their own because they have become accustomed to having others making decisions for them. If they do not acquire this skill, they may be likely to develop dependent personality disorder.

Additional Psychological Disorders

Substance-related disorders are psychological disorders of intoxication, dependence, abuse, and withdrawal caused by various substances that can be legal or illegal (APA, 2000). Substance abuse includes the overindulgence in a drug, while substance dependence includes individuals who become physiologically or psychologically reliant on a substance (D. Sue, D. W. Sue, & S. Sue, 2005). Using the *DSM-IV-TR*, individuals can be diagnosed with an array of substance abuse or dependence disorders, with substances ranging from alcohol, cannabis, to cocaine. Given the information presented in Chapter 6, it is likely that many Filipino Americans exhibit the symptoms of substance-related disorders, and many may turn to alcohol, methamphetamines, and narcotics as ways of coping with psychological stress.

Many other psychological disorders may exist in the Filipino American community but cannot be discussed fully due to the lack of research on this population (Nadal, 2004). For example, eating disorders may be prevalent in the Filipino American population, as a result of the pervasiveness of colonial mentality. One study revealed that Filipino American males may develop higher rates of body dissatisfaction than males in all other racial/ethnic groups (Yates, Edman, & Arguete, 2004), and Filipino American elementary school girls were likely to believe that they were overweight and have body dissatisfaction (Robinson, Chang, Haydel, & Killen, 2001). These issues with body image may be a result of Filipino American parents who teach their children (in direct or indirect ways) they are too dark, too fat, or too ugly, with messages that they need to find ways to become lighter-skinned, slim, or beautiful. Accordingly, many individuals may desire to be more like the colonial images of the Spanish or Americans, leading to low self-esteem or engaging in unhealthy eating behaviors (e.g., restricting, bingeing, purging) as ways of dealing with body image issues.

CULTURALLY COMPETENT COUNSELING FOR FILIPINO AMERICANS

Many authors have suggested that psychologists, counselors, social workers, and other mental health clinicians must become multiculturally competent when working with individuals of racial, ethnic, and sexual minority groups (see D. W. Sue & Sue, 2008, for a review). Accordingly, multicultural guidelines have been established within all of the major mental health associations, including the American Psychological Association (APA) and the American Counseling Association (ACA). The APA has established multicultural guidelines which assert that in order to be effective and ethical clinicians, individuals need to become multiculturally competent by increasing their knowledge, awareness, and skills in working with culturally diverse populations (APA, 2003; Sue & Sue, 2008). "Knowledge" refers to the counselor's or clinician's learning about various cultural groups, including cultural values, traditions, histories, beliefs, and behaviors. "Awareness" denotes the counselor's or clinician's insight into her or his own attitudes, biases, and beliefs that may impact work with clients; "awareness" also includes relational dynamics that may occur between both parties. Finally, the skills component refers to the actual techniques utilized to provide effective treatment with culturally diverse populations. The next section highlights previous literature on mental health treatment with Filipino Americans, revealing the various ways in which counselors and clinicians can increase their multicultural knowledge, awareness, and skills.

Multicultural Knowledge

In addition to the comprehensive knowledge on Filipino Americans emphasized throughout this text (e.g., history, cultural values, colonial mentality, family and community dynamics), there are a few other aspects about which counselors and clinicians should be well informed when working with Filipino American clients. It is important to recognize that many Filipinos and Filipino Americans value their personal space, so one should maintain a reasonable distance of one or two feet from Filipino American clients (Sanchez & Gaw, 2007). Additionally, Filipino Americans may engage in limited eye contact with strangers and authority figures. As a result, counselors and clinicians should make attempts to make brief and frequent eye contact while recognizing that limited eye contact is not a sign of disinterest or avoidance (Sanchez & Gaw, 2007). Moreover, previous literature has indicated that Filipino American clients may defer to authority figures and sometimes may convey understanding or agreement to authority figures when they in fact do not understand or do not agree (Sanchez & Gaw, 2007). An example would be when a Filipino individual utters a mild, hesitant "yes," which is meant to be understood by another as a "no" or a polite refusal (D. W. Sue & D. Sue, 2008). Clinicians or practitioners who do not understand Filipino communication styles may assume that the person was really in agreement. Thus, it is important for counselors and clinicians to ask questions several times and ask Filipino American clients to repeat what they are agreeing to, as a way of clarifying and ensuring understanding.

When working with Filipino American clients, it is also imperative to recognize that family members often may be directly and indirectly involved in counseling relationships. Counselors and clinicians should recognize that decision making about health and mental health issues is often a family affair, in which Filipino Americans at any age may collectively turn to their families for assistance and guidance (Nadal & Monzones, 2010; Sanchez & Gaw, 2007). For example, if an individual has a terminal illness or is on life support, the entire family (including parents, children, siblings, aunts, uncles, and cousins) makes a collective decision about the family member's life. Similar decisions may be made for mental health issues for family members who are diagnosed with dementia, schizophrenia, depression, anxiety, substance abuse disorders, or eating disorders. Counselors and clinicians may anticipate involvement from family members when working with Filipino American clients (Nadal & Monzones, 2010; Sanchez & Gaw, 2007). It is common for Filipino Americans to seek advice and guidance from non–immediate family members regarding personal concerns (e.g., after being diagnosed with a medical illness or condition, seeking opinions from a distant cousin who is a medical doctor). When these individuals are sought out, they often may return with the patient as a "spokesperson" for the family, or as someone who can disseminate and acquire information on the family's behalf (Nadal & Monzones, 2010). The spokesperson role can be designated to someone who is the most educated, who is the oldest or has the most seniority, or the individual who is perceived as the most rational, least emotional, and most capable of managing the situation.

Another issue that may arise in counseling or psychotherapy is the notion of "Filipino time." Filipino Americans may have a different time orientation from the general American population and often may arrive late to appointments and meetings. According to the author, many Filipino Americans abide by Filipino time because they knew and expected meetings to start late (Bonus, 2000). This type of behavior is not viewed as bad or disrespectful but rather as culturally normal. Many Filipino Americans may believe that meetings and appointments "will start when they need to start" (Bonus, 2000, p. 98). Accordingly, counselors and clinicians must be knowledgeable that lateness may be analyzed in some cases (e.g., examining if the client is late because of resistance to therapy and not because of any other practical reason). However, lateness also may be viewed as more culturally acceptable in other cases (e.g., Filipino American clients show up late to everything because lateness is culturally normal or acceptable in their families and communities).

In terms of grieving, many Filipino Americans have conflicting messages about death and dying. While they may learn from Catholicism that death is one's way of returning back to God or the creator (Braun & Nichols, 1997), they also may engage in several types of rituals in order to protect their loved ones from entering "hell" or "purgatory." Some of these rituals include praying a novena (prayer for the soul) for nine days as a way of asking God to allow their loved one to enter heaven (Braun & Nichols, 1997). Moreover, many Filipino Americans may have a difficulty "moving on" after death, as they fear that their deceased loved ones are watching them or that they are being disrespectful for not grieving long enough. (For example, among Filipino Americans, it is common to grieve and avoid parties for at least one year.) Given these practices, counselors who work with grieving clients recognize these intricacies in Filipino and Filipino American culture, which may affect their clients' coping skills and overall mental health.

Multicultural Awareness

In order for counselors and clinicians to gain awareness, they must become insightful about their own attitudes, beliefs, assumptions, and biases, which may impact their work with others who are culturally different from them. Individuals must become reflective of how their member-ship in privileged or dominant groups may impact their interactions with members of oppressed or target groups (D. W. Sue & Sue, 2008). White practitioners must understand how they are perceived by their clients of color, male psychotherapists must recognize how they are per-ceived by their female clients, and heterosexual counselors and clinicians must identify how they are perceived by their lesbian, gay, bisexual, and transgender clients. These perceptions may impact factors such as clinician-client rapport, trust, and openness in psychotherapy sessions.

Clinicians also must be aware of how their subtle biases and beliefs may impact their interactions with culturally diverse clients. For exam-ple, if a counselor or clinician holds stereotypes that Asian Americans are supposed to be a certain way (e.g., passive, submissive, intellec-tual, asexual), their biases may be revealed when a client displays the opposite values, beliefs, or behaviors. This type of bias often manifests when clinicians misdiagnose African Americans with paranoid person-ality disorder or antisocial personality disorder while Asian Americans are misdiagnosed with schizoid personality disorder (Iwamasa, Larrabee, & Merritt, 2000). Moreover, psychologists, counselors, and clinicians must be aware of the ways in which they may, directly and indirectly, dissuade their clients from becoming more acculturated or Americanized. For example, one author notes that it is important for Filipino Americans not to be criticized for their language dispari-ties and should not be persuaded to "lose their accents" (Nadal, 2008b). By encouraging a Filipino American client to speak English with an American accent, the counselor or clinician is sending the indirect mes-sage that being Filipino is negative and being American is positive.

For Filipino Americans specifically, counselors and clinicians must be aware of the influences of racial/ethnic identity development and ways this may impact counseling dynamics and relationships (see Chapter 3 for a review). For example, a Filipino American who can be classified as "ethnocentric" may have difficulty trusting a counselor or clinician who is White; thus, it would be important for the counselor or clinician to be able to discuss racial dynamics and ways in which race impacts their relationship. For counselors and clinicians of color, it would be important to realize the ways in which they do (or do not) identify with their clients' racial identity statuses and how these countertransference reactions may influence their therapeutic relationships.

Multicultural Skills

According to the literature, many skills and techniques are effective when working with Filipino American clients. For example, the literature cites that counselors and clinicians should be more "personable" with Filipino American clients because of the cultural importance of social acceptance and emotional closeness (Okamura & Agbayani, 1991). Other literature from Filipino psychology (which is based on Filipinos in the Philippines) suggests that counselors and clinicians should be indirect in psychotherapy sessions, utilizing a *pagtatanung-tanong* (or asking around) approach that uses informal and nonjudgmental inquiries (Enriquez, 1982). This method is considered effective because it relies on the Filipino American value of indirect communication, in which individuals may have difficulty in being open or straightforward with acquaintances. Filipino psychology literature also suggests that a *pakapa-kapa* (blank slate) method is most effective when working with Filipino clients. In using this technique, the counselor or clinician proceeds in a total state of ignorance, allowing clients to share the entirety of their problems. This allows clients not to feel judged and gives them an opportunity to build openness, honesty, and trust.

Several other methods can be utilized when working with Filipino American clients. For example, group or peer counseling can be effective because of *pakikasama* (social acceptance; Salvador, Omizo, & Kim, 1997). Group counseling might include Filipino Americans participating in homogenous Filipino American groups (in order to promote cultural pride and validation of one's experiences) or joining heterogeneous, mixed groups (in order to promote openness in sharing

Figure 9.3 A Filipino American father and his two adolescent sons
Photo courtesy of Ian Tamayo

with non-Filipinos without shame or guilt). Peer counseling may include other Filipino Americans providing social support to other individuals in the community. This may allow for increased openness for Filipino Americans, since many individuals feel comfortable talking to others of the same ethnic group. Peer counseling also may normalize experiences and promote other Filipino Americans as models of positive mental health. It is recommended that counselors and clinicians be familiar with Filipino community organizations (e.g., churches, businesses, support groups, clubs) in order to promote community involvement (Salvador et al., 1997). This may prove to be a useful skill for developing rapport with clients while providing them with alternative, affirmative influences.

CULTURALLY APPROPRIATE UTILIZATION OF THEORETICAL ORIENTATIONS

This section underscores the various theoretical orientations utilized most in psychology and mental health treatment. These theories include psychoanalytic and psychodynamic therapies, cognitive-behavioral therapies, humanistic and person-centered therapies, and family-system therapies. Although these are merely a sample of the various psychological theories currently utilized, they indicate the spectrum of methods that may be used in mental health treatment. By briefly reviewing these theories, cultural implications are introduced in order to promote culturally competent services for Filipino American clients.

Psychoanalytic and Psychodynamic Therapies

Psychoanalytic and psychodynamic therapies originally were conceptualized by Sigmund Freud. Their main goals are to make the unconscious conscious (Corey, 2009). Counselors and clinicians utilize several methods to uncover repressed emotions that may impact clients' current psychological state and mental health. Some of the main methods utilized are free association (when clients relate whatever comes into their minds without censoring their thoughts), dream analysis, hypnosis, and the analysis of transference and countertransference (Corey, 2009; Sue et al., 2005). "Transference" is defined as unconscious redirection of a client's feelings toward a counselor or clinician, while "countertransference" is defined as unconscious redirection of a counselor's feelings toward a client (Corey, 2009; Sue et al., 2005). Analyzing transference and countertransference can be helpful in building a therapeutic alliance and also in developing an understanding of the unresolved issues with other individuals that exist in the client's life. For example, if a client appears to be angry toward an older male psychotherapist, it may be helpful to explore the client's transference (e.g., feelings toward her or his father or male authority figures).

In psychoanalytic or psychodynamic therapies, another goal is to understand one's "defense mechanisms," which are described as unconscious psychological strategies in which individuals attempt to relieve anxiety and distort reality. Some common defense mechanisms include repression (forcing painful thoughts or memories into the unconscious and preventing painful or forcing painful thoughts or memories from entering one's conscious state of mind), denial (refusing to accept external reality because it is anxiety-provoking), reaction formation (converting unconscious wishes, impulses, or emotions into their opposites), or rationalization (creating a logical justification to cover one's true feelings about something; Corey, 2009; Sue et al., 2005). Filipino Americans may utilize these defense mechanisms as a way of saving face and avoiding *hiya* (shame). For example, they may repress their emotions to appear as if they can handle their problems, and they also may rely on reaction formation (e.g., laughing when they are actually sad) in order to relieve themselves of anxiety or depressed feelings.

Utilizing psychoanalytic or psychodynamic therapies can be effective for Filipino American clients. Because it is common for Filipino Americans to deny and repress their emotions, the use of free association can be helpful in allowing clients to speak freely about issues and reactions they may have difficulty thinking about or discussing. Free association would be similar to the *pagtatanung-tanong* (asking around) approach described in Filipino psychology. Moreover, dream analysis may be useful because Filipino Americans may be able to connect to their repressed emotions and feelings in their unconscious states. Examining dreams (e.g., discussing symbols of dreams and feelings during dream states) can be valuable in making the unconscious conscious. This tool may be especially effective for Filipino American men, who commonly repress their emotions and may be emotionally restrictive in their everyday lives and relationships.

Cognitive-Behavioral Therapy

Cognitive-behavioral therapy emphasizes cognitions (i.e., how one thinks) and behaviors (i.e., how one behaves). The focus in cognitive-behavioral therapy is to combat faulty cognitions (or cognitive distortions) while changing behaviors that impact an individual's mental health. For example, if a woman holds the cognition distortion that she is worthless, ugly, or unintelligent, psychotherapy may focus on understanding how she has learned those cognitive distortions and on preventing these distortions from continuing. If an individual is diagnosed with an eating disorder, sessions may focus on changing her or his cognitive distortions and eating behaviors. The interventions utilized most in cognitive-behavioral therapy include various relaxation techniques (e.g., breathing exercises, guided imagery) as well as cognitive restructuring (refuting cognitive distortions and replacing them with more accurate and beneficial ones; Corey, 2009; Sue et al., 2005). It is also common for counselors and clinicians to assign their clients "homework assignments" to work on outside of psychotherapy sessions.

Cognitive-behavioral therapies can be effective for Filipino American clients in many ways. Such therapies may be helpful in examining a client's cognitive distortions and how these may be related to colonial mentality and internalized racism. For example, if an individual does not feel worthy, attractive, or intelligent, one might wonder if she or he has developed colonial mentality that has affected self-esteem and mental health. Cognitive-behavioral therapies also may be advantageous for those Filipino Americans who may prefer more therapeutic structure and who may have difficulties in expressing their emotions. For example, if a Filipino American client struggles in talking with a counselor or clinician whom she or he may not fully trust, it may be beneficial to provide a homework assignment as a way of initiating conversation in psychotherapy.

Humanistic and Person-Centered Therapies

Humanistic psychology originated in the 1950s as a response to the growth of psychoanalytic and behavioral theories (Corey, 2009; Sue et al., 2005). The theory concentrates on the human dimension of psychology and emphasizes the importance of human development and self-actualization (or the process of individuals reaching their fullest potential psychologically, emotionally, spiritually, etc.). One of the best-known humanistic psychologists is Carl Rogers, who created person-centered counseling and psychotherapy, which is sometimes known as Rogerian therapy. Person-centered therapy is one of the most utilized theories in mental health counseling and focuses on three components:

1. Congruence (genuineness of both the counselor or clinician and client)
2. Empathy (the ability for the counselor or clinician to understand another person's emotional and psychological state of mind)
3. Unconditional positive regard (the ability to be compassionate toward clients regardless of the situation)

In therapy, the counselor or clinician aims to form a genuine and supportive therapeutic relationship, in order for the client to reach self-actualization (Corey, 2009; Sue et al., 2005).

Person-centered counseling can be effective for Filipino Americans in many ways. Previous literature has shown that Filipino Americans prefer emotionally warm counseling or psychotherapy (Okamura & Agbayani, 1991). This is likely due to the Filipino value of *pakikasama* (social acceptance) in which Filipino Americans desire getting along with others at all costs. Additionally, because of the influence of Spanish values, Filipino Americans may be more interpersonally warm and emotionally expressive, like Latinos (and prefer insight- or feeling-oriented counseling), unlike East Asian Americans, who may prefer structured counseling approaches (Nadal, 2004). Finally, Filipino Americans may benefit from person-centered approaches due to the Filipino value of *kapwa* (fellow being). Because Filipino Americans attach importance to feeling personal connectedness with others, using person-centered techniques can be helpful in forming trusting therapeutic relationships, which can lead to self-actualization for clients.

Family Systems Therapy

Clients of all racial and ethnic backgrounds may prefer to use family therapy, in which all members of a family see a counselor or clinician at once. When engaging in family therapy, counselors and clinicians are following the tenets of family systems therapy, which analyzes the family unit as a source of individuals' psychological distress and problems (Corey, 2009). In counseling or psychotherapy, clients learn about how their family systems operate and gain knowledge about the various roles different family members play. Furthermore, individuals learn how to make personal changes in the family system instead of trying to "fix" individual family members. Family systems therapy also looks at the extended family field, which refers to the nuclear family and various generations. In analyzing the extended family, clients can recognize the intergenerational transmission of attitudes, problems, and behaviors, which may reflect the family's current state of being (Corey, 2009).

Family systems therapy can be beneficial for Filipino Americans in a variety of ways. Because Filipino Americans are collective and value their families significantly, it would be beneficial for a counselor or clinician to grasp how family dynamics impact their everyday lives and psychological states. Additionally, in analyzing the extended family, clients can learn about the types of interpersonal issues and family dynamics that have been pervasive across various generations. For example, in a family, perhaps there have been several generations of grudges between siblings, substandard communication, or unhappy marriages. A family systems counselor or clinician may find it necessary to involve the entire family (e.g., parents, siblings, aunts, uncles, cousins, and grandparents) to understand ways individuals communicate with each other while also understanding dynamics that occur within the entire system. In doing this type of exploration, clients may see the importance of changing their role in the system instead of fixating on current, problematic family relationships.

INDIGENOUS AND SPIRITUAL COUNSELING METHODS

Using nontraditional, indigenous, or spiritual counseling methods may be important when working with Filipino American clients. "Indigenous counseling" can be defined as a system of psychological thought and practice rooted in a particular cultural tradition (Harley, 2005). In other words, indigenous counseling involves recognizing the cultural values, beliefs, and practices of a given group and integrating those practices into mental health treatment. Previous authors have found that Asian Americans (including Filipino Americans) endorse indigenous methods of coping that emphasize talking with family and community members rather than seeking traditional mental health treatment (Yeh & Wang, 2000). Given this, in order to be most effective with Filipino American clients, it is important to be familiar with and integrate Filipino American traditions and alternative coping mechanisms into traditional counseling or psychotherapy.

It is essential for counselors and clinicians to recognize the fact that many Filipino Americans may turn to folk leaders, faith healers, or shamans when they experience mental health problems (Demetrio, 1991; Henry, 1986; Hwang et al., 2007). Shamans are common in the Philippines, particularly in rural areas, where they are well respected and often considered as valuable as medical doctors (Hwang et al.,

2007). Moreover, although Filipinos and Filipino Americans tend to be Catholic, they also maintain other spiritual beliefs and engage in animistic practices that others may view as pathological or illogical (Shimabukuro et al., 1999). For example, some Filipinos and Filipino Americans may believe in mythical creatures known as *dwendes* (dwarves), who can bring bad luck if individuals cross their paths (Hwang et al., 2007). Accordingly, counselors and clinicians must be able to incorporate spiritual practices into their work with Filipino American clients and be comfortable with the spiritual beliefs their clients (particularly elderly or immigrant clients) may have.

It is also common for many Filipino Americans to be superstitious, particularly in their ideas about health and mental health. Several authors cite various superstitious beliefs that Filipinos and Filipino Americans may have about the body and illness, including:

- Rapid changes from hot to cold cause illness.
- Cold food and drink in the morning can cause illness.
- An overheated body is vulnerable to disease, and a heated body can get "shocked" and lead to illness when cooled quickly.
- Imbalance from worry and overwork create stress and illness.
- Emotional restraint is a key element in restoring balance (Becker, 2003; Sanchez & Gaw, 2007).

Counselors and clinicians must be comfortable with clients who hold these superstitious beliefs and may find it useful to ask Filipino American clients about these beliefs as a way of gaining insight to their thought processes, worldviews, and values. Moreover, inquiring about superstitions in a nonjudgmental way can be a method of developing rapport with Filipino American clients while initially establishing the importance of culture in counseling relationships.

Finally, Filipino Americans also may seek Catholic religious leaders for guidance when dealing with mental health issues. Hence, Filipino Americans may benefit from pastoral counseling. Pastoral counseling is a field in which ordained ministers, priests, and other religious leaders provide mental health services to laypersons (Strunk, 2000). Pastoral counselors are trained in contemporary psychological theories and techniques and are educated on various religious traditions. Although pastoral counselors are not licensed mental health professionals, they may have contact with a spectrum of clients, particularly clients of color, who maintain cultural mistrust for traditional mental health treatment. As a result, many Filipino American clients, specifically those who are older and of immigrant backgrounds, may seek help from pastoral counselors instead of searching for traditional mental health treatment.

DISCUSSION QUESTIONS

1. What do you think are the main reasons Filipino Americans and other people of color have difficulty seeking mental health treatment?
2. Which psychological disorders are you most familiar with? Which psychological disorders are you least familiar with? What are some reasons that you are familiar or not familiar with certain disorders?
3. What counseling or psychotherapy methods do you think would be most effective in working with Filipino American clients? Explain.
4. Which theoretical orientation would you use in working with Filipino American clients?
5. How do you feel about indigenous or spiritual counseling methods?
6. For counselors and clinicians: When working with clients, which psychological disorders would you be most comfortable with? Which psychological disorders would you be least comfortable or afraid of?

SUMMARY

This chapter focused on the various mental health experiences of Filipino Americans. By examining the help-seeking behaviors of Filipino Americans, the chapter cited the numerous obstacles in providing mental health treatment for Filipino Americans. Various psychological disorders that are common for Filipino Americans were reviewed, while cultural implications for each disorder were provided. Next, culturally competent counseling methods were introduced, and various theoretical orientations for counseling or psychotherapy were examined and applied to working with Filipino American clients. Finally, indigenous and spiritual counseling methods were mentioned to promote techniques that could be utilized with the Filipino American population.

This chapter presents two final case studies that demonstrate how psychological disorder may manifest in two Filipino American clients. In learning about these clients, readers may find it useful to pay attention to the ways culture may impact their behaviors, psychopathologies, or both. Furthermore, in reviewing the methods and theories presented in this chapter, individuals may be able to devise the methods and theories that would be most effective in working with these clients.

Case Studies

Case 1: Maria and Her Panic Attacks

Maria is a 54-year-old Filipina American who immigrated to the United States over 25 years ago. She met her husband in the Philippines, and they raised three children in a multiracial neighborhood in Portland, Oregon. She has been a devout Catholic all of her life, attending church on a weekly basis and forcing her children to pray the rosary with her every Friday night. She also forbade her children from dating, stating that they needed to concentrate on school and because she was afraid they would "ruin their lives" if they got pregnant. When her children would argue with her for being so strict, especially with religion, Maria would tell them they were "ungrateful" and they were giving her high blood pressure. Sometimes these arguments would end with Maria complaining of chest pain, difficulty breathing, and fainting briefly. Her children would be forced to help her up, which would halt the immediate dispute, without it being discussed again. These consistent arguments have led to a conflicting relationship with her children, particularly with her eldest daughter, Lorial, 23, who moved to a different state when she graduated from high school to pursue a career in fashion. Her two other children, Riya, 20, and Rodolfo, 18, also moved out of the house to attend college. As a result, Maria always felt like her children were abandoning her because she was a bad mother.

(Continued)

Recently, Maria's husband, Emilio, 53, was laid off from his job as a mechanic, due to troubles in the economy. As a result, Maria is the sole source of income in the family with her job as a post office worker, where she worked for 20 years. This has caused a strain on Maria because she has to pay for their family's mortgage, bills, and her children's college tuition. Additionally, when she gets home, she is expected to take care of household chores, to do grocery shopping, and to cook for her husband. As a result, Maria is exhausted most of her weekdays and sleeps only about 6 to 7 hours a night. She ends up fighting a lot with her husband, which often ends in her "feeling high blood pressure" (exemplified by breathing difficulty and chest pains), and sometimes needing to lie down because she feels faint. Maria does not have any friends or family members to whom she talks about her problems; although she sees her sisters and cousins on a fairly regular basis, she pretends everything is fine and she is living a happy life with her husband.

Recently, Maria went to her primary care physician to complain of back and chest pains and difficulty breathing. She also told the doctor that sometimes when she is stressed she gets dizzy and faints. She admits this usually occurs after major arguments with her family members (arguments in which she is involved or uninvolved). Her doctor runs medical tests and assumes her symptoms are psychosomatic. He talks to her about his assessment and refers her to a psychologist. Maria insists she does not need to seek any help from a psychologist or any other counselor. Instead, she goes home and prays to God and asks for help in eliminating these medical symptoms. The next morning, she makes an appointment with her priest to discuss her problems.

Case 2: Arthur and His Hallucinations

Arthur is a 22-year-old second-generation Filipino American who grew up in a predominantly working-class Filipino American neighborhood in San Diego, California. When he was 18, he graduated from high school and got a job working in a retail electronics store. He wanted to go to college, but he did poorly in high school and felt like no one in his family or school really encouraged him. He worked at the retail store for several years, where he felt like he was "wasting his life away." He tried to apply for different types of jobs (e.g., administrative assistant positions for various corporations). However, when he was invited for and attended various job interviews, he was never offered a position (or a second interview), despite believing that he interviewed very well each time. Arthur decided to "settle" with his job at the retail store and hated going to work every day. Due to embarrassment and fears of being judged or criticized, Arthur never shared these feelings with anyone—not his parents, his sibling, or the few friends he had from high school. Eventually Arthur became depressed, with symptoms including difficulties in sleeping, loss of appetite, and feelings of hopelessness and worthlessness.

For the past six months, Arthur began to hear voices that told him he was "no good." These voices spoke to him randomly throughout the day, and Arthur tried to ignore them as much as he could. However, the voices became increasingly louder and more frequent, causing him to start to believe the negative messages they were sending. He also began to believe his boss was planting small video cameras to "catch him making mistakes." He said he thought his boss was "out to get him" and he was going to get fired at any time, even though he "didn't do anything wrong." Arthur became increasingly agitated at work, particularly during busy customer times, and began "talking strangely" to customers. For example, when one customer asked for help in purchasing a television, Arthur discouraged the customer by saying "There was a video camera inside the TV that secretly records your every move." Because of this behavior and interactions with customers, Arthur's boss asked him to take a leave of absence; Arthur reacted by screaming uncontrollably and saying "Don't you dare spy at me at home!"

Arthur went home, where he lived with his parents, and he stayed in his room for two days straight. His parents noticed that he had stopped going to work and that he was despondent and unresponsive when they tried to talk to him. Most of the time, he would look at them with a blank face; other times, he told them he did not want to leave his room because it was the only place where "he was safe" and where "people couldn't spy on him." Because they were concerned with his odd behavior, Arthur's parents took him to the hospital to be examined for any potential brain injuries or health concerns. After several days of psychological evaluations and observations, Arthur was given a preliminary diagnosis of paranoid schizophrenia. His family was extremely

(Continued)

255

distressed by the whole situation and is confused as to how he may have developed this disorder. The hospital psychiatrist tells his family that Arthur may need to take psychotropic medication. His family is hesitant about this and is conflicted about what to do. The hospital staff also offers counseling services to the family as a resource.

Case Study Discussion

In reviewing these two cases, one must recognize that several cultural factors may influence how these two individuals deal with their problems. First, both scenarios show several ways in which cultural stigmas impact how Filipino American individuals cope with stress and view mental health treatment. Counselors and clinicians may recognize how cultural stigmas may prevent Maria from recognizing that she has psychological or emotional issues and seeking appropriate treatment. Moreover, culture influences Maria in the ways she handles her problems. She does not have any support systems that she can talk to about her problems. Although she sees some family members regularly, she may feel shameful about her marriage, her relationship with her children, or her other stressors. She feels a need to "save face" and to hide what she is really experiencing. It also appears that she simply represses or compartmentalizes her emotions. By not dealing with these problems, psychosomatic systems may manifest and lead her to believe she has physical health issues.

Culture also influences Arthur's psychological health. Arthur seems to have accumulated feelings of low self-esteem, disappointment, and shame for several years, yet he has never discussed these feelings with anyone in his life. Perhaps gender role expectations, in which Arthur is expected to be strong and self-sufficient as a male, have prevented him from learning how to express his emotions in healthy ways or turning to others for help. Accordingly, Arthur may have learned to repress his emotions altogether, which may have led to the development of his schizophrenic symptoms. Additionally, cultural stigmas may affect the difficulty his family has in accepting his diagnosis of schizophrenia as well as the conflict they feel about whether he should take psychotropic medications. Because Filipino Americans typically view people with mental health problems as "crazy," "weak," or shameful, they may not want to admit or accept that Arthur is psychologically unhealthy, as they want to protect the reputation of Arthur and their family.

There are a few other cultural considerations to take into account in understanding the manifestations of these individuals' psychological problems. Maria often says she has "high blood pressure" as a way of coping with her problems, particularly during times of conflict. This can be a common ploy for Filipino Americans who may or may not have high blood pressure. If they do have high blood pressure, they may be using the physical ailment as a way of avoiding stressful situations. If they do not really have high blood pressure, they may convince themselves that they do (consciously or unconsciously) to divert emotional distress. When Maria sees her doctor, he tells her that her back and chest pains and difficulty breathing may be psychosomatic and may be indications of psychological stress. Given the symptoms she is presenting, it is possible that Maria may be diagnosed with some form of an anxiety disorder (e.g., generalized anxiety disorder or panic disorder). However, her dizziness and fainting spells also may be psychosomatic manifestations that match the Latino phenomenon of ataques de nervios in which individuals may unconsciously falsify panic attacks as a means to seek attention or deal with stress.

Arthur has been given the preliminary diagnosis of paranoid schizophrenia, which is likely due to his symptoms of auditory hallucinations (e.g., the voices telling him he is "no good"), delusions (e.g., the paranoia that his boss set up video cameras "to catch him doing something wrong" or the notion others are spying on him or "trying to get him"), and anhedonia (e.g., the fact that he stays in his room without expressing any interest or desire to do anything else). When working with Filipino Americans who are diagnosed with schizophrenia, it is essential to rule out any cultural factors that may influence the symptoms. For example, a mental health practitioner may want to assess whether the hallucinations are culturally based (e.g., does the individual hear voices from a deceased family member she or he believes is visiting from the afterlife?)

Although it does not appear that Arthur's symptoms are culture based, culture may be helpful in understanding how to conceptualize a treatment plan for Arthur. A counselor or clinician might be aware of how hiya (shame) may have led to detrimental impacts on his self-esteem,

(Continued)

his inability to admit to his problems, or his failure to seek help from others. Moreover, one might speculate how institutional racism or racial discrimination may have led to Arthur's development of schizophrenic symptoms. One might argue that Arthur was not hired for a job or was not being encouraged to pursue higher education by his teachers and counselors due to institutional racism (see Chapter 6 for a review). Therefore, it may be helpful to discuss issues of race with Arthur, as a way of understanding its potential impact on his life situation, psychological being, and worldview.

In Arthur's case, one can also observe how the family has a strong involvement in the decision-making process. Medical doctors, counselors, and clinicians should recognize that this is a common practice in working with Filipino Americans. Although Arthur's family is given the option to administer psychotropic medications to minimize his hallucinations and delusions, it is likely that his family will consult with another family member (either nuclear or extended) who may have some knowledge about psychological disorders and psychotropic medications. It can even be expected that an outside family member will come to the hospital to meet with the doctor and discuss the situation, as a way of being the spokesperson who reports back to the family and translates information. With a patient's consent, a medical doctor, counselor, or clinician should be prepared to talk with this individual regardless of the closeness of blood relation or actual expertise.

In Maria's case, one may observe she does not want to obtain traditional mental health treatment and instead opts to seek guidance from a priest from her church. This rejection of traditional mental health counseling and the acceptance of religious, spiritual, or pastoral counseling is a common practice for Filipino Americans. In fact, counselors and clinicians should expect Filipino American clients to search for these nontraditional and indigenous methods. As a result, it may be helpful for culturally competent counselors and clinicians to offer nontraditional and indigenous counseling or psychotherapy as an additional resource for Filipino American individuals. For example, the medical doctor may have referred Maria to a psychologist but also recommended that she discuss the situation with her family, friends, a religious leader, or a pastoral counselor. In doing so, Maria may have become more trustful of the doctor and may have been a bit more open to acquiring information about traditional mental health counseling and psychotherapy.

Summary

Finally, in reviewing the theoretical orientations for counseling and psychotherapy, many recommendations can be made in working with these clients. In Maria's case, the various theoretical orientations would approach counseling and psychotherapy in a variety of ways. The goal of a psychoanalytic or psychodynamic counselor or clinician would be to make the unconscious conscious. It would be important for Maria to understand how she has repressed her emotions and how this repression may have led to her current psychological problems. In counseling and psychotherapy, one can use methods like free association or dream interpretation to uncover repressed emotions (e.g., Maria's sadness about her marriage or children, her distress about her job and being the only source of income, her loneliness, or her anger toward her husband and children). The goals of a cognitive-behavioral counselor or clinician would be to change cognitive distortions and behaviors. For Maria, this would include changing her cognitive distortions (e.g., she is always right and her children are always wrong, or it is bad to admit to one's problems to others) as well as her faulty behaviors (e.g., not being able to listen to others' perspectives or unconsciously falsifying panic attacks). A family-systems counselor or clinician might encourage Maria to bring other family members to counseling or psychotherapy settings as a way of promoting healthy communication and understanding. Additionally, Maria's extended family tree may be analyzed in order for her to identify transgenerational patterns that may impact her current thoughts, feelings, and behaviors. Finally, a humanistic or person-centered counselor or clinician may focus on Maria's strengths and provide her with unconditional positive regard, empathy, and genuineness as ways of promoting her self-actualization.

The use of these various psychological theories may prove difficult with a patient who is diagnosed with schizophrenia, particularly if the person chooses not to take medication or has had recurrent psychotic episodes. Although these theories may prove helpful in conceptualizing the etiology of a client's problems, it may be difficult to provide traditional mental health counseling or psychotherapy for a lower-functioning individual. However, many studies have found that individuals with single episodes of schizophrenia can recover with the uses of psychodynamic or cognitive-behavioral psychotherapy (e.g., Bateman, 2007;

(Continued)

Gottdiener, 2006; Tarrier et al., 2004). In fact, individuals who experience schizophrenic symptoms of less than a month may be diagnosed with brief psychotic episode instead of schizophrenia and often have a full recovery (Sue et al., 2005).

Given this fact, counseling and psychotherapy may prove effective with Arthur, particularly if combined with medication and other forms of psychoeducation. Psychoanalytic or psychodynamic counseling or psychotherapy may include revealing Arthur's unconscious thoughts, emotions, and psychological processes; it would likely include analyzing memories and feelings Arthur may have repressed. These include his feelings of failure, disappointment, anger, and anxiety about not being successful or pursuing a career he loves. Cognitive-behavioral counseling or psychotherapy may include disputing Arthur's cognitive distortions (e.g., he is "no good") and Arthur's behaviors (e.g., staying in his room all day long). Finally, family systems therapy may be helpful in getting Arthur's whole family involved. A counselor or clinician can assist family members to understand the problem in the "system" that may have led to Arthur's mental health problems (e.g., communication patterns between members or lack of emotional expression). By examining various generations of Arthur's family and encouraging that changes be made by all family members, it is expected family dynamics will modify and increased mental health will be achieved for all.

Case Study Discussion Questions

For undergraduate students and general readers, please consider these questions:

1. What psychological disorder do you believe Maria can be diagnosed with? What symptoms does she exhibit that lead you to believe this?
2. What psychological disorder do you believe Arthur can be diagnosed with? What symptoms does he exhibit that lead you to believe this?
3. What do you think are the causes of Maria's and Arthur's psychological problems?
4. What cultural factors should counselors and clinicians become most aware of when working with Maria? With Arthur?

For helping professionals and graduate students of psychology, please consider these questions:

1. What theoretical orientation would be most helpful in working with Maria? Why?
2. What theoretical orientation would be most helpful in working with Arthur? Why?
3. What techniques or methods would you use in working with Maria? What techniques or methods would you use in working with Arthur?
4. What would be your countertransference issues in working with Maria? What would be your countertransference issues in working with Arthur?

CONCLUSION

Through these past nine chapters, I hope that you have been able to gain some insight about the Filipino American community and the nuances of the Filipino American psyche. You may have learned about Philippine and Filipino American history—ranging from the colonization of the Philippines by Spain and the United States as well as the various immigration patterns of Filipinos in the United States, beginning as early as the year 1587. You also may have discovered the various cultural values that govern Filipino American family systems and individual psychological processes, including indigenous Filipino values like *kapwa* (fellow being) and *utang ng loob* (debt of reciprocity), Spanish influences from Catholicism, and American values like competition or individualism. You may have gained knowledge about the racial and ethnic identity development of Filipino Americans, particularly how Filipino Americans may view themselves as Filipino American or Asian American, and how they may interact or identify with Whites, Latinos and other people of color, other Asian Americans, and other Filipino Americans. You may have learned about colonial mentality and how Filipinos and Filipino Americans often may denigrate indigenous Filipino qualities and favor or glorify Spanish and American values and standards of beauty. You also may have been exposed to the various disparities that Filipino Americans may face—from lower educational attainment, higher prevalence of physical health problems such as car-diovascular disease and diabetes, and various mental health problems such as depression or substance abuse. And you may have learned about the myriad of ways that Filipino and Filipino American culture may detrimentally impact the ability to identify and cope with mental health problems.

As you can see, there are a number of ways to be Filipino American. As exemplified by the various case studies, Filipino Americans are of different genders, skin colors, sexual orientations, and social classes, and come from different provinces in the Philippines. Filipino Americans are religious and nonreligious, monoracial and multiracial, and rich, poor, and middle class. Some Filipino Americans are adopted, some Filipino Americans are immigrants, and some Filipino Americans have family histories in the United States for centuries. Thus, it is important to recognize that not every concept in this handbook can be applied, nor should be expected to apply, to every single Filipino American. Rather, the concepts presented in this book can help to further understand the greater concepts of the Filipino American to help better conceptualize various problems and dynamics that may occur within communities, within families, and internally within individuals.

To the practitioners who have read these past nine chapters, I hope you are encouraged to become more multiculturally competent in work-ing with your clients and patients. I hope you have gained knowledge and awareness of different concepts to consider in understanding your clients and patients that will lead to creating new and effective strate-gies for working with them. Perhaps this is a book that you can refer to as you continue your work with your Filipino American clients. I also hope that you can use this text as an opportunity to educate your colleagues who work with Filipino Americans too.

To the Filipino Americans who have completed these nine chapters, I hope that you have gained some insight about the various values that have impacted your personality development, your worldviews, your communication styles, your self-esteem, and your ability to navigate your everyday lives. I hope you will be encouraged to share the knowl-edge you have gained from this text with your families and friends. Perhaps if we talk more about some of these experiences negatively impacting our community (e.g., colonial mentality, crab mentality), we can prevent some of these negative mental health outcomes in our community. Perhaps if we could talk about our feelings and concerns with each other (particularly across generations), we can minimize some of the health and mental health disparities in our community.

And to everyone who has read this book, I hope you have learned the importance of giving the Filipino American community a voice. Because so little has been written about this population, it is important that everyone (both Filipino and non-Filipino) does their part to teach others about the rich culture and unique experiences that Filipino Americans have. In doing so, it is hoped that we will no longer be referred to as the forgotten Asian Americans but rather as a group that is remembered, appreciated, revered, and celebrated.

References

Abe-Kim, J., Gong, F., & Takeuchi, D. (2004). Religiosity, spirituality, and help-seeking among Filipino Americans: Religious clergy or mental health professionals? *Journal of Community Psychology, 32,* 675–689.

Agbayani-Siewert, P. (2004). Assumptions of Asian American similarity: The case of Filipino and Chinese American students. *Social Work, 49*(1), 39–51.

Alsaybar, B. D. (1999). Deconstructing deviance: Filipino American youth gangs, party culture, and ethnic identity in Los Angeles. *Amerasia Journal, 25*(1), 116–138.

Alvarez, A. N. (1996). Asian American racial identity: An examination of world views and racial adjustment. *Dissertation Abstracts International, 57*(10-B), 6554.

Alvarez, A. N., & Juang, L. (2010). Filipino Americans and racism: A multiple mediation model of coping. *Journal of Counseling Psychology 57*(2), 167–178.

Alvarez, A. N., Juang, L., & Liang, C. T. H. (2006). Asian Americans and racism: When bad things happen to "Model Minorities." *Cultural Diversity and Ethnic Minority Psychology, 12*(3), 477–492.

Alvarez, A. N., & Kimura, E. F. (2001). Asian Americans and racial identity: Dealing with racism and snowballs. *Journal of Mental Health Counseling, 23*(13), 192–207.

Alvarez, A. N., & Yeh, T. L. (1999). Asian Americans in college: A racial identity perspective. In D. Sandhu (Ed.), *Asian and Pacific*

Islander Americans: Issues and concerns for counseling and psychotherapy (pp. 105–119). Huntington, NY: Nova Science.

American Psychiatric Association. (2000). *Diagnostic and statistical manual of mental disorders* (4th ed., text revision). Washington, DC: Author.

American Psychological Association. (2003). Guidelines on multicultural education, training, research, practice, and organizational change for psychologists. *American Psychologist, 58*(5), 377–402.

Ancheta, A. N. (1998). *Race, rights, and the Asian American experience.* New Brunswick, NJ: Rutgers University Press.

Araneta, E. (1993). Psychiatric care of Pilipino Americans. In A. Gaw (Ed.), *Culture, ethnicity and mental illness* (pp. 377–412). Washington, DC: American Psychiatric Press.

Araneta, M. R., Wingard, D. L., & Barrett-Connor, E. (2002). Type 2 diabetes and metabolic syndrome in Filipina-American women: A high-risk non obese population. *Diabetes Care, 25*(3), 494–499.

Asian American Federation of New York. (2004). Census profile: New York City's Filipino American population. New York, NY: Asian American Federation of New York Census Information Center.

Atkinson, D. R., Morten, G., & Sue, D. W. (1998). *Counseling American minorities. A cross-cultural perspective.* Dubuque, IA: Brown.

Balisacan, A. M. (1994). *Poverty, urbanization and development policy.* Quezon City, Philippines: University of the Philippines Press.

Bankston, C. L. (2006). Filipino Americans. In P. G. Min (Ed.), *Asian Americans: Contemporary trends and issues,* 2nd ed. (pp. 180–203). Thousand Oaks, CA: Sage.

Barnes, J. S., & Bennett, C. E. (2002). The Asian population, 2000. U.S. Census Brief. Retrieved December 20, 2010, from http://www.census.gov

Bateman, A. W. (2007). Psychotherapy in psychiatry: Integration and assimilation. *International Review of Psychiatry, 19*(1), 1–4.

Becker, G. (2003). Cultural expressions of bodily awareness among chronically ill Filipino Americans. *Annals of Family Medicine, 1,* 113–118.

Bell, T. J., & Tracey, T. J. G. (2006). The relation of cultural mistrust and psychological health. *Journal of Multicultural Counseling and Development, 34*(1), 2–14.

References

Bem, S. L. (1981). *Bem Sex Role Inventory: Professional manual.* Palo Alto, CA: Consulting Psychologists Press.

Berganio, J., Tacata, L., & Jamero, P. (1997). The prevalence and impact of alcohol, tobacco, and other drugs on Filipino American communities. In M. P. P. Root (Ed.), *Filipino Americans: Transformation and identity* (pp. 272–286). Thousand Oaks, CA: Sage.

Bergman, M. (2004). Census bureau projects tripling of Hispanic and Asian populations in 50 years; Non-Hispanic Whites may drop to half of total population. *U.S. Census Bureau News.* Washington, DC: U.S. Department of Commerce. Retrieved April 1, 2008, from http://www.census.gov/Press-Release/www/releases/archives/population/001720.html

Bernstein, R. (2008). U.S. Hispanic population surpasses 45 million, now 15 percent of total. *U.S. Census Bureau News.* Washington, DC: U.S. Department of Commerce. Retrieved December 2, 2008, from http://www.census.gov/Press-Release/www/releases/archives/population/011910.html

Bonus, R. (2000). *Locating Filipino Americans: Ethnicity and the cultural politics of space.* Philadelphia, PA: Temple University Press.

Boydell, J., van Os, J., McKenzie, K., Allardyce, J., Goel, R., McCreadie, R. G., & Murray, R. M. (2001). Incidence of schizophrenia in ethnic minorities in London: Ecological study into interactions with environment. *British Medical Journal, 323,* 1336–1338.

Brady, S., & Busse, W. J. (1994). The Gay Identity Questionnaire: A brief measure of homosexual identity formation. *Journal of Homosexuality, 26*(4), 1–22.

Braun, K. L., & Nichols, R. (1997). Death and dying in four Asian American cultures: A descriptive study. *Death Studies, 21*(4), 327–359.

Cabato, A. L. (1995). PASACAT became my whole life. In Y. L. Espiritu (Ed.), *Filipino American Lives* (pp. 143–156). Philadelphia, PA: Temple University Press.

California Asian Pacific Islander Joint Legislative Caucus (2009). The State of Asian American, Native Hawaiian and Pacific Islander Health in California Report. Retrieved on July 1, 2009, from http://democrats.assembly.ca.gov/members/a49/pdf/AANHPI_report_091.pdf

Cass, V. C. (1979). Homosexual identity formation: A theoretical model. *Journal of Homosexuality, 4*, 219–235.

Central Intelligence Agency. (2008). *Philippines: The world factbook*. Retrieved September 23, 2008, from https://www.cia .gov/library/publications/the-world-factbook/geos/rp.html#People

Chen, X., Unger, J. B., Cruz, T. B., & Johnson, C. A. (1999). Smoking patterns of Asian-American youth in California and their relationship with acculturation. *Journal of Adolescent Health, 24*(5), 321–328.

Chesney-Lind, M., Pasko, L., Marker, N., Freeman, S., & Nakano, J. (2004). Arrest trends, gang involvement, and truancy in Hawaii: An interim report to the twenty-second Hawaii State Legislature. Manoa, HI: Public Policy Center at University of Hawai'i.

Choi, K.-H., Han, C.-S., Hudes, E. S., & Kegeles, S. (2002). Unprotected sex and associated risk factors among young Asian and Pacific Islander men who have sex with men. *AIDS Education and Prevention, 14*(6), 472–481.

Choi, Y. (2008). Diversity within: Subgroup differences of youth problem behaviors among Asian Pacific Islander American adolescents. *Journal of Community Psychology, 36*(3), 352–370.

Chung, P. J., Travis, R., Kilpatrick, S. D., Elliott, M. N., Lui, C., Khandwala, S. B., . . . Schuster, M. A. (2007). Acculturation and parent-adolescent communication about sex in Filipino-American families: A community-based participatory research study. *Journal of Adolescent Health, 40*(6), 543–550.

Church, T. A. (1986). *Filipino personality: A review of research and writings*. Manila, Philippines: De La Salle University Press.

Church, T. A., & Katigbak, M. S. (2002). Indigenization of psychology in the Philippines. *International Journal of Psychology, 37*(3), 129–148.

Clinton, W. J. (2000). Statement on signing legislation designating the Joseph Ileto Post Office. *Weekly Compilation of Presidential Documents, 36*(15), 833.

Cohn, A., & Zeichner, A. (2006). Effects of masculine identity and gender role stress on aggression in men. *Psychology of Men & Masculinity, 7*(4), 179–190.

Combs, D. R., Penn, D. L., & Fenigstein, A. (2002). Ethnic differences in subclinical paranoia: An expansion of norms of the Paranoia Scale. *Cultural Diversity and Ethnic Minority Psychology, 8*(3), 248–256.

References

Conerly, G. (1996). The politics of Black, lesbian, gay, and bisexual identity. In B. Beemyn & M. Eliason (Eds.), *A lesbian, gay, bisexual, and transgender anthology* (pp. 133–145). New York: New York University Press.

Constantino, R. (1975). *The Philippines: A past revisited (pre-Spanish-1941)*, vol. 1. Quezon City, Philippines: Tala.

Consunji, R. J., & Hyder, A. A. (2004). The burden of injuries in the Philippines: Implications for national research policy. *Accident Analysis & Prevention, 36*(6), 1111–1117.

Cordova, F. (1983) *Filipinos: Forgotten Asian Americans*. Dubuque, IA: Kendall/Hunt.

Corey, G. (2009). *Case approach to counseling & psychotherapy*. Florence, KY: Cengage Learning.

Cross, W. E. (1971). The Negro-to-Black conversion experience. *Black World, 20*, 13–27.

Darbes, L. A., Kennedy, G. E., Peersman, G., Zohrabyan, L., & Rutherford, G. W. (2002). *Systematic review of HIV behavioral prevention research in Asian Americans and Pacific Islanders*. HIV InSite Knowledge Base Chapter. San Francisco: University of California San Francisco.

David, E. J. R. (2008). A colonial mentality model of depression for Filipino Americans. *Cultural Diversity and Ethnic Minority Psychology, 14*(2), 118–127.

David, E. J. R. (2010). Cultural mistrust and mental health help-seeking attitudes among Filipino Americans. *Asian American Journal of Psychology, 1*(1), 57–66.

David, E. J. R., & Okazaki, S. (2006a). Colonial mentality: A review and recommendation for Filipino American psychology. *Cultural Diversity and Ethnic Minority Psychology, 12*(1), 1–16.

David, E. J. R., & Okazaki, S. (2006b). The Colonial Mentality Scale (CMS) for Filipino Americans: Scale construction and psychological implications. *Journal of Counseling Psychology, 53*(2), 241–252.

De Leon, L. M. (2004). Filipinotown and the DJ scene: Cultural expression and identity affirmation of Filipino American youth in Los Angeles. In J. Lee & M. Zhou (Eds.), *Asian American youth: Culture, identity, and ethnicity* (pp. 191–206). New York, NY: Routledge.

Delucchi, M., & Do, H. D. (1996). The model minority myth and perceptions of Asian-Americans as victims of racial harassment. *College Student Journal, 30*(3), 411–414.

de Mendelssohn, F. (2008). Transgenerational transmission of trauma: Guilt, shame, and the "heroic dilemma." *International Journal of Group Psychotherapy, 58*(3), 389–401.

Demetrio, F. R. (1991). Engkantos and spirits. *Encyclopedia of Philippine folk beliefs and customs* (vol. 1.; pp. 587–670). Cagayan de Oro, Philippines: Xavier University.

Downing, N. E., & Roush, K. L. (1985). From Passive acceptance to active commitment: A model of feminist identity development for women. *Counseling Psychologist, 13*(4), 695–709.

Ellison, N. B., Steinfield, C., & Lampe, C. (2007). The benefits of Facebook "friends": Social capital and college students' use of online social network sites. *Journal of Computer-Mediated Communication, 12*(4), 1143–1168.

Enright, J. B., & Jaeckle, W. R. (1963). Psychiatric symptoms and diagnosis in two subcultures. *International Journal of Social Psychiatry, 9*, 12–17.

Enriquez, V. G. (1982). *Decolonizing the Filipino psyche: Philippine psychology in the seventies.* Quezon City, Philippines: Philippine Psychology Research House.

Enriquez, V. G. (1997). Filipino psychology: Concepts and methods. In H.S. R. Kao, & D. Sinha (Eds.), *Asian perspectives on psychology* (pp. 40–53). Thousand Oaks, CA: Sage.

Enriquez, V. G. (2004). *From colonial to liberation psychology: The Philippine experience.* Dasmariñas, Cavite, Philippines: De La Salle University.

Espin, O. (1987). Issues of identity in the psychology of Latina lesbians: Explorations and challenges. In Boston Lesbian Psychologics Collective (Ed.), *Lesbian psychologies: Explorations and challenges* (pp. 35–55). Urbana: University of Illinois Press.

Espiritu, Y. L. (1992). *Asian American panethnicity: Bridging institutions and identities.* Philadelphia, PA: Temple University Press.

Espiritu, Y. L. (2003). *Home bound: Filipino American lives across cultures, communities, and countries.* Berkeley, CA: University of California Press.

Espiritu, Y. L. (2004). Colonial oppression, labour importation, and group formation: Filipinos in the United States. In K. A. Ono (Ed.),

References

A companion to Asian American studies (pp. 332–349). Malden, MA: Blackwell.

Espiritu, Y. L., & Wolf, D. L. (2001). The paradox of assimilation: Children of Filipino immigrants in San Diego. In R. G. Rumbaut & A. Portes (Eds.), *Ethnicities: Children of immigrant America* (pp. 157–186). Berkeley, CA: University of California Press.

Fabella, V. I. (2002). From the forgotten Asian American to the invisible minority: Predictors of Filipino American ethnic identity and Filipino American social identity. *Dissertation Abstracts International: Section B: Sciences and Engineering, 63*(2-B), 1021.

Fisher, R. J. (1993). Social desirability bias and the validity of indirect questioning. *Journal of Consumer Research, 20,* 303–315.

French, J. P. R., & Raven, B. (1960). The bases of social power. In D. Cartwright & A. Zander (Eds.), *Group dynamics* (pp. 607–623). New York, NY: Harper & Row.

Fulbeck, K., Lennon, S., & Spickard, P. (2006). *Part Asian, 100% Hapa.* San Francisco, CA: Chronicle Books.

Galapon, D. L. (1997). Processes of biculturalism and ethnic identity development in second-generation Filipino-American women. *Dissertation Abstracts International: Section B: Sciences and Engineering, 58*(4-B), 2178.

Gall, T. L. (1998). *Worldmark encyclopedia of culture & daily life: Vol. 3 — Asia & Oceania.* Cleveland, OH: Eastword.

Gee, G. C., Chen, J., Spencer, M. S., See, S., Kuester, O. A., Tran, D., & Takeuchi, D., (2006). Social support as a buffer for perceived unfair treatment among Filipino Americans: Differences between San Francisco and Honolulu. *American Journal of Public Health, 96*(4), 677–684.

Ghosh, C. (2003). Healthy People 2010 and Asian Americans/Pacific Islanders: Defining a baseline of information. *American Journal of Public Health, 93*(12), 2093–2098.

Gibson, C., & Jung, K. (2002). Historical census statistics on population totals by race, 1790–1990, and by Hispanic origin, 1970–1990, for the United States, regions, divisions, and states. U.S. Census Population Division. Retrieved March 20, 2010, from http://www.census.gov/population/www/documentation/twps0056.html

Gong, F., Gage, S. L., & Tacata, L. A. (2003). Helpseeking behavior among Filipino Americans: A cultural analysis of face and language. *Journal of Community Psychology, 31,* 469–488.

271

Gonzalves, T. S. (1997). The night the dancers stayed: On Pilipino cultural nights. In M. P. P. Root (Ed.), *Filipino Americans: Transformation and identity* (pp. 316–323). Thousand Oaks, CA: Sage.

Goto, S. G., Gee, G. C., & Takeuchi, D. T. (2002). Strangers still? The experience of discrimination among Chinese Americans. *Journal of Community Psychology, 30*(2), 211–224.

Gottdiener, W. H. (2006). Individual psychodynamic psychotherapy of schizophrenia: Empirical evidence for the practicing clinician. *Psychoanalytic Psychology, 23*(3), 583–589.

Grunbaum, J. A., Kann, L., Kinchen, S. A., Williams, B. A., Ross, J. G., Lowry, R., & Kolbe, L. (2002). Youth risk behavior surveillance — United States, 2001. *Morbidity and Mortality Weekly Reports, 51*, 1–66.

Grunbaum, J. A., Lowry, R., Kann, L., & Pateman, B. (2000). Prevalence of health risk behaviors among Asian American/Pacific Islander high school students. *Journal of Adolescent Health, 27*(5), 322–330.

Guevarra, R. P. (2004). Burritos and Bagoong: Mexipinos and multiethnic identity in San Diego, California. In M. Coronado, R. P. Guevarra, J. Moniz, & L. F. Szanto (Eds.), *Crossing lines: Race and mixed race across the geohistorical divide* (pp. 73–96). Lanham, MD: Rowman & Littlefield.

Guevarra, R. P. (2008). Mexipino: A history of multiethnic identity and the formation of the Mexican and Filipino communities of San Diego, 1900–1965. *Dissertation Abstracts International Section A: Humanities and Social Sciences, 68*(7-A), 3108.

Halagao, P. E. (2004a). Holding up the mirror: The complexity of seeing your ethnic self in history. *Theory on Research and Social Education, 32*(4), 459–483.

Halagao, P. E. (2004b). Teaching Filipino American students. *Multicultural Review, 13*(1), 42–48.

Hall, C. C. I. (1992). Please choose one: Ethnic identity choices for biracial individuals. In M. P. P. Root (Ed.), *Racially mixed people in America* (pp. 250–264). Newbury Park, CA: Sage.

Hall, S. P., & Carter, R. T. (2006). The relationship between racial identity, ethnic identity, and perceptions of racial discrimination in an Afro-Caribbean descent sample. *Journal of Black Psychology, 32*(2), 155–175.

References

Han, C.-S. (2008). A qualitative exploration of the relationship between racism and unsafe sex among Asian Pacific Islander gay men. *Archives of Sexual Behavior, 37*(5), 827–837.

Harley, D. A. (2005). African Americans and indigenous counseling. In D. A. Harley & J. M. Dillard (Eds.), *Contemporary mental health issues among African Americans* (pp. 293–306). Alexandria, VA: American Counseling Association.

Harrell, S. P. (2000). A multidimensional conceptualization of racism-related stress: Implications for the well-being of people of color. *American Journal of Orthopsychiatry, 70,* 42–57.

Helms, J. E. (1990). *African American and White racial identity.* New York, NY: Greenwood Press.

Helms, J. E. (1995). An update of Helm's White and people of color racial identity models. In J. G. Ponterotto, J. M. Casas, L. A. Suzuki, & C. M. Alexander (Eds.), *Handbook of multicultural counseling* (pp. 181–198). Thousand Oaks, CA: Sage.

Henry, R. L. (1986). *Filipino spirit world: A challenge to the church.* Manila, Philippines: OMF Literature.

Heras, P. (2007). Psychotherapy with Filipinas. *Women & Therapy, 30*(3/4), 63–73.

Herman, M. (2004). Forced to choose: Some determinants of racial identification in multiracial adolescents. *Child Development, 75,* 730–748.

Horan, P. F., & DiClemente, R. J. (1993). HIV knowledge, communication, and risk behaviors among white, Chinese-, and Filipino-American adolescents in a high-prevalence AIDS epicenter: A comparative analysis. *Ethnicity & Disease, 3*(2), 97–105.

Horn, L. (1995). *Minority undergraduate participation in postsecondary education.* National Center for Education Statistics Report No. 95–166. Washington DC: U.S. Department of Education.

Hübinette, T. (2004). Adopted Koreans and the development of identity in the "third space." *Adoption and Fostering, 28,* 16–24.

Human Rights Watch. (2004). The Philippines unprotected: Sex, condoms, and the human right to health. *Human Rights Watch, 16*(6), 1–68.

Hwang, W., Miranda, J., & Chung, C. (2007). Psychosis and shamanism in a Filipino-American immigrant. *Culture, Medicine and Psychiatry, 31*(2), 251–269.

Ignacio, E. N. (2005). *Building diaspora: Filipino community formation on the Internet*. Piscataway, NJ: Rutgers University Press.

Ignacio, L. F. (1976). *Asian Americans and Pacific Islanders (Is there such an ethnic group?)*. San Jose, CA: Filipino Development and Associates.

Iwamasa, G. Y., Larrabee, A. L., & Merritt, R. D. (2000). Are personality disorder criteria ethnically biased? A card-sort analysis. *Cultural Diversity and Ethnic Minority Psychology, 6*(3), 284–296.

Iwamoto, D. K., & Liu, W. M. (2008). Asian American men and Asianized attribution: Intersections of masculinity, race, and sexuality. In N. Tewari & A. N. Alvarez (Eds.), *Asian American psychology: Current perspectives* (pp. 211–232). New York, NY: Psychology Press.

Jamero, P. M. (2006). *Growing up Brown: Memoirs of a Filipino American*. Seattle, WA: University of Washington Press.

Javier, J. R., Huffman, L. C., & Mendoza, F. S. (2007). Filipino child health in the United States: Do health and health care disparities exist? *Prevention of Chronic Diseases, 4*(2), A36.

Johnson, R. C., Nagoshi, C. T., Ahern, F. M., Wilson, J. R., & Yuen, S. H. L. (1987). Cultural factors as explanations for ethnic group differences in alcohol use in Hawaii. *Journal of Psychoactive Drugs, 19*(1), 67–75.

Johnson, R. C., Schwitters, S. Y., Wilson, J. R., Nagoshi, C. T., & McClearn, G. E. (1985). A cross-ethnic comparison of reasons given for using alcohol, not using alcohol, or ceasing to use alcohol. *Journal of Studies on Alcohol, 46,* 283–288.

Johnston, M. P., & Nadal, K. L. (2010). Multiracial microaggressions: Exposing monoracism in everyday life and clinical practice. In D. W. Sue (Ed.), *Microaggressions and marginality: Manifestation, dynamics, and impact* (pp. 123–144). Hoboken, NJ: Wiley.

Jones, J. (1991). Psychological models of race: What have they been and what should they be? In J. Goodchilds (Ed.), *Psychological perspectives on human diversity in America* (pp. 3–46). Washington, DC: American Psychological Association.

Jorge, R. (2004, October 10). Everyone's idol. *Manila Times.* Retrieved January 22, 2006, from http://www.manilatimes.net/national/2004/oct/10/

References

Keith, S. J., Regier, D. A., & Rae, D. S. (1991). Schizophrenia disorders. In L. N. Robins & D. A. Regier (Eds.), *Psychiatric disorders in America* (pp. 33–52). New York, NY: Free Press.

Kim, B. S. K., Yang, P. H., Atkinson, D. R., Wolfe, M. M., & Hong, S. (2001). Cultural value similarities and differences among Asian American ethnic groups. *Cultural Diversity and Ethnic Minority Psychology, 7*(4), 343–361.

Kim, J. (1981). The process of Asian American identity development: A study of Japanese-American women's perceptions of their struggle to achieve personal identities as Americans of Asian ancestry. *Dissertation Abstracts International, 42,* 1551A.

Kim, J. G. S. (2002). Racial perceptions and psychological well being in Asian and Hispanic Americans. *Dissertation Abstracts International: Section B: Sciences and Engineering, 63*(2-B), 1033.

Kipling, R. (1899). White man's burden. In P. Brians, M. Gallwey, D. Hughes, A. Hussain, R. Law, M. Myers, . . . S. Swan (Eds.), *Reading about the world* (3rd ed., Vol. 2). New York, NY: Harcourt Brace.

Kitano, H. H., & Daniels, R. (1995). *Asian Americans: Emerging minorities.* Englewood Cliffs, NJ: Prentice Hall.

Klatsky, A. L., & Armstrong, M. A. (1991). Cardiovascular risk factors among Asian Americans living in Northern California. *American Journal of Public Health, 81,* 1432–1438.

Klatsky, A. L., Tekawa, I. S., & Armstrong, M. A. (1996). Cardiovascular risk factors among Asian Americans. *Public Health Reports, 111,* 62–64.

Kohatsu, E. L. (1993). The effects of racial identity and acculturation on anxiety, assertiveness, and ascribed identity among Asian American college students. *Dissertation Abstracts International, 54*(2-B), 1102.

Kuo, W. H. (1984). Prevalence of depression among Asian Americans. *Journal of Nervous and Mental Disease, 172,* 449–457.

Laenui, P. (2000). Process of decolonization. In M. Battiste (Ed.), *Reclaiming indigenous voice and vision* (pp. 150–160). Vancouver, BC: UBC Press.

Langenberg, C., Araneta, M. R., Bergstro, J., Marmot, M., & Barrett-Connor, E. (2007). Diabetes and coronary heart disease in Filipino-American Women: Role of growth and life-course socioeconomic factors. *Diabetes Care, 30*(3), 535–541.

Le, C. N. (2008a). Adopted Asian Americans. *Asian-Nation: The land-scape of Asian America*. Retrieved November 15, 2008, from http://www.asian-nation.org/adopted.shtml

Le, C. N. (2008b). Interracial dating & marriage. *Asian-Nation: The landscape of Asian America*. Retrieved November 15, 2008, from http://www.asian-nation.org/interracial.shtml

Lee, D. Y. (2002). The influence of acculturation and racial identity upon Asian Americans' attitudes toward seeking psychological help. *Dissertation Abstracts International: Section B: Sciences and Engineering, 63*(5-B), 2591.

Lee, R. M. (2003). The transracial adoption paradox: History, research, and counseling implications of cultural socialization. *Counseling Psychologist, 31*, 711–744.

Lee, R. M., & Miller, M. J. (2008). History and psychology of adoptees in Asian America. In N. Tewari & A. N. Alvarez (Eds.), *Asian American psychology: Current perspectives* (pp. 337–363). New York, NY: Psychology Press.

Lengua, L. J. (2000). Gender, gender roles, and personality: Gender differences in the prediction of coping and psychological symptoms. *Sex Roles, 43*(11/12), 787–820.

Leong, F. (1985). Career development of Asian Americans. *Journal of College Student Personnel, 26*(6), 539–546.

Lewis-Fernández, R., Guarnaccia, P. J., Martínez, I. E., Salmán, E., Schmidt, A., & Liebowitz, M. (2002). Comparative phenomenology of *Ataques de Nervios*, panic attacks, and panic disorder. *Culture, Medicine and Psychiatry, 2*, 199–223.

Lin, K. M., & Cheung, F. (1999). Mental health issues for Asian Americans. *Psychiatric Services, 50*(6), 774–780.

Liu, W. M., Pope-Davis, D., Nevitt, J., & Toporek, R. (1999). Understanding the function of acculturation and prejudicial attitudes among Asian Americans. *Cultural Diversity and Ethnic Minority Psychology, 5*(4), 317–328.

Liu, W. M. (2002). Exploring the lives of Asian American men: Racial identity, male role norms, gender role conflict, and prejudicial attitudes. *Psychology of Men & Masculinity, 3*(2), 107–118.

Loo, C. M., Fairbank, J. A., Scurfield, R. M., Ruch, L. O., King, D. W., Adams, L., & Chemtob, C. M. (2001). Measuring exposure to racism:

References

Development and validation of a race-related stressor scale (RRSS) for Asian American Vietnam veterans. *Psychological Assessment, 13*, 503–520.

Lubben, J. E., Chi, I., & Kitano, H. (1988). Exploring Filipino American drinking behavior. *Journal of Studies on Alcohol, 49*(1), 26–29.

Macapagal, M. E. J. (2003). Social psychology of People Power II in the Philippines. *Journal of Peace Psychology, 9*(3), 219–233.

Manalansan, M. F., (2003). *Global divas: Filipino gay men in the diaspora.* Durham, NC: Duke University Press.

Mananzan, M. J. (2003). *The Filipino women: Before & after the Spanish conquest of the Philippines.* Manila, Philippines: Institute of Women's Studies.

Maramba, D. C. (2008). Immigrant families and the college experience: Perspectives of Filipina Americans. *Journal of College Student Development, 49*(4), 336–350.

Martin, J. A., Hamilton, B. E., Sutton, P. D., Ventura, S. J., Menacker, F., & Munson, M. L. (2003). Births: Final data for 2002. *National Vital Statistics Report 2003, 52*(10), 1–113.

Mayeda, D. T., Hishinuma, E. S., Nishimura, S. T., Garcia-Santiago, O., & Mark, G. Y. (2006). Asian/Pacific Islander Youth Violence Prevention Center: Interpersonal violence and deviant behaviors among youth in Hawaii. *Journal of Adolescent Health, 39*, 276e.1–276.e11.

Mejorada, M. P. (1996, August 11). As I see it: The crab mentality. *Filipino Express.* Retrieved February 01, 2011, from HighBeam Research: http://www.highbeam.com/doc/1P1-2814590.html

Milgram, S. (1983). *Obedience to authority: An experimental view.* New York, NY: HarperCollins.

Miller, S. C. (1982). *Benevolent assimilation: The American conquest of the Philippines, 1899–1903.* New Haven, CT: Yale University Press.

Montoya, C. A. (1997). Living in the shadows: The undocumented immigrant experience of Filipinos. In M. P. P. Root (Ed.), *Filipino Americans; Transformation and identity* (pp. 112–120). Thousand Oaks, CA: Sage.

Mossakowski, K. N. (2003). Coping with perceived discrimination: Does ethnic identity protect mental health? *Journal of Health and Social Behavior, 44*(3), 318–331.

Nadal, K. L. (2000). Filipino American substance abuse: Sociocultural factors and methods of treatment. *Journal of Alcohol and Drug Education, 46*(2), 26–36.

Nadal, K. L. (2004). Filipino American identity development model. *Journal of Multicultural Counseling and Development, 32*(1), 44–61.

Nadal, K. L. (2008a). Colonialism: Societal and psychological impacts on Asian Americans and Pacific Islanders. In N. Tewari & A. N. Alvarez (Eds.), *Asian American psychology: Current perspectives* (pp. 153–172). New York, NY: Psychology Press.

Nadal, K. L. (2008b). A culturally competent classroom for Filipino Americans. *Multicultural Perspectives, 10*(3), 1–6.

Nadal, K. L. (2008c). Ethnic group membership, phenotype, and perceptions of racial discrimination for Filipino and Chinese Americans: Implications for mental health (Unpublished doctoral dissertation). Teachers College, Columbia University.

Nadal, K. L. (2008e). Preventing racial, ethnic, gender, sexual minority, disability, and religious microaggressions: Recommendations for promoting positive mental health. *Prevention in Counseling Psychology: Theory, Research, Practice and Training, 2*(1), 22–27.

Nadal, K. L. (2010a). Gender microaggressions and women: Implications for mental health. In M. A. Paludi (Ed.), *Feminism and women's rights worldwide, Volume 2: Mental and physical health* (pp. 155–175). Santa Barbara, CA: Praeger.

Nadal, K. L. (2010b). Gender roles. In S. Goldstein, & J. Naglieri (Eds.), *Encyclopedia of child behavior and development* (pp. 687–690). New York, NY: Springer.

Nadal, K. L. (2010c). Sexual identity. In S. Goldstein, & J. Naglieri (Eds.), *Encyclopedia of child behavior and development* (pp. 1344–1345). New York, NY: Springer.

Nadal, K. L. (in press). A feminist identity development model for Filipina Americans. In P. Lundberg-Love, K. L. Nadal, & M. A. Paludi (Eds.), *Women and Mental Disorders*. Santa Barbara, CA: Praeger Publishers.

Nadal, K. L., & Corpus, M. J. H. (in press). Tomboys and baklas: Experiences of lesbian & gay Filipino Americans in higher education. In V. A. Wall & J. Washington (Eds.), *The colors of the rainbow: Lesbian, gay, bisexual & transgender people of color in the academy*. Lanham, MD:

References

University Press of America and the American College Personnel Association.

Nadal, K. L., Issa, M.-A., Griffin, K., Hamit, S., & Lyons, O. (2010). Religious microaggressions in the United States: Mental health implications for religious minority groups. In D. W. Sue (Ed.), *Microaggressions and marginality: Manifestation, dynamics, and impact* (pp. 287–310). Hoboken, NJ: Wiley.

Nadal, K. L., & Monzones, J. (2010). Filipino Americans and Neuropsychology. In D. Fujii, (Ed.), *The neuropsychology of Asian Americans* (pp. 47–70). Boca Raton, FL: Taylor and Francis.

Nadal, K. L., Pituc, S. T., Johnston, M. P., & Esparrago, T. (2010). Overcoming the model minority myth: Experiences of Filipino American graduate students. *Journal of College Student Development, 51*(6), 1–13.

Nadal, K. L., Rivera, D. P., & Corpus, M. J. H. (2010) Sexual orientation and transgender microaggressions in everyday life: Experiences of lesbians, gays, bisexuals, and transgender individuals. In D. W. Sue (Ed.), *Microaggressions and marginality: Manifestation, dynamics, and impact* (pp. 217–240). Hoboken, NJ: Wiley.

Nadal, K. L., & Sue, D. W. (2009). Asian American Youth. In C. S. Clauss-Ehlers (Ed.), *Encyclopedia of cross-cultural school psychology* (pp.116–122). New York, NY: Springer.

National Center for Health Statistics. (2000). *National Vital Statistics Report, 48*(16). Hyattsville, MD: Author.

Nayani, F. (2010). Family communication patterns and ethnic identity development of multiethnic Filipino Americans. In H. McCubbin, B. DeBarsche, M. Ripke, M. Hart, F. Takasugi, & K. Ontai (Eds.), *Multiethnicity and multiethnic families: Development, identity and resilience* (pp. 199–223). Honolulu, HI: University of Hawaii Press.

Nemoto T., Aoki, B., Huang K., Morris A., Nguyen H., & Wong, W. (1999). Drug use behaviors among Asian drug users in San Francisco. *Addictive Behaviors, 24*(6), 823–38.

Nemoto, T., Aoki, B. Huang, K., Morris, A., Le, M. N., Nguyen, H., . . . Wong, W. (2000). HIV risk behaviors among Asian drug users in San Francisco. *AIDS Education and Prevention, 12*(2), 126–140.

Office of Youth Services. (2002). Disproportionate minority confinement (DMC) in Hawaii's Juvenile Justice System, Comparing Fiscal Years 1994 and 2000. Honolulu, HI: Office of Youth Services, 13.

Okamura, J. Y. (1983). Filipino hometown associations in Hawaii. *Ethnology, 22*(4), 341–353.

Okamura, J. Y. (1998). *Imagining the Filipino American diaspora: Transnational relations, identities, and communities.* New York, NY: Garland.

Okamura, J., & Agbayani, A. (1991). Filipino Americans. In N. Mokuau (Ed.), *Handbook of social services for Asian and Pacific Islanders* (pp. 97–114). Westport, CT: Greenwood Press.

Okamura, J. Y., & Agbayani, A. R. (1997). Pamantasan: Filipino American higher education. In M. P. P. Root (Ed.), *Filipino Americans: Transformation and identity* (pp. 183–197). Thousand Oaks, CA: Sage.

O'Neil, J. M. (2008). Summarizing 25 years of research on men's gender role conflict using the Gender Role Conflict Scale: New research paradigms and clinical implications. *Counseling Psychologist, 36*(3), 358–445.

Operario, D., & Nemoto, T. (2005). Sexual risk behavior and substance use among a sample of Asian Pacific Islander transgendered women. *AIDS Education and Prevention, 17*(5), 430–443.

Phinney, J. S. (1990). Ethnic identity in adolescents and adults: Review of research. *Psychological Bulletin, 108*(3), 499–514.

Phinney, J. S. (1996). When we talk about American ethnic groups, what do we mean? *American Psychologist, 51*(9), 918–927.

Pido, A. (1986). *The Pilipinos in America: Macro/micro dimensions of immigration and integration.* Staten Island, NY: Center for Migration Studies.

Pisares, E. H. (2006). Do you mis(recognize) me: Filipina Americans in popular music and the problem of invisibility. In A. T. Tiongson, E. V. Gutierrez, & R. V. Gutierrez (Eds.), *Positively no Filipinos allowed: Building communities and discourse* (pp. 111–123). Philadelphia, PA: Temple University Press.

Posadas, B. M. (1999). *The Filipino Americans.* Westport, CT: Greenwood Press.

Posadas, B. M., & Guyotte, R. L. (1990). Unintentional immigrants: Chicago's Filipino foreign students become settlers, 1900–1941. *Journal of American Ethnic History, 9*(2), 26–48.

Prentice, D. A., & Miller, D. T. (1993) Pluralistic ignorance and alcohol use on campus: Some consequences of misperceiving the social norm. *Journal of Personality and Social Psychology, 64*, 243–256.

References

Pulido, M. E. (1991, April 10–16). Youth gangs and the Filipino community. *Philippine News Magazine*, 12.

Quismundo, T. (2008, March 25). Pacquiao hits crab mentality, voices hurt. *Philippine Daily Inquirer.*

Quiton, R. A. (2006). Prevalence and early exposure to gambling behavior among Filipino Americans. *Dissertation Abstracts International: Section B: Sciences and Engineering, 67*(3-B), 1713.

Reeves, T. M., & Bennett, C. E. (2004). We the people: Asians in the United States. U.S. Census Bureau. *Census 2000 Special Reports.* Retrieved from http:/www.census.gov

Renn, K. (2008). Research on biracial and multiracial identity development: Overview and synthesis. *New Directions for Student Services, 123*, 13–21.

Revilla, L. A. (1997). Filipino American identity: Transcending the crisis. In M. P. P. Root (Ed.), *Filipino Americans: Transformation and identity* (pp. 95–111). Thousand Oaks, CA: Sage.

Rizal, J. P. (1997). *Noli me Tangere: A novel.* Honolulu, HI: University of Hawai'i Press.

Robinson T. N., Chang J. Y., Haydel K. F., & Killen, J. D. (2001). Overweight concerns and body dissatisfaction among third-grade children: The impacts of ethnicity and socioeconomic status. *Journal of Pediatrics, 138*(2), 181–187.

Romero, R. A., Messer, K., West, J. H., White, M. M., & Trinidad, D. R. (2008). Smoking trends among Filipino adults in California, 1990–2002. *Preventive Medicine, 46*(4), 336–339.

Root, M. P. P. (1990). Resolving "other"' status: Identity development of biracial individuals. *Women and Therapy, 9*, 185–205.

Root, M. P. P. (1995). *The multiracial experience: Racial borders as the new frontier.* Thousand Oaks, CA: Sage.

Root, M. P. P. (1997a). Contemporary mixed-heritage Filipino Americans: Fighting colonized identities. In M. P. P. Root (Ed.), *Filipino Americans: Transformation and identity* (pp. 80–94). Thousand Oaks, CA: Sage.

Root, M. P. P. (1997b). Introduction. In M. P. P. Root (Ed.), *Filipino Americans: Transformation and identity* (pp. xi–xv). Thousand Oaks, CA: Sage.

Rumbaut, R. G. (1995). The new Californians: Comparative research findings on the educational progress of immigrant children. In

R. G. Rumbaut, & W. A. Cornelius (Eds.), *California's immigrant children* (pp. 17–70). La Jolla, CA: Center of U.S.-Mexican Studies, University of California, San Diego.

Rumbaut, R. G., & Ewing, W. A. (2007). *The myth of immigrant criminality.* Immigration Policy Center. Washington, DC: American Immigration Law Foundation.

Ryan, C., Shaw, R., Pliam, M., Zapolanski, A. J., Murphy, M., Valle, H. V., & Myler, R. (2000). Coronary heart disease in Filipino and Filipino-American patients: Prevalence of risk factors and outcomes of treatment. *Journal of Invasive Cardiology, 12*(3), 134–139.

Salvador, D. S., Omizo, M. M., & Kim, B. S. K. (1997). Bayanihan: Providing effective counseling strategies with children of Filipino ancestry. *Journal of Multicultural Counseling and Development, 25*(3), 201–209.

San Francisco Department of Public Health. (2008). *Quarterly AIDS Surveillance Report: AIDS cases reported through September 2008.* San Francisco, CA: Author.

Sanchez, F., & Gaw, A. (2007). Mental health care of Filipino Americans. *Psychiatric Services, 58*(6), 810–815.

Sanders, W. B. (1994). *Gangbangs and drive-bys: Grounded culture and juvenile gang violence.* Piscataway, NJ: Aldine Transaction.

Santiago, B. C. (1989). *75 Blessed years of the Iglesia Ni Cristo, 1914–1989.* Quezon City, Philippines: Iglesia ni Cristo.

Santos, A. F. (1984). *Do women really hold up half the sky? Notes on the women's movement in the Philippines.* Manila, Philippines: GABRIELA Proceedings, First National Assembly.

Shih, M., Bonam, C., Sanchez, D., & Peck, C. (2007). The social construction of race: Biracial identity and vulnerability to stereotypes. *Cultural Diversity and Ethnic Minority Psychology, 13*(2), 125–133.

Shimabukuro, K. P., Daniels, J., & D'Andrea, M. (1999). Addressing spiritual issues from a cultural perspective: The case of the grieving Filipino boy. *Journal of Multicultural Counseling and Development, 27*(4), 221–239.

Siegel, K., Schrimshaw, E. W., Lekas, H-M., & Parsons, J. T. (2008). Sexual behaviors of non-gay identified non-disclosing men who have sex with men and women. *Archives of Sexual Behavior, 37*(5), 720–735.

References

Snowden, L. R., & Cheung, F. H. (1990). Use of mental health services by members of ethnic minority groups. *American Psychologist, 45*, 347–355.

Sodowsky, G. R., Kwan, K., & Pannu, R. (1995) Ethnic identity of Asians in the United States. In J. G. Ponterotto, J. M. Casas, L. A. Suzuki, & C. M. Alexander (Eds.) *Handbook of multicultural counseling* (pp. 123–154). Thousand Oaks, CA: Sage.

Soriano, F. I., Rivera, L. M., Williams, K. J., Daley, S. P. & Reznik, V. M. (2004). Navigating between cultures: The role of culture in youth violence. *Journal of Adolescent Health 34*, 169–176.

Sparrenberger, F., Cichelero, F. T., Ascoli, A. M., Fonseca, F. P., Weiss, G., Berwanger, O., et al. (2009). Does psychosocial stress cause hypertension? A systematic review of observational studies. *Journal of Human Hypertension, 23*(1), 12–19.

Spickard, P. (1997). What must I be? Asian Americans and the questions of multiethnic identity. *Amerasia Journal, 23*(1), 43–60.

Stavig, G. R., Igra, A., & Leonard, A.R. (1998). Hypertension and related health issues among Asians and Pacific Islanders in California. *Public Health Reports, 103*(1), 28–37.

Steinberg, D. J. (2000). *The Philippines: A singular and a plural place.* New York, NY: Basic Books.

Strobel, L. M. (2001). *Coming full circle: The process of decolonization among post-1965 Filipino-Americans.* Manila, Philippines: Giraffe Books.

Strunk, O. C. (2000). Pastoral counseling. In A. E. Kazdin (Ed.), *Encyclopedia of psychology* (Vol. 6; pp. 64–66). Washington, DC: American Psychological Association.

Sue, D., Sue, D. W., & Sue, S. (2005). *Understanding abnormal behavior* (8th ed.) Boston, MA: Houghton Mifflin.

Sue, D. W., Arredondo, P., & McDavis, R. J. (1992). Multicultural counseling competencies and standards: A call to the profession. *Journal of Counseling & Development, 70*(4), 477–486.

Sue, D. W., Bucceri, J. M., Lin, A. I., Nadal, K. L., & Torino, G. C. (2007). Racial microaggressions and the Asian American experience. *Cultural Diversity and Ethnic Minority Psychology, 13*(1), 72–81.

Sue, D. W., & Capodilupo, C. M. (2008). Racial, gender, and sexual orientation microaggressions: Implications for counseling and psychotherapy. In D. W. Sue & D. Sue, *Counseling the culturally diverse* (5th ed., pp. 105–130). Hoboken, NJ: Wiley.

Sue, D. W., Nadal, K. L., Capodilupo, C. M., Lin, A. I., Rivera, D. P., & Torino, G. C. (2008). Racial microaggressions against Black Americans: Implications for counseling. *Journal of Counseling and Development, 86*(3), 330–338.

Sue, D. W., & Sue, D. (2008). *Counseling the culturally diverse* (5th ed.). Hoboken, NJ: Wiley.

Sue, S. (1977). Community mental health services to minority groups: Some optimism, some pessimism. *American Psychologist, 32*, 616–624.

Sue, S., & Sue, D. W. (1971). Chinese American personality and mental health. *Amerasian Journal,* 1, 36–49.

Suinn, R. M., Ahuna, C., & Khoo, G. (1992). The Suinn-Lew Asian Self-Identity Acculturation Scale: Concurrent and factorial validation. *Educational and Psychological Measurement, 52*, 1041–1046.

Suyemoto, K. L., & Tawa, J. (2008). Multiracial Asian Americans. In N. Tewari & A. N. Alvarez (Eds.), *Asian American psychology: Current perspectives* (pp. 381–398). New York, NY: Psychology Press.

Takaki, R. (1998). *Strangers from a different shore: A history of Asian Americans.* Boston, MA: Back Bay.

Tan, M. L. (1995). From Bakla to gay: Shifting gender identities and sexual behaviors in the Philippines. In R. G. Parker & J. H. Gagnon (Eds.), *Conceiving sexuality: Approaches to sex research in a postmodern world.* (pp. 85–96). New York, NY: Routledge.

Tan-Alora, A., & Lumitao, J. M. (2001). *Beyond a western bioethics: Voices from the developing world.* Washington, DC: Georgetown University Press, 2001.

Tanford, S., & Penrod, S. (1984) Social Influence Model: A formal integration of research on majority and minority influence processes, *Psychological Bulletin, 95*, 189–225.

Tarrier, N., Lewis, S., Haddock, G., Bentall, R., Drake, R., Kinderman, P., . . . Dunn, G. (2004). Cognitive-behavioural therapy in first-episode and early schizophrenia: 18-month follow-up of a randomised controlled trial. *British Journal of Psychiatry, 184*(3), 231–239.

Teranishi, R. T. (2002). Asian Pacific Americans and critical race theory: An examination of school racial climate. *Equity & Excellence in Education, (35)*2, 144–154.

References

Terrell, F., & Terrell, S. (1981). An inventory to measure cultural mistrust among Blacks. *Western Journal of Black Studies, 5,* 180–185.

Tewari, N., & Alvarez, A. N. (Eds.). (2008). *Asian American psychology: Current perspectives.* New York, NY: Psychology Press.

Tintiagco-Cuballes, A. (2007). *Pin@y educational partnerships: A Filipino/o American studies sourcebook, Volume 1, Philippine and Filipina/o American History.* Santa Clara, CA: Phoenix.

Tiongson, A. T. (1997). Throwing the baby out with the bath water: Situating young Filipino mothers and fathers beyond the dominant discourse on adolescent pregnancy. In M. P. P. Root (Ed.), *Filipino Americans: Transformation and identity* (pp. 257–271).Thousand Oaks, CA: Sage.

Tiongson, A. T. (2006). On the politics of Filipino youth culture: Interview with Theodore S. Gonzalves. In A. T. Tiongson, E. V. Gutierrez, & R. V. Gutierrez (Eds.), *Positively no Filipinos allowed: Building communities and discourse* (pp. 111–123). Philadelphia, PA: Temple University Press.

Tiongson, A. T., Gutierrez, E. V., & Gutierrez, R. V. (Eds.). (2006). *Positively no Filipinos allowed.* Philadelphia, PA: Temple University Press.

Tompar-Tiu, A., & Sustento-Seneriches, J. (1995). *Depression and other mental health issues: The Filipino American experience.* San Francisco, CA: Jossey-Bass.

Tracey, T. J., Leong, F. T., & Glidden, C. (1986). Help seeking and problem perception among Asian Americans. *Journal of Counseling Psychology, 33*(3), 331–336.

Trenka, J. J., Oparah, J. C., & Shin, S. Y. (Eds.). (2006). *Outsiders within: Writing on transracial adoption.* Cambridge, MA: South End Press.

Trevino, F. M. (1987). Standardized terminology for Hispanic populations. *American Journal of Public Health, 77,* 69–72.

Troiden, R. R. (1989). The formation of homosexual identities. *Journal of Homosexuality, 17,* 43–73.

Uba, L. (1994). *Asian Americans: Personality patterns, identity, and mental health.* New York, NY: Guilford Press.

U.S. Census Bureau. (1989). *200 years of U.S. census taking: Population and housing questions, 1790–1990.* Washington, DC: U.S. Government Printing Office.

U.S. Census Bureau. (1994). *1990 census of population, general population characteristics, the United States* (CP-1-1). Washington, DC: U.S. Government Printing Office.

U.S. Census Bureau (2000). *Profile of selected demographic and social characteristics: 2000. Population universe: People born in the Philippines* (FBP-1). Washington DC: U.S. Department of Commerce. Retrieved February 3, 2009, from http://www.census.gov/population/cen2000/stp-159/STP-159-philippines.pdf

U.S. Department of State, Office of Children's Issues (2008). *Detailed adoption information from Philippines to the United States*. Retrieved November 21, 2008, from http://www.adoption.state.gov/news/StarCountryData.php?country=Philippines

Valverde, K. C. (1992). From dust to gold: The Vietnamese Amerasian experience. In M. P. P. Root (Ed.), *Racially mixed people in America* (pp. 144–161). Thousand Oaks, CA: Sage.

Vergara, B. M. (2008). *Pinoy capital: The Filipino nation in Daly City*. Philadelphia, PA: Temple University Press.

Vijayakumar, L. (2004). Suicide prevention: The urgent need in developing countries. *World Psychiatry, 3*(3), 158–159.

Waters, M. C. (2001). Growing up West Indian and African American: Gender and class differences in the second generation. In N. Foner (Ed.), *Islands in the city: West Indian migration to New York* (pp 193–215). Berkeley, CA: University of California Press.

Weiner, B. P., & Marvit, R. C. (1977) Schizophrenia in Hawaii: Analysis of cohort mortality risk in a multi-ethnic population. *British Journal of Psychiatry, 131*, 497–503.

Weitz, T., Harper, C., & Mohllajee, A. (2001). *Teen pregnancy among Asians and Pacific Islanders in California: Final report*. San Francisco, CA: University of California, San Francisco Center for Reproductive Health Research and Policy.

Williams, G. (1999). *The prize of all the oceans*. New York, NY: Viking Press.

Wolf, D. L. (1997). Family secrets: Transnational struggles among children of Filipino immigrants. *Sociological Perspectives, 40*(3), 457–482.

Wong, M. M., Klingle, R. S., & Price, R. K. (2004). Alcohol, tobacco, and other drug use among Asian American and Pacific Islander adolescents in California and Hawaii. *Addictive Behavior, 29*(1), 127–141.

References

Wyatt, S. G., Williams, C. R., Henderson, F. C., Walker, E. R., & Winters, K. (2003). Racism and cardiovascular disease in African Americans. *American Journal of Medical Sciences, 325*(6), 315–331.

Yates, A., Edman, J., & Aruguete, M. (2004) Ethnic differences in BMI and body/self-dissatisfaction among Whites, Asian subgroups, Pacific Islanders, and African-Americans. *Journal of Adolescent Health, 34*(4), 300–307.

Yeh, C., & Wang, Y. (2000). Asian American coping attitudes, sources, and practices: Implications for indigenous counseling strategies. *Journal of College Student Development, 41*(1), 94–103.

Yoo, H. C., & Lee, R. M. (2005). Ethnic identity and approach-type coping as moderators of the racial discrimination/well-being relation in Asian Americans. *Journal of Counseling Psychology, 52*(4), 497–506.

Young, B. B., & Kinzie, J. D. (1974). Psychiatric consultation to a Filipino community in Hawaii. *American Journal of Psychiatry, 131,* 563–566.

Ziguras, S., Klimidis, S., Lewis J., & Stuart, G. (2003). Ethnic matching of clients and clinicians and use of mental health services by ethnic minority clients. *Psychiatric Services, 54,* 535–541.

Historical References in the Poem "Ikaw"

- When the Spanish first invaded and colonized the Philippines, they considered Filipinos *Negritos* (the Spanish word for "Black persons"). Some Americans later believed Filipinos to be Black and even referred to them as "little brown brothers."
- During Spanish colonization, Filipinos were viewed as savages, particularly because many were polytheists. Spanish friars forced Filipinos to convert to Catholicism, often using brutal means as a way of teaching. Spanish friars and military also raped and beat Filipina women who were not compliant or as a way of exerting their power.
- In 1904, at the St. Louis World Fair, 1,100 Filipinos (particularly Igorots) were recruited to live on an "exhibit" to show tourists and visitors how various "savage" cultures lived.
- The term "monkey" was a common racial slur used toward Filipinos when they first arrived in the United States.
- In California in the early 1900s, Filipino American men were considered competition for Whites, who perceived them as stealing jobs and White women away. These Filipino men worked primarily in fields and reportedly were paid only $1 for 15 hours of manual labor. At night, the men would attend nightclubs and social functions, where they would dance with White and Mexican women.

This led to anti-Filipino sentiment as well as many hate crimes (e.g., beatings, burnings of houses, and even the death of Fermin Tobera, who was killed in the 1930 Watsonville Riots).

- Due to the anti-Filipino sentiment, the Tydings-McDuffie Act of 1934 was established to allow only 50 Filipino immigrants per year to enter the United States. As a result, Filipinos were considered aliens and not able to work legally in the United States. The Filipino Repatriation Act of 1935 offered Filipinos a free trip back to the Philippines, as long as they agreed to never return.

- General Douglas MacArthur often is viewed as an American hero who led during World War II. He is known for saying "I shall return" when he left his troops in the Philippines to seek alternate help from the United States. After he left, the U.S. military surrendered, leading to the Bataan Death March, where 5,000 Filipino and 1,000 American soldiers were killed.

- César Chávez often is credited as being the leader of the United Farm Workers (UFW) movement in California in the 1960s, and Mexican Americans (or Chicanos) are viewed as the only ethnic group involved in the movement. However, Philip Vera Cruz (a Filipino) was the vice president of the UFW, and Filipino Americans were instrumental in the movement before tensions arose between Chávez and Vera Cruz.

- In 1998, the book *Blu's Hanging* by Lois-Ann Yamanaka depicted a Filipino American man as a rapist and child molester, which conforms with a historical stereotype of Filipino American men as sexual deviants. The Association for Asian American Studies presented Yamanaka with an excellence in fiction award, which later was rescinded when several Filipino American activists and academics protested. The event represented the marginalization of Filipino Americans within the Asian American community.

- In 1998, Joseph Ileto, a Filipino American postal worker, was killed in front of a synagogue in Los Angeles for being "non-White." The same year, Matthew Shepard, a gay White male was killed in a hate crime. Much media attention was focused on the Shepard case while Ileto's case was barely mentioned.

- Filipino and Filipino American World War II veterans were promised that if they fought with the U.S. Army, they would receive full benefits as American soldiers did. President Barack Obama signed a bill in 2009 that would give each surviving veteran a pension in the amount of $15,000 total. However, to secure this benefit, Filipino veterans had to fight for their rights for decades.

Further Readings and Resources

FICTION

Alumit, N. 2003. *Letters to Montgomery Clift*. New York, NY: Alyson Books.

Bacho, P. 1997. *Dark blue suit: And other stories*. Seattle, WA: University of Washington Press.

Holthe, T. U. 2003. *When the elephants dance*. New York, NY: Penguin.

Roley, B. A. 2001. *American son: A novel*. New York, NY: Norton.

NONFICTION

Bulson, C. 1946 *America is in the heart: A personal history*. New York, NY: Harcourt Brace.

Jamero, P. 2006. *Growing up brown: Memoirs of a Filipino American*. Seattle, WA: University of Washington Press.

Nadal, K. L. 2010. *Filipino American psychology: A collection of personal narratives*. Bloomington, IN: Author House.

MOVIES

Cajayon, G. Producer, director, writer. 2000. *The debut* [Motion picture]. United States: 5 Card Productions.

Ginelsa, P. Producer, director, writer. 2003. *Lumpia* [Motion picture]. United States: Kid Heroes Productions.

Imme, S. D., & Imme, J. 2010. The *Filipino experience with America from the Bataan Death March to the 21st century* [Motion picture]. United States: Lilies and Ravens.

Mallillin, E. J. Producer, director, writer. 2008. Brown soup thing [Motion picture]. United States: Malinius.

Pulido, R. Producer, director, writer. 2001. *The flipside* [Motion picture]. United States: Pure pinoy.

MUSICIANS

Abugan, Ryan "Hydroponikz." http://www.hydroponikz.com
Alfa. http://alfa-music.violago.net
Bambu. http://www.bambu.la
Deep Foundation. http://www.myspace.com/deepfoundation
Geologic. http://prometheusbrown.com/blog
Illafonte, Kiwi. http://www.illafonte.com
Koba. http://www.kobasounds.com
Legaspi, Jay. http://www.jaylegaspi.com
Sisante, John-Flor. http://www.myspace.com/johnflor

COMEDIANS

Cordova, Aivy. http://www.myspace.com/aivycordova
Guila, Joey. http://www.joeyguila.com
Koy, Jo. http://www.jokoy.com
Nadal, Kevin. http://www.kevinnadal.com
Navarrete, Rex. http://www.rexnavarrete.com
RufioWho. http://www.myspace.com/rufiowho
San Juan, Edwin. http://www.myspace.com/edwinsj
Tabigue, Air. http://www.aircomedy.com

PERFORMANCE ART, SPOKEN WORD, AND POETRY

Barrett, Kay. http://www.kaybarrett.net
Cabico, Regie. http://en.wikipedia.org/wiki/Regie_Cabico

Delacruz, Alison. http://www.myspace.com/alisonmdelacruz
Kiamco, Rich. http://www.richkiamco.com
Lawsin, Emily. http://www.emilylawsin.com
Ramos, Hanalei. http://www.hanaleihanalei.com
Salazar, Adrien. http://drepoetic.wordpress.com
Two Warriors. http://www.myspace.com/two_warriors

Glossary

1.5 generation A foreign-born individual who arrived in the United States prior to age 13, learning cultural values from the home country while learning new cultural values of the host country.

Acculturation A process in which members of one cultural group adopt the beliefs, values, and behaviors of another group.

Acculturative stress The psychological, somatic, and social difficulties that may accompany acculturation processes.

Adoptee An individual who is adopted.

American Dream The vision taught in various countries that citizens and residents of the United States can pursue their goals in life through hard work and free choice.

Anhedonia The inability to experience pleasure from normally pleasurable life events, such as eating, exercise, and social or sexual interaction.

Antimiscegenation laws Laws that banned interracial marriage and sometimes interracial sex between Whites and members of other races.

Assimilation A process in which members of one cultural group abandon their beliefs, values, and behaviors and fully adopt those of a new host group.

Biculturalism A process in which members of two cultural groups can maintain beliefs, values, and behaviors of both groups.

Biethnic A descriptor for an individual whose heritage is of two distinct ethnic groups (e.g., Filipino and Indian; Puerto Rican and Mexican)

Biracial   A descriptor for an individual whose heritage is of two distinct racial groups (e.g., Asian and White; Black and Native American).

Catholic guilt   The feeling of remorse, self-doubt, or personal responsibility that results when a Catholic engages in "sinful" or inappropriate acts.

Cognitive distortions   Inaccurate thoughts or ideas that maintain negative thinking and help to maintain negative emotions.

Cognitive restructuring   The cognitive-behavioral tool of refuting cognitive distortions and replacing them with more accurate and beneficial ones.

Collective self-esteem   An individual's overall evaluation or appraisal of the worth of her or his collective group.

Collectivism   The moral stance, political philosophy, or social outlook that stresses human interdependence and cooperative action.

Colonial mentality   The concept that the colonizer's values and beliefs are accepted by the colonized as a norm and truth of their own; that the mores of the colonizer are superior to those of the colonized.

Colonialism   The exploitation by a stronger country of a weaker one, with the use of the weaker country's resources to strengthen and enrich the stronger country.

Colonization   The act or process of establishing a colony or colonies.

Compliance   The act of doing something when someone else asks one to. People have a choice when they comply, but sometimes they may do so in fear of repercussions of choosing not to comply.

Conformity   The act of changing how one behaves in order to be more like others; people conform in order to feel a sense of belonging to groups and in order to seek the approval of others.

Coping mechanism   A behavioral tool used by individuals to offset or overcome problems without correcting or eliminating the underlying condition.

Countertransference   Unconscious redirection of feelings of a counselor or clinician toward a client.

Crab mentality   The desire to outdo, outshine, or surpass another (often of one's same ethnic group) at the other's expense.

Cultural mistrust   The inclination for people of color to mistrust Whites, particularly in the areas of education and training, business and work, interpersonal and social relations, politics and law.

Decolonization   The process of humanizing the dehumanized by promoting positive mental health and identity for persons of colonized backgrounds.

Defense mechanisms   Unconscious psychological strategies through which individuals attempt to relieve anxiety and distort reality.

Delusion   A belief that is false, fanciful, or derived from deception.

***Diagnostic and Statistical Manual of Mental Disorders, Fourth Edition, Text Revision* (*DSM-IV-TR*)**   A publication by the American Psychiatric Association that provides diagnostic criteria for mental disorders.

Enculturation   The process whereby an individual learns the accepted norms and values of an established culture.

Endogamous   The personal trait or desire to marry within one's racial group.

Ethnic enclave   A neighborhood, district, or suburb that retains some cultural distinction from a larger, surrounding area.

Ethnic identity   The extent to which one identifies with one's ethnic group through self-identification, sense of belonging or commitment, attitudes toward one's ethnic group, and ethnic and cultural involvement.

Ethnicity   The membership in a particular national or cultural group and observance of that group's customs, beliefs, and language transmitted across generations.

Ethnocentricity   The tendency to view the world primarily from the perspective of one's own culture or ethnic group; the desire for one's ethnic group to be accepted and celebrated.

Filipina   A woman of Filipino descent.

Filipino guilt   The feeling of remorse, self-doubt, or personal responsibility that results when a Filipino engages in "sinful" or inappropriate acts.

First generation   A foreign-born individual who had immigrated to a host country in late adolescence or adulthood; the person may learn cultural values in the home country while acculturating or assimilating into the host country.

Fob (or FOB)   A denigrating term that is used to signify Filipinos who are "fresh off the boat" or who have not acculturated to American culture, speech, or behaviors. "Fobby" is the adjective form of this word.

Fourth generation An individual who is born in a host country and has foreign-born great-grandparents.

Gender identity An individual's personal sense of identification as male or female.

Gender microaggressions Brief statements or behaviors that send denigrating and hurtful messages based on gender (primarily aimed toward women).

Gender role conflict The experience of psychological distress for men, which manifests through restricted emotionality, health care problems, obsession with achievement and success, restricted sexual and affectionate behavior, socialized control, power, and competition issues, and homophobia.

Gender roles The behaviors, expectations, and values defined by society as masculine and feminine.

Hallucination A perception in the absence of an actual or real stimulus, usually occurring in individuals with schizophrenia. Hallucinations can be auditory, visual, olfactory, or tactile.

Hapa A Hawaiian word that literally translates as "half" and has been used as a way of describing multiracial persons in Hawaii (by self and others). Originally derived from the Hawaiian term *hapa haole* (half-White or half-mainlander), the label currently is used even on the mainland as a term of identity and empowerment.

Heterosexism Attitudes, bias, and discrimination in favor of opposite-sex sexuality and relationships.

Homophobia An irrational fear of, aversion to, or discrimination against homosexuality.

Indigenous counseling A system of psychological thought and practice rooted in a particular cultural tradition.

Individualism The moral stance, political philosophy, or social outlook that stresses independence and self-reliance.

Internalized racism The acceptance, by members of an oppressed racial group, of negative messages about their abilities and intrinsic worth; self-hatred about one's racial group.

Locus of control An individual's belief about what causes the good or bad results in her or his life, either in general or in a specific area, such as health or career.

Mania A condition characterized by extremely elevated mood, energy, unusual thought patterns, and sometimes psychosis.

Marginalization The social process of becoming or being made to confine to a lower social standing.

Martial law The system of rules that takes effect when the military takes control of the normal administration of justice.

Mestizo A Filipino and Spanish term that originally was used to describe someone who is part Spanish but also refers to individuals who are fair-skinned and/or biracial/multiracial with Filipino and White backgrounds.

Model Minority Myth A misleading stereotype that places all Asian Americans as well-educated, successful, career-driven, and law-abiding citizens.

Monoethnic A descriptor for an individual whose heritage is of one ethnic group.

Monoracial A descriptor for an individual whose heritage is of one racial group.

Mood disorders A group of diagnoses in the *DSM-IV-TR* in which an individual experiences disturbances in emotional mood.

Multiethnic A descriptor for an individual whose heritage is of two or more distinct ethnic groups (e.g., Filipino, Korean, and Chinese; Puerto Rican, Cuban, and Dominican).

Multiracial A descriptor for an individual whose heritage is of two or more distinct racial group (e.g., Black, Asian, and White). "Multiracial" also is used as an umbrella term to include biracial and multiethnic persons.

Obedience The act of doing something that an accepted authority figure tells a person to do.

Panethnicity The grouping together and labeling of various ethnicities into one all-encompassing group.

Phenotype Physical appearance and features that impact how others perceive an individual racially. Physical characteristics that may contribute to an individual's phenotype may include skin color, eye shape, facial features, and hair texture.

Pinay A slang term used to describe a woman of Filipino descent.

Pinoy A slang term used to describe a person of Filipino descent.

Pluralistic ignorance   The concept in which a majority of individuals in a group assume that most of their peers are different in some way, while the truth is that they are more similar than they realize.

Power   The ability to change, influence others, and receive what one desires. In social psychology, there are five major forms of power: coercive power, reward power, legitimate power, referent power, and expert power.

Psychosomatic symptoms   Physical symptoms an individual experiences that are believed to be caused by psychological conflicts and not from physiological health.

Race   A classification of humans, based on any or a combination of various physical characteristics, including skin color, facial form, and/or eye shape.

Racial identity   The extent to which a people perceive themselves to share a common racial heritage with their respective racial group.

Racial microaggressions   Brief, everyday exchanges that send denigrating messages to people of color because they belong to a racial minority group.

Repression   The process of forcing painful thoughts or memories into the unconscious and/or preventing those thoughts or memories from entering consciousness.

Second generation   An individual who is born in a host country and has foreign-born parents.

Sexual identity   The understanding of one's values, beliefs, and roles as a sexual being; this understanding is developed through the comprehensive process of exploring, assessing, and committing to one's sexual orientation and gender identity.

Sexual orientation   An individual's sense of personal and social identity based on sexual attractions, behaviors expressing those sexual attractions, and membership in a community of others who share those attractions.

Sexual orientation and transgender microaggressions   Brief statements or behaviors that send denigrating and hurtful messages to gay, lesbian, bisexual, and transgender persons.

Shaman   A practitioner of shamanism with a range of traditional beliefs and practices concerned with communication with the spirit world.

Social capital Connections within and between social networks as well as connections among individuals.

Social desirability bias The concept that individuals may behave in a way they believe is socially acceptable and desirable, specifically when they know that others are watching.

Social impact theory A theory in social psychology that describes how a person will respond to social influences based on strength (importance of influencers), immediacy (time and space proximity of influencers), and number of influencers.

Social influence The change in one's behavior that usually is caused by another person's intentional or unintentional power, perspective, or persuasion.

Social norms The explicit or implicit rules that a group uses for appropriate and inappropriate values, beliefs, attitudes, and behaviors.

Third generation An individual who is born in a host country and has foreign-born grandparents.

Transference Unconscious redirection of client feelings toward a counselor or clinician.

Transgender An individual whose gender identity is different from her or his biological sex or birth sex.

Transgenerational transmission The historical contexts of racism or discrimination toward a group that are passed from generation to generation, sometimes leading to trauma, shame, or guilt.

Transracial adoptee An individual who is adopted into a family that is of a different racial group from her or his own birth race.

Transracial adoption The integration of racially different parents and children within a family unit.

Worldview The framework of ideas and beliefs through which an individual interprets the world and interacts with it.

About the Author

Kevin L. Nadal, PhD, is a professor, psychologist, performer, activist, and author, who received his doctorate in counseling psychology from Columbia University in New York City. He earned his bachelor's degrees in psychology and political science from the University of California, Irvine, and a master's degree in counseling from Michigan State University. He is currently an assistant professor of psychology at John Jay College of Criminal Justice, City University of New York, where he also serves as the deputy director of the forensic mental health counseling program.

Dr. Nadal's research focuses primarily on multicultural issues in psychology, particularly involving race, ethnicity, gender, and sexual orientation. His "Pilipino American Identity Development Model" (2004) has been cited as advocating for the understanding of Filipino Americans as a unique racial and ethnic group. His current research concentrates on microaggressions, or subtle forms of discrimination, toward people of color, women, and lesbian, gay, bisexual, and transgender (LGBT) persons. His works have been published in numerous journals and books, including the *American Psychologist, Asian American Psychology: Current Perspectives, Journal of Counseling and Development*, and the *Encyclopedia of Counseling*. He is also the editor of the book, *Filipino American Psychology: A Collection of Personal Narratives*.

Dr. Nadal is also a fellow with the Robert Wood Johnson Foundation as well as the director of the Physical Activity and Pilipino American Youth Assessment project. He currently serves as an executive board member of the Asian American Psychological Association and is a national trustee of the Filipino American National Historical Society (FANHS). He is also the current president of the metropolitan New York chapter of FANHS as well as a board member of the American Psychological Association's Committee on LGBT Concerns.

In 2007, Dr. Nadal led an international campaign against ABC Studios for the negative statements made about Filipino medical schools on the television show *Desperate Housewives*. This led to several media appearances, including an interview on Fox News Channel's *The O'Reilly Factor*, the Filipino Channel, and several print and radio interviews. He has been honored with special service awards from the Philippine Economic and Cultural Endowment Foundation, Kalusugan Coalition of New York/New Jersey, and the Filipino American Human Services, Inc.

Dr. Nadal has also been a keynote speaker for many colleges, universities, and organizations across the country and abroad. He facilitates mental health trainings with the New York Police Department and other nonprofit and corporate organizations. Dr. Nadal also is a stand-up comedian and spoken word artist who has performed across the United States since 2000. He was named one of *People* magazine's hottest bachelors in 2006 and has been featured on the History Channel, HGTV, PBS, *Philippine News*, *Filipinas Magazine*, the *Filipino Reporter*, and Forbes.com.

Author Index

Abe-Kim, J., 230
Agbayani, A. R., 47, 114, 143, 144, 244, 249
Agbayani-Siewert, P., 9, 226
Ahern, F. M., 148
Alsaybar, B. D., 139, 149, 150, 151
Alvarez, A. N., 17, 28, 65, 67, 69, 70, 71, 73
Ancheta, A. N., 69
Aoki, B., 148
Araneta, E., 235
Araneta, M. R., 25
Armstrong, M. A., 25, 149, 234
Arredondo, P., 3
Aruguete, M., 154, 239
Atkinson, D. R., 67, 75

Balisacan, A. M., 94
Bankston, C. L., 143
Barnes, J. S., 3, 4, 11, 18, 195, 198
Barrett-Connor, E., 25
Becker, G., 251
Bell, T. J., 230
Bem, S. L., 165
Bennett, C. E., 3, 4, 5, 8, 9, 11, 18, 19, 20, 21, 22, 139, 143, 195, 198, 200
Berganio, J., 148
Bergman, M., 3, 4
Bergstro, J., 25
Bernstein, R., 3
Bonam, C., 202
Bonus, R., 242
Boydell, J., 237
Brady, S., 171, 172
Braun, K. L., 242
Bucceri, J. M., 169
Busse, W. J., 171, 172

Cabato, A. L., 117
Capodilupo, C. M., 168

Carter, R. T., 70
Cass, V. C., 181
Chang, J. Y., 154, 239
Chen, X., 149
Chesney-Lind, M., 149, 151, 152
Cheung, F. H., 8, 228
Chi, I., 148
Choi, K.-H., 147, 149
Choi, Y., 152
Chung, C., 230
Chung, P. J., 147
Church, T. A., 27
Clinton, W. J., 16
Cohn, A., 166
Combs, D. R., 237
Conerly, G., 173, 178
Constantino, R., 37, 44, 94
Consunji, R. J., 233
Cordova, F., 9, 10, 14, 15, 196
Corey, G., 246, 247, 248, 249
Corpus, M. J. H., 125, 126, 147, 163, 165, 171, 172, 173, 174
Cross, W. E., 68, 75
Cruz, T. B., 149

Daley, S. P., 150
D'Andrea, M., 236
Daniels, J., 236
Daniels, R., 13, 14, 111, 112
Darbes, L. A., 146
David, E. J. R., 8, 9, 12, 23, 24, 26, 38, 91, 95, 96, 97, 226, 228, 229, 230
De Leon, L. M., 150, 151
Delucchi, M., 139
de Mendelssohn, F., 17
Demetrio, F. R., 230, 250
DiClemente, R. J., 147
Do, H. D., 139
Downing, N. E., 178

Edman, J., 154, 239
Ellison, N. B., 118
Enright, J. B., 236
Enriquez, V. G., 27, 38, 244
Esparrago, T., 17
Espin, O., 173
Espiritu, Y. L., 18, 65, 69, 70, 74, 111, 115, 116, 118, 119, 123, 126
Ewing, W. A., 139, 152

Fabella, V. I., 120
Fenigstein, A., 237
Fisher, R. J., 127
Freeman, S., 150
French, J. P. R., 123
Fulbeck, K., 201

Gage, S. L., 229
Galapon, D. L., 166, 169
Gall, T. L., 19, 43, 92
Garcia-Santiago, O., 150
Gaw, A., 228, 229, 232, 233, 235, 241, 251
Gee, G. C., 25, 139
Ghosh, C., 3
Gibson, C., 2
Glidden, C., 228
Gong, F., 229, 230
Gonzalves, T. S., 51, 114
Goto, S. G., 139
Griffin, K., 119
Grunbaum, J. A., 147, 233
Guarnaccia, P. J., 234
Guevarra, R. P., 14, 197, 198, 200, 202, 209, 210, 211
Gutierrez, E. V., 15
Gutierrez, R. V., 15
Guyotte, R. L., 115

Halagao, P. E., 100, 101, 116, 117
Hall, 201, 207
Hall, S. P., 70
Hamilton, B. E., 146
Hamit, S., 119
Han, C.-S., 147
Harley, D. A., 250
Harper, C., 146
Harrell, S. P., 17
Haydel, K. F., 154, 239
Helms, J. E., 65, 68, 75
Henderson, F. C., 25
Henry, R. L., 230, 250
Heras, P., 46, 163, 166
Herman, M., 208
Hishinuma, E. S., 150
Hong, S., 67
Horan, P. F., 147
Horn, L., 18, 66
Huang, K., 148

Hübinette, T., 214
Hudes, E. S., 147
Huffman, L. C., 26
Hwang, W., 230, 250, 251
Hyder, A. A., 233

Ignacio, E. N., 117, 118
Ignacio, L. F., 66
Igra, A., 25, 234
Issa, M.-A., 119
Iwamasa, G. Y., 243
Iwamoto, D. K., 167

Jaeckle, W. R., 236
Jamero, P. M., 148, 198
Javier, J. R., 26
Johnson, C. A., 149
Johnson, R. C., 24, 148
Johnston, M. P., 17
Jones, J., 66
Jorge, R., 98
Juang, L., 17, 73
Jung, K., 2

Kann, L., 147
Katigbak, M. S., 27
Kegeles, S., 147
Keith, S. J., 237
Kennedy, G. E., 146
Killen, J. D., 154, 239
Kim, B. S. K., 67, 244
Kim, J., 69, 71, 75
Kimura, E. F., 69
Kinzie, J. D., 235
Kipling, R., 92
Kitano, H. H., 13, 14, 111, 112, 148
Klatsky, A. L., 25, 149, 234
Klimidis, S., 228
Klingle, R. S., 148
Kohatsu, E. L., 65, 71
Kuo, W. H., 232
Kwan, K., 69

Laenui, P., 100
Lampe, C., 118
Langenberg, C., 25
Larrabee, A. L., 243
Le, C. N., 196, 199, 200, 206, 207, 213
Lee, D. Y., 65, 67, 71
Lee, R. M., 2, 195, 213, 214
Lekas, H-M., 174
Lengua, L. J., 166
Lennon, S., 201
Leonard, A. R., 25, 234
Leong, F. T., 228
Lewis, J., 228
Lewis-Fernández, R., 234
Liang, C. T. H., 73
Liebowitz, M., 234

Author Index

Lin, A. I., 169
Lin, K. M., 8
Liu, W. M., 71, 167
Loo, C. M., 234
Lowry, R., 147
Lubben, J. E., 148
Lyons, O., 119

Macapagal, M. E. J., 41
Manalansan, M. F., 172, 174
Mananzan, M. J., 38, 163
Maramba, D. C., 26, 163, 166
Mark, G. Y., 150
Marker, N., 149
Marmot, M., 25
Martin, J. A., 146
Martínez, I. E., 234
Marvit, R. C., 236
Mayeda, D. T., 150, 151
McClearn, G. E., 24, 148
McDavis, R. J., 3
Mejorada, M. P., 129
Menacker, F., 146
Mendoza, F. S., 26
Merritt, R. D., 243
Messer, K., 149
Milgram, S., 124
Miller, D. T., 127
Miller, M. J., 195, 213, 214
Miller, S. C., 93
Miranda, J., 230
Mohllajee, A., 146
Montoya, C. A., 15, 119
Monzones, J., 40, 41, 48, 230, 241, 242
Morris, A., 148
Morten, G., 75
Mossakowski, K. N., 24
Munson, M. L., 146

Nadal, K. L., 1, 2, 4, 5, 7, 8, 9, 10, 11, 12, 17,
    18, 19, 23, 28, 33, 40, 41, 43, 46, 48, 50, 52,
    53, 64, 65, 66, 69, 70, 71, 73, 74, 75, 78, 91,
    92, 95, 96, 97, 98, 110, 114, 116, 119, 125,
    126, 138, 139, 140, 142, 144, 145, 146, 147,
    148, 149, 152, 163, 164, 165, 168, 169, 170,
    171, 172, 173, 174, 176, 177, 179, 200, 201,
    202, 206, 211, 226, 230, 237, 239, 241, 242,
    243, 249
Nagoshi, C. T., 24, 148
Nakano, J., 150
Nayani, F., 202–203
Nemoto, T., 148, 149, 174
Nevitt, J., 71
Nguyen, H., 148
Nichols, R., 242
Nishimura, S. T., 150

Okamura, J. Y., 47, 74, 98, 114, 115, 139, 143,
    144, 244, 249

Okazaki, S., 8, 9, 12, 23, 24, 38, 91, 95, 96,
    97, 226
Omizo, M. M., 244
O'Neil, J. M., 163, 167
Oparah, J. C., 215
Operario, D., 174

Pannu, R, 69
Parsons, J. T., 174
Pasko, L., 149
Pateman, B., 147
Peck, C., 202
Peersman, G., 146
Penn, D. L., 237
Penrod, S., 126
Phinney, J. S., 66, 72
Pido, A., 115, 164
Pisares, E. H., 130
Pituc, S. T., 17, 43, 114, 144
Pope-Davis, D., 71
Posadas, B. M., 6, 12, 13, 14, 111, 112, 115,
    196, 197, 198, 210
Prentice, D. A., 127
Price, R. K., 148
Pulido, M. E., 151

Quismundo, T., 130
Quiton, R. A., 154

Rae, D. S., 237
Raven, B., 123
Reeves, T. M., 3, 5, 8, 9, 11, 18, 19, 20, 21, 22,
    139, 143, 200
Regier, D. A., 237
Renn, K., 201
Revilla, L. A., 11
Reznik, V. M., 150
Rivera, D. P., 171, 174, 176, 177
Rivera, L. M., 150
Rizal, J. P., 46, 92
Robinson, T. N., 154, 239
Romero, R. A., 149
Root, M. P. P., 9, 96, 98, 195, 196, 200, 201,
    202, 203, 204, 206, 210, 226
Roush, K. L., 178
Rumbaut, R. G., 66, 73, 139, 152
Rutherford, G. W., 146
Ryan, C., 25, 234

Salmán, E., 234
Salvador, D. S., 244, 245
Sanchez, D., 202
Sanchez, F., 228, 229, 232, 233, 235, 241, 251
Sanders, W. B., 139, 150
Santiago, B. C., 45
Santos, A. F., 164
Schmidt, A., 234
Schrimshaw, E. W., 174
Schwitters, S. Y., 24, 148

Shih, M., 202
Shimabukuro, K. P., 236, 251
Shin, S. Y., 215
Siegel, K., 174
Snowden, L. R., 228
Sodowsky, G. R., 69
Soriano, F. I., 150
Sparrenberger, F., 25
Spickard, P., 198, 201
Stavig, G. R., 25, 234
Steinberg, D. J., 93, 94, 95
Steinfield, C., 118
Strobel, L. M., 92, 100, 101, 113
Strunk, O. C., 251
Stuart, G., 228
Sue, D., 3, 5, 7, 9, 17, 239, 240, 241, 243, 246, 247, 248, 249
Sue, D. W., 3, 4, 5, 7, 8, 9, 17, 52, 53, 69, 75, 138, 140, 142, 168, 169, 239, 240, 241, 243
Sue, S., 69, 75, 228, 239
Sustento-Seneriches, J., 23, 24, 232
Sutton, P. D., 146
Suyemoto, K. L., 198, 201, 207, 208

Tacata, L. A., 148, 229
Takaki, R., 6, 7, 14, 196, 197, 198
Takeuchi, D. T., 139, 230
Tan, M. L., 172
Tanford, S., 126
Tawa, J., 198, 201, 207, 208
Tekawa, I. S., 25, 234
Teranishi, R. T., 144
Terrell, F., 230
Terrell, S., 230
Tewari, N., 28
Tintiangco-Cuballes, A., 116
Tiongson, A. T., 15, 113, 139, 146
Tompar-Tiu, A., 23, 24, 232
Toporek, R., 71
Torino, G. C., 169
Tracey, T. J. G., 228, 230
Trenka, J. J., 215

Trevino, F. M., 18, 64
Trinidad, D. R., 149
Troiden, R. R., 181–182

Uba, L., 7, 8, 18, 26, 28, 66, 73, 139, 228, 231
Unger, J. B., 149

Valverde, K. C., 207
Ventura, S. J., 146
Vergara, B. M., 17
Vijayakumar, L., 233

Walker, E. R., 25
Wang, Y., 250
Waters, M. C., 70
Weiner, B. P., 236
Weitz, T., 146, 147
West, J. H., 149
White, M. M., 149
Williams, C. R., 25
Williams, G., 93
Williams, K. J., 150
Wilson, J. R., 24, 148
Wingard, D. L., 25
Winters, K., 25
Wolf, D. L., 8, 111, 166, 232
Wolfe, M. M., 67
Wong, M. M., 148
Wong, W., 148
Wyatt, S. G., 25

Yang, P. H., 67
Yates, A., 154, 239
Yeh, C., 250
Yeh, T. L., 65, 67, 71
Yoo, H. C., 2
Young, B. B., 235
Yuen, S. H. L., 148

Zeichner, A., 166
Ziguras, S., 228
Zohrabyan, L., 146

Subject Index

Acculturation and assimilation:
  colonial mentality toward, 91, 97
  cultural values and, 37, 50, 52–54
  gang membership and, 150
  racial/ethnic identity development and, 70,
    71, 75, 77, 78
Adopted Filipino Americans:
  case studies on, 194–195, 219–220, 221–223
  demographics of, 195–196, 213
  discrimination against, 215–216, 219–220
  identity development of, 214–216
  mental health experiences of, 213–214
African Americans:
  Filipino American affiliations with, 73, 145,
    208–209, 237
  interracial marriages of, 199–200
  mental health experiences of, 237
  model minority myth tensions with, 140
  multiracial/multiethnic subgroups including,
    195, 204, 207–209
  population of, 2
  racial identity models for, 68
Agricultural employment, 14, 73, 210, 290
Alcohol consumption. See Substance use/abuse
American colonization:
  colonial mentality from (see Colonial
    mentality)
  cultural influence of, 12, 36, 48–52
  education influenced by, 48, 49–50, 95
  gender roles influenced by, 163–164
  history of, 92–93
  individualism and competition influenced
    by, 49, 50–52, 163–164
  societal influences of, 93–96, 239–240
Antimiscegenation laws, 14, 196–197, 198
Anxiety disorders, 233–235, 253–254, 256–261
Arts:
  colonialism impacting, 95

communities and groups related to, 114, 117
hip-hop culture and, 73, 151, 208–209
Asian Americans, generally. See also specific
    groups (e.g. Filipino Americans)
  definition of, 4–5
  education of, 8–9, 143–144
  ethnic groups of, 5–6
  experiences of, 4–10
  generational status of, 7–8
  history and demographics of, 6–8
  income of, 9, 22–23, 142
  languages of, 5
  marginalization among, 9–10, 74,
    144–145, 290
  mental health experiences of, 8–10,
    227–228
  model minority myth about (see Model
    minority myth)
  multiethnic subgroups including, 195, 204,
    211–212
  panethnic Asian American consciousness,
    76, 77, 78
  physical characteristics of, 5
  population of, 2–3, 4, 6
  racial identity development of, 69–71
  refugees becoming, 7
  religions of, 5
Asian Exclusion Act (1924), 14, 15
Asian Indian Americans:
  interracial marriages of, 199
  population of, 6

Bahala na (fatalistic passiveness), 40, 41
Bayanihan (community), 43
Beauty standards, 95–96, 206
Biculturalism, 37, 53–54. See also Acculturation
    and assimilation
Bipolar disorder, 231–232

Biracial Filipino Americans, 195, 204. *See also* Multiracial/multiethnic Filipino Americans
Black Americans. *See* African Americans
Body image, 153–154, 239–240

Cardiovascular disease, 25
Case studies:
  on adopted Filipino Americans, 194–195, 219–220, 221–223
  on colonial mentality, 90, 103–108
  on communities and groups, 109–110, 131–136
  on cultural values, 35–36, 55–61
  on gender roles, 162, 186–187, 188–189, 190–191
  on LGBT experience, 162, 187–188, 189–191
  on model minority myth, 138, 155–160
  on multiracial/multiethnic issues, 193–194, 217–219, 221–223
  on psychopathologies, 225–226, 253–261
  on racial and ethnic identity, 63–64, 80–86
Catholicism, 12, 19–20, 43, 44–45, 92, 126, 230, 233
Chávez, César, 210, 290
Children, Filipino American:
  adopted, 194–196, 213–216, 219–220, 221–223
  education of (*see* Education)
  gangs/juvenile crime involvement of, 139, 144, 145, 149–153
  physical health of, 26
  teen pregnancies of, 139, 146–147
  youth and student organizations for, 113–114, 116
Chinese Americans:
  discrimination faced by, 73, 144
  education of, 22, 143–144
  immigration of, 6
  interracial marriages of, 199
  population of, 6
Chinese Exclusion Act (1882), 6
Christianity, 12, 19–20, 43, 44–45, 92, 126, 230, 233
Cognitive-behavioral therapy, 247–248
Collectivism, 36, 37, 38–39, 43, 49. *See also Kapwa* (fellow being)
Colonial mentality. *See also* American colonization; Spanish colonization
  case studies on, 90, 103–108
  communities and groups impacted by, 120
  cultural values influenced by, 38, 43, 49, 91–92, 97, 98
  decolonization frameworks, 100–102
  defined, 96
  Filipino American, 12, 38, 43, 49, 90–108, 120, 154, 164, 167–168, 200, 239–240, 248
  gender roles impacted by colonialism, 38, 43, 45–47, 163–164, 167–168, 230
  hierarchies from, 98–99
  history of colonialism, 91–93

interracial marriages/multiracialism impacted by, 200, 206
self-esteem/self-respect influenced by, 12, 38, 90–91, 96–97, 100, 103–108, 239–240, 248
societal influences of colonialism, 93–96, 154, 206, 239–240
Communities and groups:
  bayanihan (community), 43
  case studies on, 109–110, 131–136
  colonial mentality impacting, 120
  contemporary, 113–122
  crab mentality in, 128–130
  cultural and regional associations as, 115–116
  Filipino American settlement patterns in, 19, 112–113
  generational issues in, 118, 125
  history of, 111–113
  immigration status impacting, 119
  impact of, 120–122
  individualism/competition impacting, 50–52, 115–116, 128–130
  marginalization in, 120, 121
  online, 117–118
  pluralistic ignorance in, 127–128
  political interest groups as, 114, 116–117
  power in, 122–124
  religious tensions in, 119–120
  social and organizational psychology on, 122–128
  social class impacting, 112–113, 118–119
  social desirability bias in, 127
  social influence in, 124–127
  special interest groups as, 116–117
  tension in, 112–113, 118–120
  tsismis (gossip) dividing, 116, 125, 130
  youth and student organizations as, 113–114, 116
Competition. *See* Individualism and competition
Compliance, 124, 125, 126
Conformity:
  communities and groups influenced by, 123, 124–125, 126
  cultural values influenced by, 40 (*see also Pakikisama*)
Crab mentality, 128–130
Culturally competent counseling, 240–245
Cultural mistrust, 230–231
Cultural values:
  acculturation, assimilation and biculturalism impacting, 37, 50, 52–54
  American influence on, 12, 36, 48–52
  bahala na (fatalistic passiveness) influencing, 40, 41
  bayanihan (community) influencing, 43
  case studies on, 35–36, 55–61
  collectivism and, 36, 37, 38–39, 43, 49

colonial mentality and, 38, 43, 49, 91–92, 97, 98
communities and groups reflecting (*see* Communities and groups)
culturally competent counselor's awareness of, 240–245
education and, 48, 49–50
ethnicity based on (*see* Ethnicity)
Filipino, 12–13, 36, 37–43
hiya (shame) influencing, 39–40
individualism/competition and, 49, 50–52
kapwa (fellow being) influencing, 38–39, 41
lakas ng loob (inner strength) influencing, 40–41
mental health experiences impacted by, 229, 232–233, 236, 238–239, 240–250
pakikasama (social acceptance) influencing, 40
Spanish influence on, 12, 36, 43–47
utang ng loob (debt of reciprocity) influencing, 39, 41

Debt of reciprocity (*utang ng loob*), 39, 41, 123, 126, 239
Decolonization framework, 100–102
Demographics. *See also* Population
adoptee, 195–196, 213
Asian American, 6–8
Filipino, 11–12
Filipino American, 17–23, 141–142
interracial marriage, 199–200
multiracial/multiethnic, 195
Depression, 24, 96–97, 165–166, 231–233
Diabetes, 25–26
Discrimination:
adoptees facing, 215–216, 219–220
education as basis for, 49–50, 95
ethnic identity influenced by, 72–73, 76
Filipino Americans facing, 14–15, 16–17, 65, 73, 144, 197–198
hate crimes and, 16, 198
immigrants facing, 6, 14–15, 196–198
mental health experiences impacted by, 16–17, 237
microaggressive, 73, 119–120, 168–169, 176–178
multiracial, 204, 207–209
sexism as, 168–169
sexual orientation, racial and ethnic, 173–174, 176–178
transgenerational transmission of racism, 17
within-group (Filipino), 97, 98
Divorce, 20–21, 44, 141
Drug use. *See* Substance use/abuse

Eating disorders, 154, 239–240
Economy, Filipino, 93–94
Education:
Asian American, 8–9, 143–144
Chinese American, 22, 143–144

colonialism impacting, 48, 49–50, 95
discrimination based on level of, 49–50, 95
Filipino, 48, 49–50, 95
Filipino American, 13, 19, 21, 22, 48, 49–50, 139, 142–145
Japanese American, 22, 144
Korean American, 22, 144
model minority myth about, 138–139, 142–145
women's, 21, 143
Elders, 42. *See also* Generational issues
Employment:
agricultural, 14, 73, 210, 290
Filipino American, 13–14, 15–16, 21, 111–112, 141, 142, 165, 210, 290–291
gender roles influencing, 21, 165
income from (*see* Income)
military, 14, 290–291
professional, 15, 112–113
women's, 21, 141, 165
Enriquez, Jocelyn, 130
Ethnicity. *See also* Racial issues
Asian American ethnicities, 5–6
colonial mentality impacting ethnic identity, 98
communities and groups reflecting (*see* Communities and groups)
ethnic awareness, 75, 76–77
ethnic identity development, 71–74, 75–79, 179–181, 182–184, 201, 214–216, 243–244
ethnocentric realization, 76, 77, 244
feminist identity development and, 179–181
Filipino American ethnic categorization, 18–19, 66–67
multiethnic issues (*see* Multiracial/multiethnic Filipino Americans)
panethnic Asian American consciousness, 76, 77, 78
race and ethnicity, defined, 66–68
racial identity overlap with, 70–71
sexual orientation, race and ethnicity, 171, 173–174, 182–184

Family relations:
cultural values influencing, 41–42
elders in, 42 (*see also* Generational issues)
family systems therapy, 249–250
marriage and (*see* Marriage)
mental health treatment, family involvement in, 241–242, 249–250
Fatalistic passiveness (*bahala na*), 40, 41
Fellow being (*kapwa*), 38–39, 41, 239, 249
Feminist identity development model, 178–181
Filipino Americans:
adopted, 194–196, 213–216, 219–220, 221–223
children of (*see* Children, Filipino American)
colonial mentality of (*see* Colonial mentality)
communities and groups of (*see* Communities and groups)
crab mentality of, 128–130

Filipino Americans *(Continued)*
cultural values of (*see* Cultural values)
demographics of, 17–23, 141–142
education of, 13, 19, 21, 22, 48, 49–50, 139, 142–145
employment of, 13–14, 15–16, 21, 111–112, 141, 142, 165, 210, 290–291
experiences of, 11–13
family relations of (*see* Family relations)
gambling by, 153–154
gangs and juvenile crime among, 139, 144, 145, 149–153
hierarchies among, 49–50, 98–99
history and immigration of, 6, 13–17, 20, 30–33, 111–112, 119, 196–198, 289–291
income of, 22–23, 139, 141, 142
languages of, 21, 49–50, 141
LGBT (*see* LGBT (lesbian, gay, bisexual, transgender) Filipino Americans)
marginalization of, 9–10, 74, 120, 121, 140, 144–145, 290
marriage of, 14, 20–21, 41, 111–112, 141, 196–201
men as (*see* Men, Filipino American)
mental health experiences of (*see* Mental health experiences)
military service of, 14, 290–291
model minority myth about (*see* Model minority myth)
multiracial/multiethnic (*see* Multiracial/ multiethnic Filipino Americans)
physical characteristics of (*see* Physical characteristics/phenotype)
physical health of, 25–26, 139, 146–147, 149, 229, 234
political interests of, 52, 76, 77, 114, 116–117, 130
population of, 4, 6, 11, 17–18
poverty rates of, 21–22, 141
racial and ethnic issues facing (*see* Ethnicity; Racial issues)
religions of (*see* Religions)
substance use/abuse by, 24–25, 139, 148–149, 165–166, 239
women as (*see* Women, Filipina)
Filipino Repatriation Act (1935), 290
Filipinos (in Philippines):
art of, 95
beauty standards of, 95–96, 206
cultural values of, 12–13, 36, 37–43
demographics of, 11–12
economic status of, 93–94
education of, 48, 49–50, 95
food of, 95
government of, 94
languages of, 12, 21, 48, 95
mental health experiences/psychology of, 27–28, 227
physical characteristics of, 66, 95–96

poverty rates of, 94, 214
religions of, 19–20, 43, 44–45, 92
Food, 95

Gambling, 153–154
Gangs/juvenile crime, 139, 144, 145, 149–153
Gay Filipino Americans. *See* LGBT (lesbian, gay, bisexual, transgender) Filipino Americans
Gender roles:
case studies on, 162, 186–187, 188–189, 190–191
colonial influences on, 38, 43, 45–47, 163–164, 167–168, 230
cultural influences on, 38, 43, 45–47
education impacted by, 21
employment impacted by, 21, 165
expectations and conflict, 166–168
feminist identity development model and, 178–181
gender identity and (*see* LGBT (lesbian, gay, bisexual, transgender) Filipino Americans)
gender microaggressions, 168–169
influences of, 163–169
mental health impacts of, 165–168, 230
sexism and, 168–169
Generational issues:
Asian Americans generational status, 7–8
communities and groups impacted by, 118, 125
cultural values and, 42
education differences between generations, 143
interracial relationships and, 209
teen pregnancy statistics related to, 146
transgenerational transmission of racism, 17
Generosity, cultural values influencing, 39, 42–43
Gossip *(tsismis)*, 50–51, 110, 116, 125, 130, 229
Government, colonialism impacting, 94
Grief counseling, 242–243
Groups. *See* Communities and groups
Guilt, Filipino or Catholic, 126

Hate crimes, 16, 198
Hip-hop culture, 73, 151, 208–209
Hispanic Americans:
Filipino American affiliations with, 73, 145, 210, 290
Filipino American categorization as, 18, 64
interracial marriages of, 14, 196–197, 199–200
mental health experiences of, 227
model minority myth tensions with, 140
multiracial/multiethnic subgroups including, 195, 204, 209–211
population of, 2–3
History:
of Asian American experience, 6–8

of colonialism, 91–93
of Filipino American communities and groups, 111–113
of Filipino American experience, 13–17, 30–33, 289–291
of interracial relationships with Filipino Americans, 196–198
HIV/AIDS, 139, 146–147
Hiya (shame):
  community/group pressure through, 123–124, 126, 127, 128
  cultural values influenced by, 39–40
  defined, 39–40
  mental health experiences impacted by, 229, 232–233, 236
Homosexual Filipino Americans. *See* LGBT (lesbian, gay, bisexual, transgender) Filipino Americans
Hospitality, cultural values influencing, 42–43
Humanistic and person-centered therapies, 248–249
Hypertension, 25, 149, 234

Identity development:
  adoptive, 214–216
  ethnic, 71–74, 75–79, 179–181, 182–184, 201, 214–216, 243–244
  feminist, 178–181
  multiracial and multiethnic, 201–205
  racial, 68–71, 75–79, 179–181, 182–184, 201, 243–244
  sexual, 181–184
"Ikaw" (poem), 30–33, 289–291
Ileto, Joseph, 16, 290
Immigration:
  Chinese American, 6
  communities and groups impacted by immigration status, 119
  discrimination against immigrants, 6, 14–15, 196–198
  Filipino American, 6, 13–17, 20, 111–112, 119, 196–198
  Japanese American, 6
  refugees', 7
  undocumented immigrants, 11, 15–16, 119
Immigration Act (1924), 6
Immigration Act (1965), 6, 15
Income:
  Asian American, 9, 22–23, 142
  Filipino American, 22–23, 139, 141, 142
Indigenous and spiritual counseling methods, 229–230, 236, 250–252
Individualism and competition, 49, 50–52, 115–116, 128–130, 163–164
Inner strength *(lakas ng loob)*, 40–41
Interracial marriage/relationships:
  antimiscegenation laws on, 14, 196–197, 198
  contemporary, 198–201
  demographics of, 199–200

generational issues with, 209
history of, 196–198
immigrants in, 111–112, 196
Introspection, 76, 77, 79
Itliong, Larry, 210

Japanese Americans:
  education of, 22, 144
  immigration of, 6
  multiracial, 198
  population of, 6

Kapwa (fellow being), 38–39, 41, 239, 249
Korean Americans:
  education of, 22, 144
  population of, 6

Lakas ng loob (inner strength), 40–41
Languages:
  accents and, 49–50, 97, 99, 103–105, 243
  Asian American, 5
  colonialism impacting, 95
  Filipino, 12, 21, 48, 95
  Filipino American, 21, 49–50, 141
Latinos. *See* Hispanic Americans
"Leave it up to God" attitude, 40, 41
Legislation:
  Asian Exclusion Act (1924), 14, 15
  Chinese Exclusion Act (1882), 6
  Filipino Repatriation Act (1935), 290
  Immigration Act (1924), 6
  Immigration Act (1965), 6, 15
  Tydings-McDuffie Act (1934), 290
  Walter-McCarran Immigration and Naturalization Act (1952), 14, 15
LGBT (lesbian, gay, bisexual, transgender) Filipino Americans:
  bisexuals, specifically, 174–175
  case studies on experiences of, 162, 187–188, 189–191
  "coming out" by, 171, 172–173
  definitions related to, 170–171
  discrimination faced by, 173–174, 176–178
  experiences of, 163, 170–178
  HIV/AIDS among, 146–147
  race, ethnicity and sexual orientation of, 171, 173–174, 182–184
  religion impacting, 172–173
  sexual identity development models for, 181–184
  social influence over, 125
  substance use/abuse among, 148–149
  transgenders, specifically, 174–175
Loving v. Virginia, 198

Marcos, Ferdinand, 94
Marriage:
  antimiscegenation laws on, 14, 196–197, 198
  divorce from, 20–21, 44, 141

Marriage *(Continued)*
  Filipino American, 14, 20–21, 41, 111–112,
    141, 196–201
  interracial, 14, 111–112, 196–201, 209
  out-of-wedlock pregnancy issues, 139,
    146–147
  wedding traditions, 41
Men, Filipino American:
  body image and eating disorders of, 154, 239
  colonial influences on, 38, 43, 45–47,
    163–164, 167–168, 230
  education of, 143
  gang/crime involvement of, 149, 152
  gender roles impacting, 163–168, 230
  homosexual (*see* LGBT (lesbian, gay,
    bisexual, transgender) Filipino Americans)
  immigrant, 6, 13–14, 111–112, 196–198
  income of, 23, 142
  marriage of (*see* Marriage)
  mental health experiences of, 230, 235, 247
  substance use/abuse by, 24, 148–149
Mental health experiences:
  adoptees', 213–214
  anxiety disorders and, 233–235, 253–254,
    256–261
  Asian American, 8–10, 227–228
  bipolar disorder and, 231–232
  case studies on (*see* Case studies)
  cognitive-behavioral therapy, 247–248
  culturally appropriate theoretical orientation
    utilization, 245–250
  culturally competent counseling, 240–245
  cultural mistrust in, 230–231
  cultural values impacting, 229, 232–233,
    236, 238–239, 240–250
  depression and, 24, 96–97, 165–166, 231–233
  discrimination impacting, 16–17, 237
  eating disorders and, 154, 239–240
  family systems therapy, 249–250
  Filipino, 27–28, 227
  Filipino American, 16–17, 23–27, 225–261
  gender roles impacting, 165–166, 230
  help-seeking behavior, 227–231
  humanistic and person-centered therapies,
    248–249
  indigenous and spiritual counseling
    methods, 229–230, 236, 250–252
  personality disorders and, 238–239
  physical health and, 25–26, 229, 234
  psychoanalytic and psychodynamic
    therapies, 246–247
  psychopathologies and, 24, 96–97, 154,
    165–166, 225–226, 231–240, 253–261
  schizophrenia and, 235–237, 254–261
  substance use/abuse and, 24–25, 239
Mexican Americans. *See also* Hispanic
    Americans
  Filipino American alliances with, 73
  interracial marriages of, 14, 196–197

multiracial/multiethnic subgroups including,
    195, 204, 209–211
Microaggressions:
  gender, 168–169
  racial, 73
  religious, 119–120
  sexual orientation and transgender, 176–178
Military service, 14, 290–291
Model minority myth:
  body image and, 153–154
  case studies on, 138, 155–160
  education and, 138–139, 142–145
  Filipino American statistics and, 140–142
  gambling and, 153–154
  gangs/juvenile crime and, 139, 149–153
  HIV/AIDS and teen/out-of-wedlock
    pregnancy and, 139, 146–147
  impacts of, 8–9, 140
  substance use/abuse and, 139, 148–149
Multiracial/multiethnic Filipino Americans:
  biracial, specifically, 195, 204
  case studies on, 193–195, 217–219, 221–223
  communities and groups impacted by, 120
  demographics of, 195
  discrimination against, 204, 207–209
  interracial relationships and, 14, 111–112,
    196–201, 209
  multiracial and multiethnic identity
    development, 201–205
  physical characteristics/phenotypes of, 204,
    207, 208, 211, 212
  subgroups of, 195, 205–212
Muslim/Islamic faith, 20, 44, 45

Navy, U.S., 14
Nigrescence Model for Black Americans, 68

Obedience, 124, 125, 126
Older adults, 42. *See also* Generational issues
Online groups and communities, 117–118
Overweight/obesity, 25

Pacific Islanders:
  Filipino American categorization as, 18, 64
  population of, 2
Pacquiao, Manny, 130
Pakikasama (social acceptance):
  communities and groups influenced by, 123,
    124–125, 126, 127, 128
  cultural values influenced by, 40
  defined, 40
  mental health experiences impacted by,
    244, 249
Personality disorders, 238–239
Philippines:
  arts in, 95
  beauty standards in, 95–96, 206
  colonization of (*see* American colonization;
    Spanish colonization)

cultural values in, 12–13, 36, 37–43
demographics of, 11–12
economy of, 93–94
education in, 48, 49–50, 95
food in, 95
government of, 94
languages in, 12, 21, 48, 95
mental health experiences/psychology of
  Filipinos, 27–28, 227
physical characteristics of Filipinos, 66,
  95–96
poverty rates in, 94, 214
religions in, 19–20, 43, 44–45, 92
Physical characteristics/phenotype:
  Asian American, 5
  beauty standards of, 95–96, 206
  body image based on, 153–154, 239–240
  colonial mentality toward, 97, 98–99, 154,
    239–240
  multiracial, 204, 207, 208, 211, 212
  racial definitions based on, 66
Physical health:
  cardiovascular disease and, 25
  diabetes and, 25–26
  Filipino American, 25–26, 139, 146–147,
    149, 229, 234
  HIV/AIDS and, 139, 146–147
  hypertension and, 25, 149, 234
  mental health and, 25–26, 229, 234
Pluralistic ignorance, 127–128
POCRIAS (People of Color Racial Identity
  Attitudes Scale), 68–69
Politics:
  lack of cohesion in Filipino American
    politics, 52, 130
  political corruption, 94
  political interest groups, 114, 116–117
  social political awakening, 76, 77
Population. See also Demographics
  African American, 2
  Asian American, 2–3, 4, 6
  Asian Indian American, 6
  Chinese American, 6
  Filipino American, 4, 6, 11, 17–18
  Hispanic American, 2–3
  Japanese American, 6
  Korean American, 6
  Pacific Islander, 2
  Vietnamese American, 6
Poverty rates:
  Filipino, 94, 214
  Filipino American, 21–22, 141
Power, in communities and groups, 122–124
Pregnancy, teen/out-of-wedlock, 139, 146–147
Psychology. See also Mental health experiences;
  Psychopathologies; Psychotherapy
  Filipino, 27–28, 227
  social and organizational, of groups and
    communities, 122–128

Psychopathologies:
  anxiety disorders as, 233–235, 253–254,
    256–261
  bipolar disorder as, 231–232
  case studies on, 225–226, 253–261
  depression as, 24, 96–97, 165–166,
    231–233
  eating disorders as, 154, 239–240
  personality disorders as, 238–239
  schizophrenia as, 235–237, 254–261
  substance abuse disorders as, 239
  suicide as, 232–233
Psychotherapy. See also Mental health
    experiences
  cognitive-behavioral therapy, 247–248
  culturally competent, 240–245
  family systems therapy, 249–250
  humanistic and person-centered therapies,
    248–249
  psychoanalytic and psychodynamic
    therapies, 246–247

Racial issues. See also Ethnicity
  case studies on racial/ethnic identity,
    63–64, 80–86
  colonial mentality impacting racial
    identity, 98
  discrimination as (see Discrimination)
  feminist identity development and,
    179–181
  Filipino American racial categorization,
    18–19, 64–65, 66
  historical view of race, 2–3
  interracial marriages/relationships as, 14,
    111–112, 196–201, 209
  multiracial/multiethnic (see Multiracial/
    multiethnic Filipino Americans)
  race and ethnicity, defined, 66–68
  racial identity development, 68–71, 75–79,
    179–181, 182–184, 201, 243–244
  sexual orientation, race and ethnicity, 171,
    173–174, 182–184
Refugees, 7
Religions:
  Asian American, 5
  bahala na ("Leave it up to God") attitude,
    40, 41
  colonial influence on, 12, 19–20, 43, 44–45,
    91–92
  communities' and groups' religious tensions,
    119–120
  Filipino, 19–20, 43, 44–45, 92
  guilt, Catholic, 126
  religious microaggressions, 119–120
  sexual orientation impacted by, 172–173
  spiritual/pastoral counseling methods,
    229–230, 236, 250–252
  suicide views of, 233
Rogers, Carl/Rogerian therapy, 248

Schizophrenia, 235–237, 254–261
Self-esteem/self-respect:
  colonial mentality impacting, 12, 38, 90–91,
    96–97, 100, 103–108, 239–240, 248
  cultural values impacting, 47
  marginalization impacting, 9–10, 74, 120,
    121, 140, 144–145, 290
Self-reflection activities:
  on colonial mentality, 108
  on Filipino American experience, 30–33,
    289–291
  on gender and sexual orientation, 191–192
  on multiracial Filipino American
    experience, 224
  on racial and ethnic identity, 87
Sexual issues:
  model minority myth about, 139, 146–147
  sexism as, 168–169
  sexual identity development models,
    181–184
  sexual orientation as (*see* LGBT (lesbian,
    gay, bisexual, transgender) Filipino
    Americans)
Shame. *See Hiya* (shame)
Smoking. *See* Substance use/abuse
Social acceptance. *See Pakikasama* (social
  acceptance)
Social class:
  communities and groups impacted by, 111,
    112–113, 118–119
  educational achievement and, 145
  gang/juvenile crime involvement and,
    150–151
  hierarchies of, 49–50, 98–99
  socioeconomic demographics, 17–23,
    141–142
Social desirability bias, 127
Social influence, in communities and groups,
  124–127
Social networking, 118
Social political awakening, 76, 77
Spanish colonization:
  colonial mentality from (*see* Colonial
    mentality)
  cultural influence of, 12, 36, 43–47
  gender roles influenced by, 38, 43, 45–47,
    163–164, 167–168
  history of, 91–92

religion influenced by, 12, 19–20, 43,
  44–45, 92
societal influences of, 93–96, 239–240
Substance use/abuse, 24–25, 139, 148–149,
  165–166, 239
Suicide, 232–233

Tago ng tago (TNTs/undocumented
  immigrants), 11, 15–16, 119
Teen/out-of-wedlock pregnancy, 139,
  146–147
Time, Filipino, 242
Tobacco use. *See* Substance use/abuse
Tobera, Fermin, 198, 290
Transgenerational transmission of racism, 17
Tsismis (gossip), 50–51, 110, 116, 125, 130, 229
Tydings-McDuffie Act (1934), 290

Undocumented immigrants, 11, 15–16, 119
United Farm Workers Movement, 73, 210, 290
Utang ng loob (debt of reciprocity), 39, 41, 123,
  126, 239

Vera Cruz, Philip, 210, 290
Vietnamese Americans, population of, 6

Walter-McCarran Immigration and
  Naturalization Act (1952), 14, 15
White Americans:
  interracial marriages of, 14, 196–200
  multiracial/multiethnic subgroups including,
    195, 201, 205–207
Women, Filipina:
  colonial influences on, 38, 43, 45–47,
    163–164
  education of, 21, 143
  employment of, 21, 141, 165
  feminist identity development model for,
    178–181
  gender roles of, 21, 38, 43, 45–47, 162–163,
    163–169, 178–181, 186–187, 188–189,
    190–191, 230
  lesbian (*see* LGBT (lesbian, gay, bisexual,
    transgender) Filipino Americans)
  marriage of (*see* Marriage)
  sexism impacting, 168–169
  teen/out-of-wedlock pregnancy of, 139,
    146–147